AN INTRODUCTION TO SAID NURSI

To the precious memory of Bediuzzaman Said Nursi in the 51st anniversary year of his death

An Introduction to Said Nursi
Life, Thought and Writings

IAN MARKHAM AND SUENDAM BIRINCI PIRIM

ASHGATE

Published by
Ashgate Publishing Limited
Wey Court East
Union Road
Farnham
Surrey, GU9 7PT
England

Ashgate Publishing Company
Suite 420
101 Cherry Street
Burlington
VT 05401-4405
USA

www.ashgate.com

British Library Cataloguing in Publication Data
Markham, Ian S.
  An introduction to Said Nursi : life, thought and writings
  1. Nursi, Said, 1873–1960. 2. Islam–Doctrines.
  I. Title II. Birinci Pirim, Suendam.
  297.2'092–dc22

Library of Congress Cataloging-in-Publication Data
Markham, Ian S.
  An introduction to Said Nursi : life, thought and writings / Ian S. Markham and Suendam Birinci Pirim.
    p. cm.
  Includes index.
  ISBN 978-1-4094-0769-0 (hardcover : alk. paper) — ISBN 978-1-4094-0771-3 (pbk. : alk. paper) — ISBN 978-1-4094-0770-6 (ebook) 1. Nursi, Said, 1873–1960. 2. Nurculuk. I. Birinci Pirim, Suendam. II. Title.
  BP253.Z8N8765 2010
  297.8'3—dc22

2010040818

ISBN 978-1-4094-0769-0 (hbk)
ISBN 978-1-4094-0771-3 (pbk)
ISBN 978-1-4094-0770-6 (ebk)

Printed and bound in Great Britain by the
MPG Books Group, UK

Contents

EXTRACTS FROM THE WRITINGS OF SAID NURSI

Acknowledgements

Collaborating on this book has been important and precious work. In an age when Islam is so frequently misunderstood, it is essential that the insights of distinguished Islamic scholars are made accessible. We appreciate very much our time together at Hartford Seminary in Connecticut. This is an institution that has pioneered the importance of the Christian–Muslim dialogue for decades. To our friends, colleagues (both on the Faculty and on the Staff), we are deeply grateful.

We are grateful to Sarah Lloyd, the Commissioning Editor for Ashgate. She has recognized the importance of this moment—the need for accessible texts that explain in a systematic way the insights of Islamic scholars. Her care with this project is much appreciated. As the book moved into production, Nick Wain provided an outstanding service to the authors.

We are grateful to those who helped us with the glossary, especially Lynn Campbell, Whitney Kirby, and Audrey O'Brien. Christine Faulstich did a wonderful job on the index and Christine Peel read the proofs carefully. Katie Glover and Catric Whaley helped organize the project.

We are grateful to our respective life partners—Harun and Lesley. For your love and support, we are forever grateful.

The editors are grateful for the following permissions: Şükran Vahide for the translations of the *Risale-i Nur*; Ashgate Publishing for permission to use sections from Ian Markham, *Engaging Bediuzzaman Said Nursi*, (Ashgate 2009).

Suendam Birinci Pirim and Ian Markham

Introduction

There are very few books on Islamic thinkers. With Christian theologians, there are companions, encyclopedias, dictionaries, introductions, textbooks, and surveys. There are accessible introductions to the thought of such theologians as Karl Barth and Paul Tillich. But when it comes to Islam, there is virtually nothing. With the exception of some good work on classical thinkers (for example, Al-Ghazali), contemporary Islamic thinkers are treated sociologically rather than as theologians. A book on Muhammad Iqbal is more likely to focus on his contribution to the emergence of Pakistan than his highly innovative account of God. This needs to change; we need to start engaging at the level of ideas with the rich depths of contemporary Islamic theology.

This book is written for the student in the academy. We are interested in the student in "Introduction to Islam" course that wants to understand the worldview of a distinguished and hugely influential Islamic thinker. We want to see courses emerge that compare and contrast Muslim and Christian theologians. This is a book that is intended to be accessible and, at the same time, demanding. It is accessible because the opening chapters ease the reader into the context of our thinker and provide an accessible overview of the theology. It is demanding because then the reader is invited into the primary text. To look closely at the challenge of interpretation and to enjoy exploring the nuance and detail embedded in the extracts. At moments when the text is difficult, the reader is invited to turn to the end of the book and use the glossary. And at the end of every chapter, there are study questions to orientate and reflect on the material.

This book is an exploration of the thought of Bediuzzaman (this means "Wonder of the Age") Said Nursi (1878–1960). His thought has birthed a major worldwide Islamic movement of approximately 6 million followers. While the Egyptian Muslim Brotherhood (a group committed to the realization of a Muslim State, which observes *sharia*) is numerically small yet has spawned a vast literature, the Nur community (the community formed out of Nursi's thought) has produced a vast movement, which has had virtually no attention. We list under the further reading sections all the books that have been written on Nursi available in English. One of our tasks in this book is to start correcting the imbalance: instead of focusing on small Muslim movements, let us start taking more interest in the mainstream ones.

While the need to understand the inspiration behind a major Muslim movement may be our place to start, there are many other reasons for this book on Said Nursi. The first is that he is a remarkably compelling thinker and writer. The underlying project is renewal. At a time when a modern Turkey is emerging that can compete effectively in twentieth century Europe, Nursi sees the danger. Islam is being associated with the "old" and "irrelevant". He is determined to illustrate that this is not the case. He illustrates that Islam, properly understood, is compatible with the best that modernity brings. One can be a Muslim and an advocate for technology and science; one can be a Muslim and operate effectively in a secular state; and one can be a Muslim and commit to peaceful co-existence with those who disagree with Islam. Furthermore the arguments for these positions are all found in the Qur'an. The embrace of science, pluralism, and dialogue are not, for Nursi, a betrayal of the teaching of the Qur'an and the Prophet Muhammad. Instead this constructive attitude to modernity is directly derived from these Muslim sources. The second reason is that Nursi is a writer who wants to reconnect human life with God and eternity. There is a deep piety in his writing. Any person of faith coming to his major work the *Risale-i Nur* (the Treatise of Light) cannot help admire the passion and manifest love for God pulsating through the text. Nursi writes movingly about seeing God in the creation; he is a spiritually sensitive thinker.

This is an invitation to those interested in interfaith dialogue to move beyond the "sociology" of dialogue to a real engagement with the other. The dialogue movement tends to avoid doctrinal differences. Instead we are told that the task of dialogue is simply to listen not to judge. This is an invitation to think of dialogue differently: let us "cross over" and seek to understand the thought of the other from the inside. Let us read the primary sources and understand the worldview. To make this possible, a Christian priest and professor has teamed up with a doctoral candidate and member of the Nur community to write this book. We wanted to model what we are after. Every sentence of this book is shared. We wanted to offer a compelling, accurate, portrait of this remarkable mind. This is our shared goal. Having done the exercise, we then have our own positions, which naturally are different from each other. However, we are both deeply committed to the exercise. We need to enter into each other's worlds much more effectively. We need to be able to give an account of what each other thinks, which is fair, accurate, and respectful. This approach to interfaith dialogue is both more interesting and more productive.

We are now at the point where the journey should begin. We start by placing Said Nursi in context. We start with his remarkable life — a soldier, prisoner, political commentator, scholar of the Qur'an, and leader. It is to his life that we turn next.

Chapter 1
Life and Times of Said Nursi (1878–1960)

"I consider Said Nursi's thought to be one of the foremost assemblages of important ideas among Islamic thinkers. It is not simply Nursi's intellectualism and piety that touch the reader, but the deep human respect inherent in his ideas."[1]

Known through his vibrant legacy in Turkey and in the Middle East, not much attention has been paid to Said Nursi and his ideas in the West. His name has only recently started to appear in books dedicated to modern Islamic thought and Muslim intellectuals. One major reason for the growing interest toward Nursi and his teachings in the West is due to his faith-based understanding of Islam and his insistence on keeping Islam distinct from politics. Nursi was deeply concerned with the challenges facing humanity, believers, and the Muslim *ummah* in particular. He had a faith-centered understanding of Islam, not a state-centered one. Consequently, he did not see the solution in establishing an Islamic state, a position advocated by many of his contemporaries. Even though he was often misunderstood in Turkey, he never lost hope or fell into despair in his loneliness, and continued to spell out what he thought to be right and beneficial for all. At times, he turned toward the future, addressing upcoming generations in his work and writings.

Having lived through one of the most significant periods in recent history, Nursi witnessed and participated in key events that affected the world. These include two World Wars, the collapse of the Ottoman Empire which gave birth to the secular Republic of Turkey, the continuing colonization of Muslim lands, the partition of the Muslim world after gaining independence through nationalist ideologies, the emergence of major ideologies such as communism and capitalism, and major movements like atheism, materialism, and anarchism. People, cultures, religion, science; in short, the entire globe was re-shaped during the years covering Nursi's life span.

Nursi was born in 1878[2] in a small village called Nurs in the city of Bitlis located in southeastern Anatolia. He grew up and received his education around districts considered periphery to the Ottoman Empire. In his youth, he effectively

---

[1]   Şerif Mardin, "Reflections on Said Nursi's Life and Thought" in Ibrahim M. Abu-Rabi, *Islam at the Crossroads: On the Life and Thought of Bediuzzaman Said Nursi*, (New York: State University of New York Press, 2003), 45.

[2]   Biographies of Said Nursi may refer to several different dates regarding his birth year, which was reported according to official calendars used by the Ottoman Empire; *Rumi* 1290 and *Hijri* 1293. Differences occur while converting these dates to a Gregorian calendar

moved to the center of the empire and became an intellect not only contributing to but shaping the agenda of Turkey. It is a remarkable life. Before proceeding toward details of his life, it will be helpful to look at his environment in order to locate Nursi in the world of his times and gain a better insight to his theology and thinking.

Anatolia during Nursi's Early Years

The geography and political landscape of the globe in the nineteenth century was different from what it is today. Nursi was born in the lands of the Ottoman Empire, and grew into his youth through the last decades of this old domain. His environment was predominantly composed of Sunni Muslims, most of whom were ethnically Kurdish.

Established to realize a long held dream of uniting Turks under the same flag, the Ottoman Empire maintained its rule for over six centuries from 1299 to 1923. Its lands spread from Asia Minor to the Middle East, Northern Africa, and Southeastern Europe. It operated through a state system with different provinces composed of people from different religions and races. The empire was located in the center of three continents and bridged different cultures and religions. Istanbul, historically known as Constantinople, was the capital of the empire for about five centuries. The city continues to be the most dynamic metropolitan area of modern day Turkey, continuing to reflect the diversity of the nation and its population.

Even though a leading motivation for the establishment of the empire was the unification of Turks, Ottoman was known as the greatest empire of Islamic civilization. After an overwhelming majority of Turks accepted Islam starting from the eighth century on, religious fellowship was regarded as higher than any ethnic bond. The concept of *ummah* in Islam, referring to the community of Muslims, includes all races and ethnicities as equal creation of God announcing that the most honored in the sight of God is the most righteous (Q, 49:13).[3] In light of this teaching, the Prophet of Islam stated in his last sermon that no race could be superior over the other since all humankind is created from the same couple, Adam and Eve.[4]

---

date. Based on a profound research, 1878 will be referred as his birth year throughout the book. Said Nursi, *Tarihçe-i Hayatı*, (Istanbul: Söz Press, 2009), 959-960.

[3]   Qur'an, 49:13 "O humankind! We created you from a single (pair) of a male and a female, and made you into nations and tribes, that ye may know each other (not that ye may despise (each other). Verily the most honored of you in the sight of God is the most righteous of you. And God has full knowledge and is well acquainted (with all things)."

[4]   "All mankind is from Adam and Eve, an Arab is not superior over a non Arab nor a non Arab is superior over an Arab; also a white is not superior over a black nor a black is superior over a white except by piety and good action. Learn that every Muslim is a brother to every Muslim and that the Muslims constitute one brotherhood. Nothing shall

The Ottoman Empire is almost synonymous with the notion of Muslim *caliphate*, which is known as the dominion of the *Caliph*. In the *Sunni* tradition, this was a title given to Muslim leaders mostly concerned with political leadership and state affairs. *Caliphs* would be supervised by *sheikh al-Islam*, a leading religious scholar given the highest authority of legislation and guidance. According to *Shi'a* Islam, spiritual and political leadership is united in the same leader, or *Imam*. From the sixteenth century on, Ottoman Sultan's received the title of *Caliph* as leaders of the Muslim *ummah*. The empire was a monarchic dynasty and the same system was applied throughout the years of *caliphate*.

Similar to a living organism, this great empire had its establishment, expansion, and decline periods. Its most remarkable years are regarded as the fifteenth to seventeenth centuries. In contrast to the darkness of the Western Middle Ages, arts and sciences were flourishing in the Ottoman lands. Mathematics, astronomy, geography, navigation, philosophy, mysticism, visual arts such as calligraphy, miniatures, and illumination, music and literature were among the leading fields of productivity.[5] One visible legacy of Ottoman is the fascinating architecture, most notably visible in mosques and bazaars, such as the Blue Mosque and the Grand Bazaar.

The nineteenth century marked the decline and eventual downfall of the Ottoman Empire. Modernization and reform within the empire began in the first 40 years of this century. This was followed by a period called *Tanzimat* (1839–1876), known as a time of reorganization or reforms. Moving away from monarchy, under *Meşrutiyet*, Constitutional Monarchy, the establishment of a parliament restricted the Sultan's absolute power. While people, particularly the educated, were ready and eager for this shift, a major concern was the representation of all ethnicities and religions in the parliament.

Islamic unity was the building block of the Ottoman Empire and kept it empowered until the strong force of nationalism, which was mostly advocated by the Western educated intelligentsia, confronted the empire. The nineteenth century elite were mostly educated in Paris where nationalism was a major trend. It was a period when remedies to heal the falling empire were being sought. More importantly, it was not a single dynasty or nation being affected, but a representation of the unity of Islam and its fall would give birth to many more problems. The early version of nationalism promoted by the Young Turks was Ottomanism similar to current day "American identity" claimed by the citizens of the United States. It was promoted as the ideology of the First Constitutional Era (1876–1877). However, it did not survive long as wars within the empire and around the world were waged to preserve national identities. Although Islam and

---

be legitimate to a Muslim which belongs to a fellow Muslim unless it was given freely and willingly. Do not, therefore, do injustice to yourselves."

5   "1001 Inventions" is a project supported with a book and mobile exhibitions aiming to reintroduce Muslim discoveries impacting today's world. More information could be obtained at: www.1001inventions.com/

Ottomanism were the strongest currents at the time, the Second Constitutional Era (1909–1922) was the period when Turkish nationalism and Turkification became trendy, leading the country toward becoming a national republic.

The early twentieth century saw the beginning of wars and the fall of the empire. Nursi witnessed all these transformations in the last phase of the Ottoman rule as an adolescent and youth during the decline, and an adult throughout the descent of the empire and Caliphate. Throughout this period, Nursi's primary aim was preserving the integrity of Islam. Even though earlier he believed that unity could be achieved through Ottoman identity, as events moved on, he moved toward a pan-Islamic outlook. a pan-Islamic outlook. While pan-Islam would support political and social unity of all Muslim states, Nursi's support was towards spiritual and economical unity of the Muslim world. He wrote and gave sermons about uniting features of Islam and potential dangers of nationalism, materialism, and philosophy contradicting to teachings of the Qur'an. Among the popular trends of the time, Ottomanism, nationalism, and Islamic unity, Nursi was an advocate of Islamic unity.

After World War I and the Independence War, a new secular republic was established in 1923 over the ashes of the Ottoman Empire. Its founder, Mustafa Kemal, was among the supporters of nationalism. He named the country Türkiye, the land of Turks. From the nineteenth century on, such monolithic nationalism has never been fully accepted or appreciated by the country's ethnically diverse population. Despite the regard of the populace, nationalism has been instituted and enforced by the state since the formation of modern Turkey.

Turkey's population still protects the richness of its ethnic diversity including Turkic, Kurd, Arab, Assyrian, Circassian, Laz, and others. The county's 99 percent Muslim population hosts a variety of practices varying from religious movements to Sufi orders. While the country's regime is strictly secular, a significant orthodox[6] presence of religious practice continues to take place, often triggering debates and research in regards to the existence of religious communities and practices in secular systems.

Nursi's Childhood and Early Adolescence

Going back to the late nineteenth century, the years of Nursi's infancy, a major war broke out between Russia and the Ottoman Empire in 1877–1878, known as "The 93 War." The empire lost its provinces in Europe and part of the Balkans and was faced with a dramatic decline in economic activity. The migration and relocation of communities from lost provinces increased economic hardship and the empire struggled to maintain stability. This was the environment that shaped Nursi's

---

[6]   Orthodox will be used as an appositive term referring to practicing individuals and communities.

childhood. As the fourth child born to a family of seven children, his humble home did not escape the growing problems of the empire.

Nursi's father Mirza and mother Nuriye[7] were practicing Muslims known for carefully preserving their piety. His remarkable memory, bright intelligence, and brave personality intrigued his family and village community. Nursi wanted to study and teach like his elder brother Abdullah, who was among Nursi's first instructors.

Nursi was going to be his last name , used following the establishment of the Turkish republic, declaring his affiliation to the village of his birth. The word *nur*, an Arabic noun meaning light, is used in modern day Turkish. This word would come to hold great significance in Said's life. Nursi's village , a little hamlet of 20 houses, was Nurs, accordingly his official last name was Nursi, and his mother's name was Nuriye, meaning woman of light. Mentioning several other instances that the word *nur* came across his life, Nursi notes that the Divine Name *an-Nūr*, The Light, was the one which provided him guidance through troubles he faced regarding understanding divine truths. He also noted that a Qur'anic verse known as 'the *nur* verse' of the chapter *an-Nūr*[8] occupied his thought, enlightened his mind and heart the first.[9] Most importantly his life's major work was entitled the *Risale-i Nur*, the Treatise of Light; its followers are called *Nurcu*, advocates of light; and the community founded on his teachings, despite being fragmented, is known as the *Nur* community.

Nursi received his education in the eastern provinces of Turkey. He started his *medrese*,[10] religious school, education when he was about ten years old, leaving his home for the first time. Nursi's commitment to knowledge and scholarship, led him to travel to the leading *medāris*, plural for *medrese*. He continued to study with different *ulemā*, scholars, so that he might benefit from the different perspectives and expertise. Nursi had a remarkable capacity for learning. He managed to appreciate and understand the distinctive approach of a particular *medrese*, within weeks or months of staying there. His gift for learning and capacity for retaining detailed knowledge caught the attention of many. the attention of many. Following his pursuit, Nursi moved on searching new venues for learning.

One dominant feature of Nursi's character was apparent from his early years; *parrhesia*, speaking candidly. He was always willing to offer his views and challenge a perceived injustice. There were occasions when he challenged older students or corrected scholars. This behavior carried into his later life; leading

---

[7]   Nure or Nura according to one of his biographers. (Şükran Vahide, *Islam in Modern Turkey: An Intellectual Biography of Bediüzzaman Said Nursi*, (New York: SUNY Press, 2005), 3).

[8]   Qur'an: 24:35.

[9]   Said Nursi, *Barla Lahikası*, (Istanbul: Söz Press, 2006), 383.

[10]   Arabic transliteration of the word could be found as *madrasah*. In order to be consistent with the original references, Turkish transliteration of the word will be used.

Nursi to defy injustices and develop a keen understanding of justice based on the Qur'an.

His travels around the *medāris* continued for about five years and left Nursi unsatisfied with his experience. He did not fit in the education system of the time, and was disappointed with not finding the type of quality and attentive education he sought. He turned back to his village Nurs. In despair, he saw a vision of the Prophet Muhammed (peace be upon him) in his dream. Kissing the Prophet's hands to show his respect, Nursi asked for *ilm*, knowledge. The Prophet answered "Knowledge of the Qur'an will be given you on the condition you ask no questions of any of my community".[11] Filled with the spiritual empowerment of this dream, Nursi was back on track to pursue education.

Nursi was settled and content with the *medrese* in Bayezit, in Erzurum where he received his education from Shaykh Muhammad Celali and was given *icazet*, an authorization diploma, earning the title of *Molla*. He is reported to be fourteen or fifteen years old at the time. The form of education by then was studying with distinguished scholars until reaching a satisfactory level deserving of receiving a diploma. Under this open system of education, *mollas* could start their own schools, providing a formal education to any interested student.

Revolutionary Ideas and Activism

Nursi received his diploma in three months, accomplishing the equivalent of what could take up to 15 years of studying. He was able to do this by skipping large chunks of the syllabi and following his own course. Along with the books and material presented to him in three months at this *medrese*, Nursi had already read and memorized an astonishing body of work, including many books considered the building blocks of Islamic theology and philosophy. He was distinguished as having an unusual photographic memory, which allowed him to remember many things he saw only once. One of his biographers, Şükran Vahide notes:

> During his time in Bayezit, Said completed the entire course of study then current in *medreses*. The works studied were heavily annotated with commentaries, commentaries on commentaries, and even commentaries on those commentaries and further explanations, so that to complete the course under normal conditions took the average student fifteen to twenty years. The method was to completely master one book and one subject before passing onto the next.[12]

In 1891, when he was 15 years old, fully accredited as a *molla*, and freshly graduated, Nursi started his own *medrese* in Mardin, a city in southeast Anatolia.

---

[11]   Şükran Vahide, Islam in Modern Turkey: An Intellectual Biography of Bediuzzaman Said Nursi, (New York: SUNY Press, 2005), 9.

[12]   Vahide, *Islam in Modern Turkey*, 10.

He was dynamic and engaged with his students both in and out of the classroom. Beyond their normal curriculum, Nursi and his students took part in hiking, wrestling, and a number of other sports and games.

Nursi traveled around eastern districts, including the cities Bitlis, Siirt, Mardin, Van, and Erzurum. His fame was spreading around eastern provinces and he came to be known as a remarkably clever young scholar. As word of him spread, Nursi was invited by scholars to meet and be tested via debates. He engaged in conversations with *ulemā*; rapidly, he was recognized as a scholar who not only had thoughtful answers, but also could illuminate and contribute to contemporary discussions.

Amazed with this sharp young mind, Molla Fethullah of Siirt gave him the title *Bediüzzaman*, nonpareil or wonder of the age resembling his cleverness to Bediuzzaman Hamadānī (968–1008). As Nursi continued to attract popular attention, governors of eastern provinces decided to protect and support him. In 1895, when he was 19 years old, Nursi was invited to reside at a regional governor's residence in Bitlis.

During his stay in Bitlis, Nursi met with regional governors and other politicians. Through these engagements, he developed an interest in questions about society, politics, and economics.

In 1897, Nursi was invited to Van by Hasan Pasha. He stayed 10 years in Van, first resided with Hasan Pasha for a year, then continued his residence for 9 more years forming a close relationship with the newly appointed governor of the time, Tahir Pasha. Nursi and Tahir Pasha formed a friendship based on mutual respect, whereby Nursi's endeavors in learning and teaching were supported by Tahir Pasha, who in turn received guidance and counseling from him.

His stay and companionship with Tahir Pasha helped Nursi relate with the world at large. He followed newspapers regularly, learning more about the events in the capital of the empire, Istanbul, and the conditions of the world. His biography reports of news he read in these years that significantly shaped Nursi's aims and sharpened his dedication and commitment to serve the Qur'an. In 1898, Tahir Pasha, shared with Nursi a quote in a newspaper from the British secretary for the colonies stating, "So long as the Muslims have the Qur'an, we shall be unable to dominate them. We must either take it from them, or make them lose their love of it." As a response Nursi asserts, "I shall prove and demonstrate to the world that the Qur'an is an undying, inextinguishable Sun!".[13]

A noteworthy development during Nursi's stay in Van came from his access to Tahir Pasha's library, where he studied sciences. He studied math, physics, astronomy, chemistry, biology and geology, and gained depth into history and philosophy. He wrote a book on math, which was destroyed by a fire in the governor's residence prior to its publishing. He also wrote commentaries on logic.

---

[13] Vahide, *Islam in Modern Turkey*, 10.

The intellectual image of nineteenth century Ottoman depicts a clear division among the educated class, educated class, reflected as a polarization of ideas. Of the many types of schools built by Sultan Abdulhamid all over the empire, some attempted to provide training in both modern sciences and religious subject. However, due to a deep social cleavage, only a small minority benefited from these schools. Education was mostly given through given through dual institutions; *mekteb* and *medrese*. The system offered by the former was western oriented, with a focus on a positivist approach to sciences, whereas the latter instituted a classical Islamic education. Nursi received and completed a *medrese* education excelling to its highest ranks, yet continued to improve himself in the sciences of the time. He often expressed his frustration toward traditional religious scholars, whose discussions could not provide solutions to the major problems of the time. For Nursi, religion did not consist solely of faith matters; instead, he argued that due to its comprehensive nature, religion was connected with sociology, politics, and economics.

During this time there was no system of education in the country offering both scientific and religious training. Indeed, *Mekātib and medāris*, as the places of popular education of the time, seemed to carry pride in their separate curricula, each being critical of the other. Nursi was deeply troubled with this schism. While developing his knowledge in these two essential areas, he formed his ideal system of education. Rooted as a teaching scholar in the field of religion Nursi composed a proposal for a university to be established in eastern Anatolia offering a joint education in religion and the sciences.

> The religious sciences are the light of the conscience and the modern sciences (lit. "the sciences of civilization") are the light of the reason; the truth becomes manifest through the combining of the two. The students' endeavor will take flight on these two wings. When they are separated it gives rise to bigotry in the one, and wiles and skepticism in the other.[14]

Moving from the Periphery to the Center

In 1907, Nursi traveled to Istanbul to present his proposal for a university to the empire's Sultan. His petition was presented to the Palace. As the outcome Nursi was going to praise the Sultan's efforts while noting their inapplicability. The university he proposed would offer joint studies of science and religion. He named it *Medresetü'z Zehrā*, to be a sister university to the Azhar University in Cairo.[15] Another intention he had was also to engage with a broader spectrum of

---

[14]   Said Nursi, *Münāzarāt in Bediüzzaman Said Nursi'nin İlk Dönem Eserleri*, (Istanbul: Söz Press, 2007), 508. As translated by Şükran Vahide in Islam in Modern Turkey, 45-56.

[15]   Nursi, *Münāzarāt*, 507.

scholars, intellectuals, and politicians there. Istanbul was the heart of Ottoman intelligentsia, the center of the Muslim world, and an important axis in the world's power balance.

Concerned with the growing gap between *mekteb* and *medrese* scholars and students, Nursi wanted to share his apprehension and warn against the dangers of such a split among the educated of the nation. According to his proposal, all students would have to study both science and religion; it could either be a major in science with a minor in religion or the other way round. The goal was interdisciplinary study, with graduates literate in both realms. The location of the proposed university was also important. Nursi suggested eastern Anatolia, with two major campuses in two important cities. He wanted to connect the distant communities of the empire to the center. Rebellions were growing in every corner of the empire and for Nursi the solution was to provide an enriched education for all.

After being hosted as a guest of Ferik Ahmed Pasha, Nursi rented a room in Şekerci Han, in the Fatih district. The building was a large commercial center providing hostel services used frequently by the scholars and thinkers of the time. This residence marked Şekerci Han as a center for intellectuals of Istanbul. Not having adopted western clothing, which was the trend of the time, coming from the east in traditional clothing Nursi provoked some curiosity. He hung a sign on his door stating, "Here all questions are answered, all problems are solved, but no questions are asked" with the intent to attract attention to the problems of the time, specifically of the backward eastern provinces, and promote occasions to meet and engage with scholars.[16] He was eager to explore the possibility of collaboration with the hope of healing the problems of a much wounded nation and the Muslim world.

Achieving this goal, shortly after his arrival Nursi was engaged with Istanbul's *ulemā*. At the time, Shaykh Muhammad Bakhīt, a grand *mufti*, interpreter and expert of Islamic law, of Egypt and a leading member of the Muslim world's recognized al-Azhar University, was in Istanbul. Shaykh Bakhīt posed a question asking young thinker's view on "freedom and the Ottoman state, and European civilization." He responded that the Ottoman was pregnant with Europe, and Europe with Ottoman. And one day each would deliver the birth of what they carry. Upon this answer, confirming Nursi's title Bediuzzaman, Shaykh Bakhīt said that he had similar opinions, "[b]ut only Bediuzzaman could express it so succinctly and eloquently".[17]

Van's governor Tahir Pasha wrote a letter to Sultan Abdulhamid informing him of Nursi's coming and his high reputation among eastern provinces. Nursi applied for an appointment to meet the Sultan; however, his bold confidence as an eastern scholar coming to the center of the empire to propose a new program on education was not taken well. He was sent to a mental hospital for presenting "this much courage" which was not found to be "conformable with sanity" by the officials.

---

16   Vahide, *Islam in Modern Turkey*, 39.

17   Ibid., 39-41.

Nursi was cleared by a doctor who was left in amazement with his "intelligence and knowledge, courage and bravery." The doctor concluded that the accusation of insanity was due to Nursi's courageous and frank behavior not matching "the refined manners of the age".[18] The ruling was not open to being criticized or challenged, especially by someone coming from its distant periphery.

Nursi found himself in the center of the pre-Second Constitutional Era arguments. Though he was closely engaged in educational and cultural endeavors, Nursi was following the challenges faced by the Empire and the Muslim world. He took to writing. As well as writing many articles, he delivered public speeches to inform people. He strongly rejected any form of despotism, was a staunch supporter of freedom, constitutionalism, and a participatory regime, what would later be called democracy. Advocating constitutionalism, Nursi provided an Islamic justification for it. And as constitutionalism mutated into a call for democracy, Nursi supported this call and described himself as a religious republican. In this context, republic implies the election of the representatives by the people and the importance of the freedom of expression.

As a devoted religious scholar, with a striking charisma, Nursi was in favour of freedom and constitutionalism leaving some surprised. His fondness of freedom was at a level that he said, "I can live without bread, but I can't live without freedom."[19] Nursi took a stand against violent rebellions and played a significant role in stopping some internal conflicts in the empire. His biography notes numerous accounts of these efforts. In 1910, Bediuzzaman Said Nursi traveled to the eastern provinces to meet with local leaders about the conditions of the time, answering their questions about new freedom movements, and informing them of benefits of freedom and constitutional regime versus monarchy. Actually, and importantly, his concern was with 'the common man', in this case the Kurdish tribesmen. His work *Münāzarāt* is composed of these exchanges. Some questions and hesitations about the constitutional era were concerned with the involvement of non-Muslims as leaders and representatives in the parliament. When he was asked about how Armenians could be the head of an official district or governor, Nursi replied that as watchmakers, machine repairmen, or janitors they provided a service to people, which is what he saw as the true purpose of government.[20]

In 1911, Nursi went to Damascus in response to an invitation from the area's religious authorities. He was asked to offer a sermon in the historical Umayyad Mosque. Nursi presented a more elaborate picture of the Muslim world and condition in relation to the west. He identified six severe ailments that marred this condition and offered six remedies for their healing. The sermon was well received and immediately published as *the Damascus Sermon*. To this day, it is regarded as a helpful source and receives much attention both from the Muslim world and abroad.

---

[18] Vahide, *Islam in Modern Turkey*, 51.

[19] Said Nursi, *Emirdağ Lahikası*, (Istanbul: Söz Press, 2006), 41.

[20] Nursi, *Münāzarat*, 507.

Moving toward the epicenter of the events and the empire, in 1911 Bediuzzaman was invited to attend Sultan Reshad's Rumeli trip as the official representative of the eastern provinces. He was also given the aid and promise for his university project in eastern Anatolia. Its construction started, but was interrupted by the First World War. Nursi assembled a defense team of his students and volunteers in protection of the eastern provinces. He served as the general of this volunteers' regiment which was attached to the army as a militia force. It was composed of approximately 5,000 members. He continued teaching his students at any possible occasion and started writing an exegesis *Ishārāt-al Ī'jāz, Signs of Miraculousness*, in 1913.

Post World War I

In 1915, Bediuzzaman was taken captive by Russians after being wounded in Bitlis And was sent to Kostroma camp for prisoners of war. After spending about 20 months there, he escaped through St. Petersburg. He traveled through Poland, Germany, and Bulgaria spending some months in these European countries, once again improving his knowledge. He returned to Istanbul in 1918.

Nursi's return to Istanbul was met with a "hero's welcome" that echoed in the empire's capital and districts. He was chosen to be a member of a new initiation named *Dārü 'l-Hikmet 'il-Islāmiye*, a learned council or Islamic academy seeking solutions of growing problems of the *ummah*.[21] He completed *Ishārāt-al Ī'jāz, Signs of Miraculousness* and composed several other books namely *Tülüāt, Sünūhāt, Lemaāt,* and *İşārāt* during his service at *Dārü 'l-Hikmet* between the years 1918 and 1922.

Bediuzzaman Said Nursi was deeply troubled by the British occupation of Istanbul, as he witnessed the reoccupation in March, 1920. He invited the people of Istanbul to unite and resist against the occupation. He also became a strong supporter of the independence movements in Anatolia known as *Kuva-yi Milliye*. He published a pamphlet entitled *Hutūvāt-ı Sitte* against British occupation aiming to inform people of its dangers not only in regard to Ottoman provinces, but also toward the unity of Islam. He opposed the *shaykh al-Islam*'s *fatwa*, legislation justifying the occupation and issued a statement against it calling for resistance. *Shaykh al-Islam* held the official highest rank of opinion in the Sunni world, comparable to the archbishop in the Anglican Church; Nursi's attitude posed a significant challenge.

It was not surprising that the newly instituted parliament in Ankara started taking an interest in Nursi. Nursi was opposed to the occupation of Istanbul and encouraging a movement of national independence. He was invited to Ankara in 1922 where he spent eight months which was going to be the dawn of a remarkable change in his life.

---

21   Vahide, Islam in Modern Turkey, 133.

Transformation: From Old Said to New Said and Composition of the Risale-i Nur

Nursi supported the constitutionally formed republic from the beginning. However, he was disappointed with the way the republic was evolving in Ankara. Refusing to be affiliated with the politics of the time, he declined the positions he was offered, such as being a member of the parliament, the chief religious official of eastern provinces (*şark umûmi vâizliği*), and membership in the religious affairs department of the government. Seeing dangers surrounding this new formation, he issued 10 articles as a warning to members of parliament in 1923, reminding them of the causes that had required the nation to enter into wars and the sacrifices that people made. He felt that these issues were not being taken seriously by the slowly developing government. He was critical of the lack of religious piety among the parliamentarians. Nursi turned back to Van, to his *medrese* with an intention to teach. However, his life was about to face a dramatic shift that would change everything. The newly founded government was disappointed in Nursi's decision not to support the new regime; and the government feared Nursi's charisma and influence. Keeping him suppressed and under tight control seemed a safe and legitimate solution.

In 1925, around the age of 50 and suffering from chronic illnesses from his days of World War I and captivity in Russia, Nursi was sent into exile in western Anatolia. He was accused of supporting a rebellion in the eastern provinces. This was the beginning of many misconceptions and misunderstandings about his work and ideas leading to 35 years of exile and imprisonment that would dominate the rest of his life. These years of being cast out and in custody were intended to isolate Said from society.

He was deported to little villages where the occupants were forbidden to speak to him or offer any help. Even though he was careful with his food, his biography accounts that he was poisoned 19 times; each time he became ill. Due to his age and other illnesses, he continued to get sick often and kept a light diet consisting of a simple soup and a small amount of bread.

Since the time of his return from Russia, Said was going through a transition period toward a more settled phase in his life. He began referring to himself as New Said after 1926, when he started to write the *Risale-i Nur*. Retrospectively, he referred to himself in his earlier days as Old Said. This marked the transition from his enthusiastic years actively involved with social and political events. Through reflections from his works like *Qatre*, *Zerre*, and later *Mesnevî-i Nuriye*, it can be traced that the New Said had emerged in Istanbul, in 1920 and 1921s. He wrote *Mesnevî-i Nuriye* in Arabic in 1922 to 1923. He later referred to this book as the seed of the *Risale-i Nur*. It is important to note that Nursi's transition from Old to New Said was not a rupture; rather it could be understood as a passage from the restlessness of rivers to the stillness of oceans.

In 1925, after staying for 20 days in Istanbul, he was sent to Burdur, a small town in southwestern Anatolia. Burdur was a location of exile where Nursi resided for 7 months. During his stay, he wrote *Nurun İlk Kapısı, The First Door to Light.*

In 1926, Nursi was sent to Isparta, a small city in the east of Burdur. He was located in the city center and started to engage with people and teach. He was deported again within 20 days, this time to one of the littlest villages of the district named Barla, where he started to write the major work of his life, the *Risale-i Nur*, the Treatise of Light. Nursi lived in Barla for nine years composing most of the *Risale* during this time.

Barla was an isolated village with no connecting roads. Transportation was mainly by boats and animals. Nursi was under tight custody and was banned from even speaking with the few villagers residing in this secluded remote place. A few people attempting to talk him were warned. He was about 50 years old and was going through maybe the most significant transformation in his life. He was left with no book other than the Qur'an he carried. Even though most were scared of its consequences, one by one people started to interact with him. Villagers, farmers, and shepherds would learn matters of faith and religion from him. When Nursi started to write, they were eager to assist him in his efforts.

Their help came in the form of transcribing text and later multiplying it by hand. Nursi would edit any initial transcripts before the process of multiplication. He would go through each written copy for editing after their completion. Since it was restricted by the government to even talk with him, this process was done in remote areas outdoors and in homes behind curtains. Nursi was not allowed to be given nor sold paper or ink. Later this embargo was applied to anyone related to him. Publishing any of his writings was not even an option to be explored due to such restrictions. It was a period when religious education had faded and independent efforts were banned by government. The demand from local people toward these hand written pieces on faith, morality, and religious practices was growing. Soon the town turned to a school with its men, women, and children reading from and transcribing or copying the *Risale*.

In 1934, Nursi was taken from Barla back to Isparta. He was accused of starting a subversive organization intent on challenging the government. In 1935, he was sentenced to one year in prison in Eskişehir with 120 of his students where they were kept under harsh conditions.

In 1936 he was exiled to Kastamonu, a city located in central northern Anatolia, where he spent about seven and a half years. He continued to exchange letters with his students. These letters were collected and later published as *Lahika*. *Āyet-ül Kübrā, The Supreme Sign*, was also written during his stay in Kastamonu. It was also within this period that the *Risale* became known throughout communities and was recorded by pen within multiple districts.

In 1943, Nursi was taken to Ankara, deported back to Isparta and was imprisoned for a year in Denizli with 126 students. *The Fruits of Belief* was written during this period of exile.

In a court in Denizli, the *Risale* was analyzed in its entirety by a group of experts who approved that they were focused on faith matters and did not include anything challenging toward the regime. In 1944 the court ruled in favor of Nursi, his students, and 130 pieces of the *Risale*.

The little hope for freedom that the court's decision brought would not last. Nursi was exiled to Emirdağ, Afyon in 1944 where he continued to write. Though he and his writings were legally available, Nursi was banned from going to the mosque. Even his attire was held against him. The new secular regime's revolutions included changing the alphabet and style of dress, both of which were Westernized. The traditional turban was banned and Western hats were legally required to be worn. Constantly harassed, even by his security guards, to adopt the new way of dress and abandon his own, Nursi notes the psychological pressure of this particular exile.

In 1948, he and 80 of his students were sentenced to imprisonment in Afyon for 20 months. The court in Afyon claimed to not accept the decision of the Denizli court which was in favor of Nursi, his books, and students. Prison conditions were severe. He was slightly over 70 years and was sick at this time and Afyon's harsh winters worsened his condition. Nursi was placed in a cell in the cold winter with no heating, no bathroom, and in total isolation. Nursi recalls his imprisonment in Afyon as the toughest of his experiences, equaling one day's pressure to a month's hardship in the Denizli prison.

Political developments within the Republic at this time played a part in Nursi's work and the way he was received. The Republic existed as a one party government from its establishment in 1923 until 1946 and parliament consisted of only the members of the Republican party. After its shift to a multiple party representation, the Democrat party won the elections in 1950. As one of their earliest actions, they published a general amnesty freeing thinkers of the time. Nursi benefited from this amnesty and some of restrictions on him were lifted. Most importantly, the *Risale* started to be printed in publishing houses and be sent all around the nation and some important centers around the world such as the Vatican. In 1951, Nursi received a thank you letter from the Vatican as a response to the section of the *Risale* that the Vatican recieved.

Even though the *Risale* was analyzed and considered non-subversive by the Denizli court in 1944, prejudiced, baseless, and unjust accusations continued for eight more years. Nursi and his works were fully acquitted by Afyon court in 1956. Nursi called this as "the *Risale-i Nur*'s 'festival'." Even after this date, he was not left alone by security officials of the country.

Nursi remained committed to social justice, but at the same time insisted that his students must not use violence. Nursi, himself, modeled appropriate behavior: even though he had to cope with 35 years of hardship, there is no record that he ever behaved inappropriately towards his accusers. He was invited by the scholars around the Muslim world to reside in their countries as he faced ongoing injustice and his message was suppressed. Nursi responded to them kindly, declining their invitations and insisted on staying in Turkey.

In 1960, he asked his students to take him to Urfa, a city in southeast Turkey affiliated with the Prophet Abraham (Peace be upon him). He chose this location to spend the last days of his life. Nursi was ill, and his stay in Urfa was not long. On March 23, he passed away. His funeral was a major event. The military government that came to rule via coup after his death still considered him a threat and his corpse was removed from his grave and relocated to an undisclosed location. His body was at rest in Urfa for only 111 days. The empty tomb still lies in the *dergah*, shrine, of Abraham in Urfa.

Said Nursi's Legacy: The Risale-i Nur and the Nur Community

While his empty tomb still lies in the shrine of Abraham in Urfa, Nursi lives on in the minds and hearts of those, who read the *Risale-i Nur*. Many are influenced by his life, thoughts, and writings. A newspaper article published at the time of his death noted that students of Nursi were more than one and a half million (Akşam, 24.03.1960). Arguably the number of his followers today is more than 6 million.[22] As a recently emerging formation, about half a century old, the Nur community continues to grow. There have been no specific studies dedicated to the statistical data on the community, perhaps due to its expansion in many different parts of the world and difficulty in collecting concrete statistics. One thing can be confidently noted that the community is visibly enlarging on local and global scales as Bediuzzaman Said Nursi and the *Risale-i Nur* collection are attracting attention both in various parts of the Muslim world and the West.

The Nur community is a text-based formation with a strong emphasis on community. Nursi advised his students to construct study circles to read, learn, and have discussions of the *Risale*. Simultaneous to the composition stage of the *Risale*, numerous study circles and discussion groups were formed by scribes, readers, and students of this text. This community was organically established as followers of Nursi continued to multiply manuscripts by handwriting and sharing them with people in their families and neighborhoods. These circle or discussion group meetings continue to be held, mostly in homes or locations called *dershane*, study-homes that often serve as student housing dedicated to the study of the *Risale*. *Dershanes* can be found in Turkey or elsewhere around the world where followers of the community live. Bringing people from different professions and backgrounds together, a typical community is composed of men and women of every age, including elderly and children, all of whom actively participate in various ways.

The Nur community gained its identity and was shaped through correspondences between Nursi and his students as well as exchanges among his students. Of the 15 volumes of the *Risale-i Nur*, three consist of selected letters from these exchanges. Named as *Lāhikalar*, appendixes, these writings serve as a guide to the community and are used to this day. Letters included in these *Lāhikalar* are often written in question and answer format and deal with various topics from theological conversations to jurisprudential matters, mostly on topics regarding ways to

---

[22] M. Hakan Yavuz, *Islamic Political Identity in Turkey*, (Oxford: Oxford University Press, 2003), 11.

strengthen faith. Central to the *Risale* is the theme of transforming imitative belief to a conscious and verified belief, righteousness, preserving a pious life, ethics and social relationships, methods of serving the religion, intellectual and spiritual struggle, and politics.

The development and distribution of this way of thinking and its implication for matters of faith continued with the emergence of various publishing houses, organizations, foundations, educational institutions, press and media, publications and journals, and academic studies. These developments included the translation of the *Risale-i Nur* collection. Starting with Arabic and English translations in 1990s, the majority of the text has been translated into more than 35 languages including most European and Asian languages, and African dialects.

The *Risale* encourages critical thinking and fosters variations in thought. This feature of the text and teachings of the *Risale* is both characteristic of and conducive to a community that is not monolithic. The community has about 10 fragmentations. Partitioning happened through a divergence of ideas around participation in social arenas, that is, political involvement, the use and mission of media organs, prioritizing areas of service, and similar concerns. Each of these matters was rooted in a particular understanding of the text leading toward different stances and nuanced practices. Of the main fragmentations, most of these groups support one another through collaborative projects and attend events organized by one another. A major example of this is international symposiums on Bediuzzaman Said Nursi held in Istanbul, where thousands of *Nurcus* from most groups attend.

The largest partition of the community is the *Gülen* group named after its founder Fethullah Gülen (b.1941). With education as its primary goal, the group has established approximately 200 schools around the world. This branch also stands out as having the most media outlets, including television channels, a newspaper, several journals and publishing companies, along with other non-profit and profit oriented organizations such as hospitals.

What makes Bediuzzaman Said Nursi and the Risale-i Nur important?

Bediuzzaman Said Nursi was a Muslim theologian who wrote a thematic commentary of the Qur'an. This characteristic of his exegesis, the *Risale-i Nur*, is unique compared to traditional commentaries of the Qur'an which interpret the verses of the text according to the order in which they appear. This makes the *Risale* more accessible to people who are not students or scholars of religion, who can still follow the exegete's arguments and grasp the topics being discussed. For Muslim scholars and students of religion, this provides a contemporary and fresh outlook to the scripture. For non-Muslims, this exegesis provides an insight into different themes of Islamic scripture, providing a thematically organized presentation of the way these topics are addressed throughout the Qur'anic text. Concepts of belief and God, scripture, revelation, purpose of life and creation, life after death, human responsibility and accountability, justice and worship are among the themes to be found in the *Risale*.

Nursi believed that the exegesis of the *Risale* should reflect this tone of the Qur'an, emphasizing the universality of the message and language of the scripture. If the audience of the Qur'an is all conscious creation, for Nursi, a commentary of this scripture should reflect this inclusivity by addressing not only Muslims, but all believing and non-believing individuals.

Having the Qur'an as the source and the teacher, Nursi was highly concerned about reflecting the scripture's characteristics fairly by staying honest to its nature. He noted that although the scripture deals with many different topics, there are four major themes within the Qur'an that serve as an undertone to all other topics addressed by the text. These are *tawhid*, oneness of God, prophethood, afterlife, and the significance of justice and worship. The main themes in the *Risale* are in accordance with these four concepts. A strong emphasis is placed on faith, ways to obtain knowledge of God, the purpose of creation, and humankind's responsibility in relation to this cosmic purpose. Nursi repeatedly challenges views describing the condition of human beings as coincidental, unattended or neglected. He defines creation and the universe as a book, like the Qur'an, teaching us of our Creator.

Another important feature making Said Nursi's *Risale* pertinent for today's reader is its reflection of the life he lived, from the challenges he faced to the interactions he had with people of different faiths. Readers of the *Risale*, no matter the generational gap between themselves and Nursi, may find elements of his experience that they can relate to or may have shared.

Having struggled to observe a devout life while experiencing a harsh application of secularism targeting any form of religious expression, Said Nursi asserted that a true practice of secularism should protect freedom of conscience and one's right to practice religion freely. He was a dedicated advocate of positive action and strongly challenged the use of violence. By encouraging constructive behavior, Bediuzzaman Said Nursi interpreted *jihad* as spiritual struggle or struggle with words.

Nursi's interactions with both religious and secular conservatives, Muslims of various schools of thought, believers of other faiths, and those who make no claim to faith are reflected in his writings. His openness to various ways of thinking and believing characterizes the *Risale* and demonstrates his support for freedom of speech, freedom of conscience, and preserving the dignity of humanity and their rights.

Reflection Questions

1. What were the important factors that shaped the worldview of Bediuzzaman Said Nursi?
2. What is the Nur community? Identify some of the main subgroups?
3. How does the approach of Said Nursi compare to the approaches taken by other major twentieth-century thinkers?

Chapter 2
The Concepts of God and the Qur'an

In this chapter, we shall explore the concepts of God and the Qur'an, which are central to an Islamic worldview. Due to the confines of space, the discussion of these major themes, about which Said Nursi had much to say in his voluminous corpus, is difficult. However, we shall provide an overview of both the picture of God in Islam and the text on which that picture is based.

Concept of God in Islam

Islam is a monotheistic religion with a great emphasis on *tawhid*, oneness and unity of God whose divine nature is considered beyond the comprehension of individual or collective human understanding. God communicates through messengers and prophets, revealing through them books that serve as guides. Gaining knowledge of the Divine is not only possible through channels that God reveals, but also through sound reasoning.[1]

A key component of knowledge of the Divine nature is the Names. A Qur'anic verse states "To Him belong the most Beautiful Names,"[2] revealing that a way to know God is through His names and attributes. An understanding of this verse is that Names of God are infinitely many visibly and invisibly filling the earth and the heavens. The 99 oft referred Divine Names are mentioned in an authentic *Hadith*. Another source is *Jawshan al-Kabīr*, a supplication of the Prophet that holds a significant importance in Nursi's understanding of the Divine names, in which God is exalted with a 1,001 names. All attributes and actions belonging to God are united in One Unique and Supreme Being, Eternal and Absolute; whom all creatures need, while God needs no one.

The following extract illustrates an example of Nursi's interpretation of the Divine Names:

A sultan has different titles in the spheres of his government, and different styles and attributes among the classes of his subjects, and different names and signs in the levels of his rule, for example, Just Judge in the judiciary, Sultan in the civil service, Commander-in-Chief in the army, and Caliph in the learned establishment. If, making an analogy with these, you know the rest of his names

---

[1]   Islamic theology considers God's Supreme Being beyond gender. Though Arabic, the language of the main sources of Islam, has gendered pronouns, the belief system does not resemble God to any creation nor affiliates with any gender.

[2]   Qur'an, 20:8.

and titles, you will understand that a single sultan may possess a thousand names and titles in the spheres of his rule and levels of government. It is as if, through his corporate personality and telephone, the ruler is present and knowing in every sphere; and through his laws and regulations and representatives, sees and is seen; and behind the veil in every degree, disposes and sees, governs and observes through his decree, knowledge, and power.

It is exactly the same for the Sustainer of All the Worlds, Who is the Ruler of Pre-Eternity and Post-Eternity; in the degrees of His dominicality He has attributes and designations which are all different but which look to each other; and in the spheres of His Godhead He has names and marks which are all different but which are one within the other; and in His magnificent activities He has representations and appellations which are all different but which resemble each other; and in the disposals of His power He has titles which are all different but which hint of one another; and in the manifestations of His attributes He has sacred appearances which are all different but which show one another; and in the displays of His acts He has wise disposals which are of numerous sorts but which complete one another; and in His multicoloured art and varieties of creatures, He has splendid aspects of dominicality which are all different but which look to one another. And together with this, in every world, in every realm of beings, the title of one of the Most Beautiful Names is manifested. In each sphere one Name is dominant and the other Names are subordinate to it, rather, they are there on account of it.[3]

Among the many names are *Allah*, the Almighty, *Rahmān* and *Rahīm*, The Most Gracious and Merciful, *Ahad*, *Samad*, the Eternally Besought, *Alīm*, the All-Knowing, Hakīm, the All-Wise, *Khaliq*, the Creator, *Ghafūr*, the Forgiver, *Rabb*, the Sustainer, *Razzāq*, the Provider, *Jalīl* the Sublime, *Nūr*, the Light, *Bāqī*, the Everlasting, and so on. In a section explaining to whom humans offer their worship and supplication, Nursi states:

> the only True Object of Worship will be One in Whose hand are the reins of all things, with Whom are the treasuries of all things, Who sees all things, and is present everywhere, who is beyond space, exempt from impotence, free of fault, and far above all defect; an All-Powerful One of Glory [*Qadīr-i Dhul Jalāl*], an All-Compassionate One of Beauty, [*Rahīm –i Dhul Jamāl*], an All-Wise One of Perfection [*Hakīm-i Dhul Kamāl*].[4]

A central element of Islamic theology that must be stressed is the love of God. This love is reciprocal between God and creation and is manifested throughout all that exists. One of the "beautiful names" of God is *al-Wadūd*, the Loving One, who loves His creation. This name implies that God created the entire cosmos in

---

[3]   Said Nursi, 'Twenty-Fourth Word, First Branch' in *The Words*, 341–342. <http://www.erisale.com/index.jsp?locale=en#content.en.201.341 >

[4]   Said Nursi, *The Words*, (Söz Press, 2009), 328. Available online at http://www.erisale.com/index.jsp?locale=en.

a loving manner. Through this insight, a believer recognizes an intimate bond of love between the Creator and creation, and among all creation for they exist by the will of the Beloved.

Reflecting on this name, Nursi concludes that all of creation is bound to one another with this Divine love. Regarding cosmic rules and laws of physics, he describes the force of mass attraction as a visible manifestation of Divine love. Describing that gravity is embedded in everything, from atoms to stars, as a signature-like law of God, a force that keeps the cosmos bound to one another and in order. Everything in creation, he says, is "adorned and decked out from top to bottom with purposes and instances of wisdom, and you know that the earth revolves and is turned like an ecstatic Mevlevi [whirling dervish] in perfect order within most exalted aims."[5] Understanding and explaining the nature of the Divine and the Divine's relationship to humanity continue to be vital tasks not only for theologians, but also for believers of various traditions.

The Qur'an

The Qur'an, the holy scripture of Islam, is the primary source of the religion. There has been a strong agreement among Muslims on the Qur'an's unique ontological status; it is believed to be the very Words of God. The Qur'an is regarded as God-speech; a channel of God's revealing Himself to humanity. It was revealed to Prophet Muhammad within the course of 23 years signifying the gradual transformation of a society and marking the duration of his prophecy. Its revelation began in AD/CE 610, when the Prophet was at the age of 40, and had made a trip to cave *Hira* on the *al-Nur* Mountain located in the east of Makkah; a place he would often go for contemplation.

Contrary to widespread early Orientalist notions that the Qur'an was authored by Prophet Muhammad, falsely considered divine as Jesus is in Christianity; Muslims accept the Qur'an as the greatest miracle given to Prophet Muhammad and regard him as fully human. Muslims regard Prophet Muhammad as the noblest of human beings, a messenger and teacher of Divine Signs that are revealed both in the Qur'an and universe. His sayings and deeds, *Hadith*, secondary to the Qur'an, are among the foundational sources of the religion.

A distinctive feature of the Qur'an is its method of preservation. Muslims hold an opinion that the message has been preserved as it was revealed and since the time of its revelation it has been preserved without change. So, the Muslim belief is that the Qur'an consists of the revealed words of God that are not authored, but only transcribed by humans. Due to this firm belief, the Qur'an is well respected and has an authoritative position in the lives of Muslims. While there are noteworthy similarities among the message of the Qur'an, Torah, and the Bible (such as the notions of faith, the Creator God, who communicates through messengers, belief

---

5   Nursi, *The Words*, 184.

in afterlife, call for righteousness, and so on), a major difference is found regarding the methods of the books' preservation.

It is important to briefly mention the meaning of the terms *revelation* and *inspiration* according to Islam for each term holds specific meanings. *Revelation* is sent by God explicitly to prophets through the angel Gabriel, the "angel of revelation." *Inspiration* is considered as a general communication of God with His creation. From dreams to scientific discoveries, wise actions to art works, any knowledge is understood to be rooted in Divine inspiration. Mentioning the difference between the two, Nursi considers revelation as "elevated, universal, and sacred" and inspiration more specific to a person and as very "insignificant" in comparison to revelation. Also, he claims that to "suppose inspiration to be like Revelation, and of similar kind to Revelation" would lead one to "fall into an abyss."[6]

Among the themes the Qur'an mentions are creation, revelation, afterlife, human soul, and society. As mentioned, four major topics could be noted as *tawhid*, Divine unity, and belief in God; prophethood, signifying the special way of God's communication with His creation through revelation; afterlife, as reminder of accountability and living a responsible life; justice and worship, as a main purpose of creation of humankind and conscious beings. All beings are created in the wisest and most just state with an intendedmapurpose. Part of the conscious beings' responsibility is understood to recognize the functions, in a way specific worship of every kind, and offer them to the Creator in the form of their prescribed worship.

Beyond considering it as "both a book of invocation, and a book of prayer, and a book of summons,"[7] Nursi defines the Qur'an as:

> both a book of wisdom and law, and a book of prayer and worship, and a book of command and summons, and a book of invocation and Divine knowledge.[8]

Miraculousness of the Qur'an is often emphasized in the *Risale-i Nur*. One of the early books of the collection *Signs of Miraculousness* is dedicated to "the inimitability of the Qur'an's conciseness" as is the Twenty-Fifth Word on "The Miraculousness of the Qur'an." It is "the treasury of miracles and supreme miracle," Nursi says, that "proves the Prophethood of Muhammad (PBUH) together with Divine unity so decisively that it leaves no need for further proof."[9]

Furthermore, he notes:

> If you look at the Qur'an with the eyes of a sound heart, you will see that its six aspects are so brilliant and transparent that no darkness, no misguidance, no doubt or suspicion, no trickery could enter it or find a fissure through which to

---

[6] Said Nursi, *The Letters*, (Söz Press, 2009), 520. Available online at http://www.erisale.com/index.jsp?locale=en

[7] Nursi, *The Words*, 250.

[8] Ibid., 250.

[9] Ibid., 250.

enter and violate its purity. For above it is the stamp of miraculousness; beneath it, proof and evidence; behind it, its point of support, pure dominical revelation; before it, the happiness of this world and the next; on its right, questioning the reason and ensuring its confirmation; on its left, calling on the conscience to witness and securing its submission; within it is self-evidently the pure guidance of the Most Merciful; its outside observedly consists of the lights of belief; and its fruits, with all certainty the purified and veracious scholars and saints, who are adorned with all the human perfections and attainments. If you fasten your ear to the breast of that tongue of the Unseen, you will hear from afar a most familiar and convincing, an infinitely serious and elevated heavenly voice equipped with proof which repeats *"There is no god but God."* It states this so certainly it is at the degree of "absolute certainty", and illuminates you with a "knowledge of certainty" resembling "vision of certainty."[10]

Nursi on God

It is important to emphasize that Said Nursi was deeply committed to Islam and its main sources, the Qur'an and *Hadith*. As the previous chapter mentioned, belief is foundational to his work, the *Risale-i Nur*. Having witnessed major changes reshaping the world, Nursi foresaw possible threats to the religion. In the face of attempts to distort or harm the foundation of religion, he aimed to preserve it by revitalizing an outlook closely linked with reason and logic. He concluded that many problems of the time were due to weakness of belief in the pillars of faith. Diagnosing the illness of the age as weakness of belief, he dedicated his writings and endeavors to the cause of strengthening faith.[11] A significant aim for Nursi was transforming cultural and implicit belief into a conscious and justified belief. He saw that cultural and implicit belief was too weak to stand before the doubt-inducing questions of the time that could be resisted only with a faith sustained by reasonable proofs.

Nursi specified "three great and universal things which make known" God to human beings; the universe, the Prophet, and the Qur'an.[12] On one account he adds a fourth, namely conscience.[13] Focused on these channels, the primary purpose of his writings is to cultivate faith and prove its vitality for human happiness both for the worldly life and in the hereafter.

Nursi states that each of these channels manifests the Necessarily Existent God, His Divine art and actions in different ways. Every reflection is a manifestation of God's Divine names through which the Almighty is known to His conscious creation. Multiplicity of reflections of the Divine names does not contradict with

---

[10]   Nursi, *The Words*, 316.

[11]   Said Nursi, *Kastamonu Lahikası*, (Istanbul: Söz Press, 2006), 133.

[12]   *The Words*, Nineteenth Word, p. 243.

[13]   *Mesnevi-i Nuriye*, Nokta, p. 208–215.

the concept of *tawhid*, Divine unity. *Tawhid*, "the mighty truth of Divine unity"[14] as Nursi refers to it, has an immense emphasis in the *Risale-i Nur* as one of the four major themes of the Qur'an:

> The Oneness of the Divine Essence together with the universality of the Divine acts, the Unity of Almighty God's person together with His unassisted comprehensive dominicality, His Singleness together with His unshared all-embracing disposal, His being beyond space and yet present everywhere, His infinite exaltedness together with being close to all things, and His being One and yet Himself holding all matters in His hand, are among the truths of the Qur'an.[15]

Oneness and unity are two indissoluble aspects of understanding God and accordingly the Divine names. An important component deserving attention is the absoluteness of Divine oneness which does not accept any fragmentation. Elaborating on this Nursi states:

> the Most Pure and Holy One is without like, Necessarily Existent, utterly remote from matter, and beyond space; His fragmentation and division is impossible in every respect as is any sort of change or alteration; His being needy or impotent is beyond the bounds of possibility.[16]

For Nursi, these two concepts are understood with the help of one another. For example "the meaning of Divine Oneness" unfolds "within the light of Divine Unity."[17] With an acknowledgement that it can be an overwhelming task to grasp the meaning of these concepts, he offers an illustration of the sun and its reflections on any thing that has a reflective surface.

In order not to overwhelm minds by Divine Unity, which is apparent in the boundless multiplicity of creatures, the Qur'an of Miraculous Exposition constantly points out the manifestation of Divine Oneness within Divine Unity. For example, the sun encompasses numberless things with its light. In order to consider the sun itself in the totality of its light, a most extensive conceptual ability and comprehensive view is necessary. So, lest the sun itself be forgotten, it is displayed in every shining object by means of its reflection. And in accordance with the capacity of each, all shining objects display the sun's qualities, such as its light and heat, together with the manifestation of its essence. And just as in accordance with their capacities, all lustrous objects show the sun together with all its attributes, so too do the sun's qualities, like its light and heat and the seven colors in its light, all encompass all the things facing it.

---

[14]　　Nursi, *The Words*, 298.

[15]　　Ibid., 209.

[16]　　Said Nursi, *The Flashes*, (Söz Press, 2009), 437. Available online at http://www.erisale.com/index.jsp?locale=en.

[17]　　*The Flashes*, 18.

In the same way, *And God's is the highest similitude*[18] -but let there be no mistake in the comparison-just as Divine Oneness and Eternal Besoughtedness have a manifestation together with all the Divine Names in everything, in animate creatures in particular, and especially in man's mirror-like essence, so too through Divine Unity does each of the Divine Names connected to beings encompass all beings. Thus, lest minds become overwhelmed by Divine Unity and hearts forget the Most Pure and Holy Essence, the Qur'an constantly puts before the eyes the Stamp of Divine Oneness within Divine Unity.[19]

The sun allegory is repeatedly used in the Risale-i Nur to exemplify Divine Unity and Oneness. Nursi mentions that every part of creation has their share according to their given ability to mirror the various manifestations of the Divine Names and accordingly a range of degrees occur in mirroring. He writes:

> The sun has manifestations from a fragment of glass, to a droplet of water, a pool, the ocean, and the moon to the planets. Each contains the sun's reflection and image in accordance with its capacity, and knows its limits. In accordance with its capacity, a drop of water says: "There is a reflection of the sun on me." But it cannot say: "I am a mirror like the ocean." ... Each of the Divine Names has manifestations like a sun, from the heart to the Divine Throne. The heart too is a Throne, but it cannot say: "I too am like the Divine Throne."[20]

Nursi asserts that there is "a sign of oneness, a stamp of unity" which could be seen over the universe and everything in it. "For while being the same, certain things are all-encompassing. And while being numerous, some display a unity or similarity, since they resemble one another and are found everywhere. As for unity, it shows One of Unity. That means that its maker, owner, lord, and fashioner has to be one and the same."[21] Pondering on the topic, he expands it with an illustration of the signs of Divine oneness:

> [God] placed many stamps of oneness on all species and numerous seals of unity on all universals, as well as the various stamps of unity on the world as a whole. Of those many seals and stamps, we shall point out one on the page of the face of the earth in the springtime. It is like this:

> The Pre-Eternal Inscriber's raising to life in the spring and summer at least three hundred thousand species of plants and animals with complete distinction and differentiation and total order and separation amid infinite intermingling and confusion, is a stamp of Divine unity as clear and brilliant as the spring itself. Yes, anyone with an iota of consciousness will understand that to create with

---

[18] Qur'an, 16:60.

[19] Nursi, *The Words*, 19–20.

[20] Nursi, *The Flashes*, 180–181.

[21] Nursi, *The Words*, 294.

perfect order while raising to life of the dead earth in the spring, three hundred thousand samples of the resurrection of the dead, and to write without fault, error, mistake or deficiency, in most well-balanced, well-proportioned, well-ordered, and perfect fashion the individual members of three hundred thousand different species one within the other on the face of the earth, is a seal particular to an All-Glorious One, an All-Powerful One of Perfection, an All-Wise One of Beauty, possessing infinite power, all-encompassing knowledge, and a will capable of governing the whole universe.[22]

Nursi on Creation and the Role of Human Beings

Throughout the *Risale-i Nur* is the Qur'anic notion that God created everything with a purpose. Based on this belief, God charged human beings with certain duties, placed them on the transient earth for a trial and examination, and gave them faculties to discover His attributes that are manifested throughout the universe in various forms. The highest aim for humanity is to complete their faith with knowledge and love of God. As Nursi states:

> Be certain of this, that the highest aim of creation and its most important result are belief in God. The most exalted rank in humanity and its highest degree are the knowledge of God contained within belief in God. The most radiant happiness and sweetest bounty for jinn and human beings are the love of God contained within the knowledge of God. And the purest joy for the human spirit and the sheerest delight for man's heart are the rapture of the spirit contained within the love of God. Indeed, all true happiness, pure joy, sweet bounties, and untroubled pleasure lie in knowledge of God and love of God; they cannot exist without them.[23]

Through Divine revelation the wisdom behind the creation of the universe and human beings is learned. Based on a Qur'anic verse, Nursi concludes that humankind is a responsible agent of God.[24] In relation to "the most beautiful names" of God, which stands out as a central theme of the *Risale-i Nur*, Nursi expands on the humans role and the purpose of creation.

The creation narrative is mentioned several times in the Qur'an, symbolizing the significance of the relationship between humanity and the Creator. These narrations depict in detail the awe-inspiring cosmic event of creation.

One narrative of creation describes God appearing before a great assembly of angels to announce that He is *"about to place a vicegerent in the earth!"*[25] As

---

22   Nursi, *The Words*, 307–308.

23   Nursi, *Letters*, 262.

24   Qur'an, 33:72.

25   Qur'an, 2:30.

the verse unfolds, humans learn that the purpose of their creation is to exist as vicegerents of God on earth, to be in relation with the rest of creation as a caretaker. Other passages describe the creation of humans from clay and make mention of the knowledge and skills humans have been equipped with for fulfilling the role of vicegerency.

The creation of humans is distinct in relation to other forms of creation, whereby their fitrah, innate nature, has been endowed with God's spirit. As the verse follows, God creates a mortal of clay and states *"When I have shaped him, and breathed into him of My spirit."*[26] To be filled with Divine spirit signifies reflecting the attributes of God.[27] The Qur'an emphasizes that along with manifesting the attributes of God, humans have been granted knowledge from God, symbolized by the teaching of Adam at the time of his creation; *"He taught Adam the names, all of them."*[28]

Knowledge of "the Divine names," Nursi notes, is the "greatest miracle in the question of the supreme vicegerency." He further elaborates that while every Prophets' miracles are related to "a particular human wonder," Adam's miracle stands out as the one impacting "all human attainment and progress, and humanity's final goals." The comprehensiveness of this knowledge, passed on through Adam, mirrors his position as the forefather of all humankind and all the Prophets.[29] The name Adam refers not only to the first human being, but also to all of humankind.

With the breath of the Divine flowing through their souls and having been granted access to the knowledge of God's nature, human beings have been prepared for taking up the role of vicegerency on earth. These Qur'anic accounts of the manner in which humans were created and granted certain gifts from their Creator set the foreground for a better understanding of the role of vicegerency in Nursi's thought.

Nursi on Vicegerency and the Trust

A central idea of Nursi's description of human beings is that they are "the choice result of the universe and the most important creature in the view of the Creator."[30] A human, he states is "the summary and result of the universe, and God's vicegerent on earth, and its delicate fruit."[31] Nursi relates the position of vicegerency, with the acceptance of the Trust,[32] which exalts human beings to an elevated rank over

---

[26]   Qur'an, 38:72.

[27]   This account of creation is understood in relation to the concept of humans being created in the image of God; a concept that is not mentioned in the Qur'an, but in *Hadith Qudsi.*

[28]   Qur'an, 2:31.

[29]   Nursi, *The Words,* 270.

[30]   Said Nursi, *The Damascus Sermon,* Translated by Şükran Vahide, 2nd ed. (Istanbul: Sozler Publication, 1996), 43.

[31]   Nursi, *The Words,* 442.

[32]   The Qur'anic verse about the offering of the Supreme Trust is as follows: *"We did indeed offer the Trust to the heavens, and the earth, and the mountains; but they refused*

the rest of creation and charges them with the duty of caretaker of other beings in the universe.[33]

Interpreting vicegerency and Trust oftentimes revolves around worldly dominion and political leadership. Particularly, since the fall of the last caliphate, numerous works have been produced solely focusing on a state-related analysis of the topic. It cannot go unnoticed that despite witnessing the major changes of the twentieth century, Nursi preferred to explain these two concepts from a more spiritual and moral perspective, revolving around love and responsibility; which have been overshadowed by state-associated interpretations.

The *Risale-i Nur*, illustrates the importance of a faith-based approach to concepts of vicegerency and Trust, expanding on the meaning of vicegerency and how this significant role is developed and nurtured, particularly in response to the human ego or self.

In his explanation of the Supreme Trust, Nursi describes the human "I" or ego, as an element of the Trust which is "the key" to the treasure of Divine Names. Nursi refers to a famous *Hadith* where God states that He was a hidden treasure and wanted to be known, therefore He created the world.[34] In relation to this *Hadith*, "the names" taught to Adam are referred to as the knowledge given to humanity of Divine attributes. This act of teaching is God revealing Himself to creation so that He may be known and loved. This Divine knowledge, Nursi notes, is both the seed and culmination of all knowledge.[35]

Among the many descriptions of human beings, Nursi notes that, human being "is such an antique work of art of Almighty God. He is a most subtle and graceful miracle of His power whom He created to manifest all his Names and their inscriptions, in the form of a miniature specimen of the universe."[36]

God equipped human beings with an "I" as Trust, "which comprises indications and samples that show and cause to recognize the truths of the attributes and functions of His dominicality."[37] Nursi introduces the "I" as "a unit of measurement" with which "the attributes of dominicality and functions of Divinity might be known."

Nursi pays great attention to this "unit of measurement," describing it as imaginary, lacking concrete subsistence like the "hypothetical lines in geometry."[38] It is a component, offering a glimpse of understanding of the unbounded and immeasurable Divine attributes. The Just God granted humans with indications and evidences of Divine attributes, opening windows of knowledge to them to know and discover their Creator. Unless humans were provided skills of comprehension,

---

to undertake it being afraid thereof. But man assumed it; indeed, he is most unjust, most foolish" (Qur'an, 33:72).

[33]   Nursi, *The Damascus Sermon*, 42.

[34]   Nursi, *The Words*, 557–558.

[35]   Nursi, *Letters*, 262.

[36]   Nursi, *The Words*, 320.

[37]   Ibid., 558.

[38]   Nursi, *The Words*, 558.

speech, seeing, hearing, and all capacities for understanding, it would not be possible for them to grasp Divine attributes and the ways they operate in the cosmos.

The "I," helps human beings "draw a hypothetical and imaginary limit." In Nursi's words, the "I,"

> imagines in itself a fictitious dominicality, ownership, power, and knowledge: it draws a line. By doing this it places an imaginary limit on the all-encompassing attributes, saying, "Up to here, mine, after that, His;" it makes a division. With the tiny units of measurement in itself, it slowly understands the true nature of the attributes.[39]

When God granted self-knowledge as a component of measurement, Nursi describes that it served as a key to unlock the hidden treasure of the knowledge of the Divine names. Expanding on "I" as the unit of understanding God's immense attributes, Nursi gives examples of a person's insight:

> "Like I am the owner of this house, so too is the Creator the owner of the universe." And with its partial knowledge, it may understand His knowledge, and with its small amount of acquired art, it may understand the originative art of the Glorious Maker. For example, the "I" says: "As I made this house and arranged it, so someone must have made the universe and arranged it," and so on. Thousands of mysterious states, attributes, and perceptions which make known and show to a degree all the Divine attributes and functions are contained with the "I". That is to say, the "I" is mirror-like, and, like a unit of measurement and tool for discovery, it has an indicative meaning; having no meaning in itself, it shows the meaning of others.[40]

Humans are nourished by the light of God's attributes; they carry manifestations of Divine names, and reflect them back to the rest of creation. While Nursi sees these manifestations as a Trust of God which is a tool for unfolding the mystery of the Divine knowledge, he warns that if the "I" abandons its imaginary state and assumes a reality to itself, claiming ownership of Divine reflections, it would betray the Trust.[41] Nursi keenly declares that the unique capacity and abilities endowed to human beings through their innate nature is nothing but manifestations of the attributes of their Creator. Including humans, the entire creation serves as a constant mirror of these attributes. However, it is only humankind that is able and expected to read and understand these reflections, and respond accordingly.

An important aspect of vicegerency is evident in the constant reminders within the Qur'an and *Hadith* about weakness, forgetfulness, and vulnerability of human beings. Nursi calls readers attention to this weakness, mentioned in

---

[39]   Ibid., 558.

[40]   Ibid., 559.

[41]   Ibid., 560.

the continuation of the Qur'anic creation scene, where Adam is lured by Satan's deception.[42] Wisdom of the Book reminds believers that while the vicegerents of the Divine are exalted above the rest of creation, human beings are in constant need of guarding themselves against any misguidance and neglect of their role. Nursi proclaims human beings ought to study Divine names continuously and take them as their guidance in progressing toward pleasing their creator.[43]

In discussing the "delicate senses" and "sensitive faculties" humans have been created with, Nursi speaks of them in relation to two main goals set for humanity. First, that they would use these faculties to give thanks and worship God in a comprehensive way; with knowledge, awareness, and appreciation of His numerous and diverse bounties. Second, that they would employ these senses and faculties to witness the manifestations of God's attributes and believe in them, responding to God's desire to make Himself known to humankind. Humanity's perfection can be achieved only through these aims. Through their attainment Nursi writes, "*insan* [human being] becomes a true human being."[44]

To be a true human being is to have faith; to come to know the Divine through His attributes, and worship God; adoring the Almighty through acts of love, such as prayer. The Qur'an declares that human beings are created for the worship of God alone. Nursi understood that being an adorer of God, is the foundation and completion of human vicegerency. Knowledge of Divine attributes, he concludes, is the vital element in the journey of human beings toward becoming a perfect adorer of their Creator.

Nursi on Reflective Thought

In Islam, worship is not only understood in its formal forms of prescribed prayers, fasting, or giving charity. Pondering on God's creation and the channels of His revelations, pursuing knowledge to gain better insights of His names, and having reflective thought about his creation are all considered within the range of worship. As Nursi calls it that would be "worship in the form of reflection."[45] Relating the importance of contemplation to the very sources of the religion, Nursi states:

> [M]y heart combined with my mind and urged me to the way of reflective thought which the Qur'an of Miraculous Exposition commands with such verses as,
>
> That you may consider.(2:219; 2:266) * Perchance they may reflect.(7:176, and so on) * Do they not reflect in their own minds, did God create the heavens and the earth?(30:8) * There are signs for those who consider.(13:3, and so on)

---

42   Qur'an, 2:36.
43   Nursi, *The Words,* 270.
44   Ibid., 139.
45   Nursi, *The Words,* 465.

The Hadith the meaning of which is "An hour's reflective thought is better than a year's [supererogatory] worship"[1] states that on occasion an hour's reflection may be equivalent to a year's worship. It also offers powerful encouragement for reflective thought.[46]

Before taking a closer look at some of the examples of the reflective thought Nursi illustrated in the *Risale-i Nur*, we will pause to review the functions of the channels revealing God mentioned above. Prophet Muhammad is a needed teacher of the two books, the Qur'an and the book of the universe. Through his teachings, he solves and expounds the strange riddle of the mystery of the world's creation; he discovers and solves the abstruse talisman which is the mystery of the universe; and he provides convincing and satisfying answers to the three awesome and difficult questions that are asked of all beings and have always bewildered and occupied minds: "Where do you come from? What are you doing here? What is your destination?"[47]

Questions such as these trigger critical thinking of nature of humankind and their role are examples of ideas leading toward reflective thought.

Nursi does not consider these channels as independent from one another, rather he deems them to be closely linked to one another coming from the same source and reflecting the same meanings in different ways. Each one helps increase the insight of the others. Mentioning the book of the universe, a key concept in the *Risale-i Nur*, he names it as the "embodied Qur'an." It is the Qur'an that is looked at, felt, and experienced. Each book is written by the same author, reflecting His eternal and everlasting attributes. While the universe is a manifestation of His attribute *al-qudrah*, power, reflecting that He is the One who is able to do what He wills as He wills; the Qur'an along with the Torah and the Bible is a manifestation of His attribute *al-kalam*, speech, meaning that the Creator communicates with His creation in the ways they are capable of comprehending. Mentioning the relationship of the Qur'an and the book of the universe, Nursi writes:

> And, for example, take a book in every line of which a whole book is finely written, and in every word of which a sura [chapter] of the Qur'an is inscribed with a fine pen. Being most meaningful with all of its matters corroborating one another, and a wondrous collection showing its writer and author to be extraordinarily skilful and capable, it undoubtedly shows its writer and author together with all his perfections and arts as clearly as daylight, and makes him known. It makes him appreciated with phrases like, "What wonders God has willed!" and, "Blessed be God!" Just the same is the mighty book of the universe; we see with our eyes a pen at work which writes on the face of the earth, which is a single of its pages, and on the spring, which is a single folio, the three hundred thousand plant and animal species, which are like three hundred thousand different books, all together, one within the other, without fault or error, without mixing

---

46 Nursi, *The Flashes*, 378.

47 Nursi, *The Words*, 244.

them up or confusing them, perfectly and with complete order, and sometimes writes an ode in a word like a tree, and the complete index of a book in a point like a seed. However much vaster and more perfect and meaningful than the book in the example mentioned above is this compendium of the universe and mighty embodied Qur'an of the world, which is infinitely full of meaning and in every word of which are numerous instances of wisdom, to that degree —in accordance with the extensive measure and far-seeing vision of the natural science that you study and the sciences of reading and writing that you have practised at school— it makes known the Inscriber and Author of the book of the universe together with His infinite perfections. Proclaiming "God is Most Great!," it makes Him known. Uttering words like "Glory be to God!", it describes Him. Uttering praises like "All praise be to God!," it makes Him loved.[48]

Contemplation and reflective thought are important steps leading one toward the attainment to a state of constantly observing and experiencing Divine presence. Nursi writes about two aspects of worship noting that "One is worship and contemplation in the absence of the Object of Worship. The other is worship and supplication in His presence and addressing Him directly."

Reflective thought for him is an important access guiding a believer to pass "from the work to the producer of the work" and enabling a worshipper to witness that "an All-Beauteous Maker wants to make himself known and acquainted through the miracles of His own art" and to respond "with knowledge and belief."[49]

There are two important concepts involved with the model Nursi developed a model for reflective thought, suggesting that the book of the universe be read at two different levels of meaning; *mānā-i ismī*, the meaning of things which refers to themselves, and *mānā-i harfī*, the indicative meaning to which things refer. In other words, the "self-referential" and the "Other-indicative"[50] meanings. He explains:

According to the apparent meaning of things, which looks to each thing itself, everything is transitory, lacking, accidental, non-existent. But according to the meaning that signifies something other than itself and in respect of each thing being a mirror to the All-Glorious Maker's Names and charged with various duties, each is a witness, it is witnessed, and it is existent.

This model provides a mindset finding a way to the Creator through creation and cultivating faith from everything in the universe, including the one's self. Nursi compares this outlook to the "staff of Moses." As water would pour out from the rock which Moses hit with his staff, this reflective outlook would harvest faith from anything it touches.

---

[48]   Nursi, *The Words*, 171.

[49]   Ibid., 339.

[50]   Colin Turner, Hasan Horkuc, *Said Nursi*, (London: I.B. Tauris, 2009), 67.

Nursi instructs employment of the "Other-indicative" viewpoint in many passages throughout the *Risale-i Nur*:

> [T]he All-Wise Qur'an is a most elevated expounder, a most eloquent translator of the Mighty Qur'an of the Universe. ... It regards beings, each of which is a meaningful letter, as bearing the meaning of another, that is, it looks at them on account of their Maker. It says, "How beautifully they have been made! How exquisitely they point to their Maker's beauty!," thus showing the universe's true beauty. But the philosophy they call natural philosophy or science has plunged into the decorations of the letters of beings and into their relationships, and has become bewildered; it has confused the way of reality. While the letters of this mighty book should be looked at as bearing the meaning of another, that is, on account of God, they have not done this; they have looked at beings as signifying themselves. That is, they have looked at beings on account of beings, and have discussed them in that way. Instead of saying, "How beautifully they have been made," they say "How beautiful they are," and have made them ugly. In doing this they have insulted the universe, and made it complain about them.[51]

The "Other-indicative" perspective guides one to pass from causes to their sources. Drawing attention to possible doubts that could be caused by causality or naturalism, Nursi offers to look at the real meanings they indicate. About the passive condition of nature, for instances, he states:

> Nature is a Divine art, it cannot be the artist. It is a dominical book, and cannot be the scribe. It is an embroidery, and cannot be the embroiderer. It is a register, and cannot be the accountant. It is a law, and cannot be the power. It is a pattern, and cannot be the source. It is a recipient and is passive, and cannot be the author. It is an order, and cannot the orderer. It is a code of creation, and cannot be the establisher of the code.[52]

Nursi points out that "the world has two faces, indeed, three faces. One is the mirror to Almighty God's Names, another looks to the hereafter and is its arable field, and the third looks to transience and non-existence."[53] He advises that focusing on the first two is necessary and the last deserves no attention, for the world is transient. This should not be understood as a rejection of worldly life or advocacy for an isolated life, but instead the world does not become one's highest priority, where one disregards the other two faces. Nursi again suggests an outlook of loving everything on the earth on behalf of God, a perspective that would comfort the sensitive human soul from the troubles of attachment to transitory beings. Human being, notes Nursi,

---

51   Nursi, *The Words*, 145.
52   Nursi, *The Flashes*, 437.
53   Nursi, *The Words*, 355.

loves firstly himself, then his relations, then his nation, then living creatures, then the universe, and the world. He is connected with all these spheres. He may receive pleasure at their pleasure and pain at their pain. However, since nothing is stable in this world of upheavals and revolutions swift as the wind, man's wretched heart is constantly wounded. The things his hands cling onto tear at them as they depart, even severing them. He remains in perpetual distress, or else plunges into heedless drunkenness. Since it is thus, my soul, if you have sense, gather together all those loves and give them to their true owner; be saved from those calamities. These infinite loves are particular to One possessing infinite perfection and beauty. When you give it to its true owner, you will be able to love everything without distress in His name and as His mirrors. That means this love should not be spent directly on the universe. Otherwise, while being a delicious bounty, it becomes a grievous affliction.[54]

For Nursi, transiency of creation mirrors the eternality of God. Using the sun allegory, he writes:

The ever-renewed instances of beauty and fairness passing over the faces of the beings in the universe show that they are shadows of the manifestations of an Eternal Beauteous One. Yes, bubbles sparkling on the surface of a river and then disappearing, and other bubbles coming after them and sparkling like those that preceded them shows that they are mirrors to the rays of a perpetual sun. In the same way, the flashes of beauty which sparkle on the traveling beings in the river of flowing time point to an Eternal Beauteous One and are signs of Him.[55]

Belief is the highest aim of the life in the view of Nursi. A true happiness he claims is only found in belief that is enriched with the knowledge of God, through reading His signs on everything, and enriching it by loving all for the sake of God. With this perception, he wrote at the age of 75 based on all his knowledge and experiences that "true enjoyment, pain-free pleasure, grief-free joy, and life's happiness are only to be found in belief and in the sphere of the truths of belief."[56]

Reflection Questions

1. What is Nursi's view of prophethood?
2. What are the Divine Names? Describe the ways in which Nursi uses the divine names to describe the nature of God?
3. For Said Nursi, why are humans significant?

---

54   Nursi, *The Words*, 368.
55   Ibid., 710.
56   Ibid., 163.

Chapter 3
Said Nursi and Spirituality

One reason why the writings of Said Nursi are so popular is the manifest "spirituality" that comes pulsating through the *Risale-i Nur*. There is a love of God—a presence of God—that permeates the pages. Nursi has a vibrant spirituality. Readers of his *magnum opus* the *Risale-i Nur* are repeatedly exhorted to experience the intimacy of God. So in the fourteenth note of the Seventeenth Flash, Nursi explains that our immortality is not for ourselves "but for the manifestation of the Enduring One of Glory."[1] And while we are here on earth, we should not be worshipping the causes (for example, ourselves), instead "man" s true object of worship, place of recourse, and savior can only be the One Who rules the earth and the heavens, and holds the reins of this world and the next.'[2] In addition to these general exhortations to experience God, there are particular moments in Nursi's life where he had certain intense experiences that conveyed insights into the ultimate nature of reality. In the *Sixth Letter*, for example, he writes about an experience which came to him while alone in the mountains; he talks about the five forms of exile. He writes:

> The first: due to old age, I was alone and a stranger away from the great majority of my friends, relations, and those close to me; I felt a sad exile at their having left me and departed for the Intermediate Realm. Then another sphere of exile was opened within this one: I felt a sad sense of separation and exile at most of the beings to which I was attached, like last spring, having left me and departed. And a further sphere of exile opened up within this, which was that I had fallen apart from my native land and relations, and was alone. I felt a sense of separation and exile arising from this too. Then through that, the lonesomeness of the night and the mountains made me feel another pitiable exile. And then I saw my spirit in an overwhelming exile, which had been prepared to journey to eternity both from this exile and from the transitory guest house of the world.[3]

In this passage, Nursi is highly sensitive to the transitory nature of life. Taken out of context, it might seem almost Buddhist (or perhaps worthy of Existentialist philosophy) in his awareness of the power of attachment (to others, to country, and to life). However, it is important to look more closely. The first exile is the sense

---

[1]   Said Nursi, 'The Seventeenth Flash – Fourteenth Note' in *The Flashes Collection* (Istanbul, 1995), 185.

[2]   Ibid., 184.

[3]   Said Nursi, 'The Sixth Letter' in *Letters* 2nd edition (Istanbul: Sözler Neşriyat A.Ş 1997), 42–3.

of loss due to old age (many who were close to Nursi are no longer alive); the second is the inevitable separation (as people come and go); the third is the sense of dislocation that Nursi felt in his country (exacerbated due to his antagonism to the secular nationalism of the government); the fourth is the contrast between the insignificant human life and nature (especially mountains and the night); and the last exile is the conflict between the spirit ready for eternity and life which must still be lived here.

Now although this is a good comprehensive description of the human predicament, it is important to note how it confronts this pervasive sense of "anxiety." He writes: "Suddenly the light of belief, the effulgence of the Qur'an, and the grace of the Most Merciful came to my aid. They transformed those five dark exiles into five luminous and familiar spheres. My tongue said: *God is enough for us, and He is the best disposer of affairs.*"[4] The point is that his intense experience of dislocation is transformed by his recollection of a verse from the Qur'an (3:173). This illustrates a central theme of Nursi. The experience of God needs to be rooted. Spirituality, for Nursi, must be grounded in the truths found in the Qur'an.

Perhaps a primary reason why Nursi wanted Muslims to recognize that faithful Islam does not depend on the continuation of the Caliphate or an Islamic State is that the "experience" of God does not depend on these things. Instead, argued Nursi, God has provided a variety of mechanisms that enable humanity to live in religiously richer and more virtuous way.

A good illustration of this is his moving description of the five daily prayers. For Nursi, this is not simply a matter of obedience to the command of God, although, of course, it is at least that. It is more. The pattern of daily prayer is an opportunity to live the rich experience of life during the course of one day. He explains:

> The time of *Fajr*, the early morning: This time until sunrise resembles and calls to mind the early spring, the moment of conception in the mother's womb, and the first six days of the creation of the heavens and the earth; it recalls the Divine acts present in them.

> The time of *Zuhr*, just past midday: This resembles and points to mid-summer and the prime of youth, and the period of man's creation in the life-time of the world, and calls to mind the manifestations of mercy and the abundant bounties in them.

> The time of *Asr*, afternoon: This is like autumn, and old age, and the time of the Final Prophet (PBUH), known as the Era of Bliss, and recalls the Divine acts and favours of the All-Merciful One in them.

---

4   Ibid., 43.

The time of *Maghrib*, sunset: Through recalling the departure of many creations at the end of autumn, and man's death, and the destruction of the world at the commencement of the Resurrection, this time puts in mind the manifestations of Divine Glory and Sublimity, and rouses man from his slumbers of heedlessness.

The time of *Isha*, nightfall. As for this time, by calling to mind the world of darkness veiling all the objects of the daytime world with a black shroud, ... it proclaims the awesome and mighty disposals of the All-Glorious and Compelling Subduer.

As for the *nighttime*, through putting in mind both the winter, and the grave, and the Intermediate Realm, it remains man how needy is the human spirit for the Most Merciful One's Mercy.[5]

So the morning prayer is analogous to birth and the early stages of life; the mid-day prayer is an invitation to stop and be still in the busyness of life—the mid-life moment; and evening prayers are an ideal opportunity to live as if it is old age. In this powerful description of prayer, Nursi understands entirely that one of the primary purposes of faithful living before God is to live life with reflection and intention. Reflection is important because the pauses in a day are what give the passing of time significance. It is so easy to live through the pattern of sleep, waking, working, television, sleeping without pausing and reflecting on the significance of the time passing. The reflective moments built into this structure of prayer ensures that the pattern of living is placed in the context of the creator. As a result of this space to be reflective, one then can live life with intention. Time is the most precious gift that God gives us. As a moment passes, it has gone forever. One wants to use every second of living aware of its special significance and ultimately use it for the glory of God. Nursi invites us to see in this discipline of the five daily prayers a vehicle that ensures that life is lived with the focus on what matters most.

With a deep commitment to celebrating the practices of Islam (and explaining their significance), Nursi also invites the reader to see the spiritual in the beauty of creation. Time after time, Nursi argues that in creation are countless indicators as to the nature of God. For Nursi, the beauty and order of the world are clear evidence of the reality of a creator. So, for example, in the Tenth Word, Nursi explains that the world does not make sense unless there is a hereafter. The marvel that makes up humanity cannot simply cease to exist; there must be a moment beyond that completes the human being. It would be a dishonor to the intricate achievement of human sophistication for it simply to cease to be. As one reads the *Risale-i Nur*, Nursi invites us to see the world a certain way. This is a world in which everything points to the source underpinning the world.

---

5   Said Nursi, 'Nineth Word, Fourth Point' in *The Words* (Istanbul, 1992), 53.

Reading Nursi as a Muslim who gained insights into the ultimate nature of reality by intense experiences makes sense in so many ways. However, his formal relationship with Sufism is much more complex. It is to the formal relationship that we turn next.

Sufism in the *Risale-i Nur*

Nursi learned and was inspired by the teachings and writings of spiritual leaders and pioneers of *tarīqah*, Sufi orders. References to them can be found throughout the *Risale*. Significant names standing out among the others include Shayk Abd al-Qadir Geylani,[6] Imam Rabbani Shaykh Ahmad Sirhindi, Imam Ghazali, and Shah Naqshband.

Acknowledging the authenticity of *tarīqah*,[7] Nursi concluded that the time was not right for them. In the Ninth part of the Twenty Ninth Letter dedicated to the paths of *velāyet*, sainthood, Nursi elaborates on beautiful intensions and aims of *tarīqah*, such as strengthening faith and purifying the soul, he also draws attention to the potential dangers of following a journey through these orders:

> Together with being very easy, the way of sainthood is very difficult. And together with being very short, it is very long. And in addition to being most valuable, it is very dangerous. And together with being very broad, it is very narrow. It is because of this that some of those who journey on the path sometimes drown, sometimes become harmful, and sometimes return and lead others away from the path.[8]

Nursi's readings and observation of the time and its necessities convinced him that his contemporaries were exposed to many doubts and were challenged to provide rational responses to skeptics who thought faith incoherent and implausible.. Otherwise their faith would be weakened by such doubts and they would have the risk of losing faith. Loss or lack of faith is the extreme detriment in Nursi's view, for its consequence would be the loss of one's eternal happiness. This is the risk involved in journeying on *tarīqah* which require lengthy training, including

---

[6]   His name is also transliterated as 'Jilani.'

[7]   The following is an example of Nursi's appreciation of *tarīqah*: "Underlying the terms 'Sufism,' 'path,' 'sainthood,' and 'spiritual journeying,' is an agreeable, luminous, joyful, and spiritual sacred truth. This truth has been proclaimed, taught, and described in thousands of books written by the scholars among the people of illumination and those who have had unfolded to them the reality of creation, who have told the Muslim community and us of that truth. May God reward them abundantly!" (*The Letters*, Twenty-Ninth Letter, p. 518).

[8]   Said Nursi, *The Letters*, Translated by Şükran Vahide, (Istanbul: Sozler Publication, 1997), 551.

some challenges that result in not all seekers successfully completing the journey. And, as the way of heart *tasavvūf*, Sufism, could fall short in resisting to doubts of the time harming belief, Nursi concluded that "compelling circumstances of the present time"[9] required belief to be the necessity and it was "not the age of Sufism."[10] Emphasizing the priority of gaining, nourishing, and strengthening belief, Nursi resembled faith to "basic sustenance" and *tasavvūf* to "fruit."[11]

Led by these motivations, Nursi cultivated a way of mutually employing reason and the heart. This, he clarifies, is a way inspired by the Qur'an, combining reason which was highly employed by *Salaf*, the early scholars of Islam, and heart which was the way followed by *Salih*, righteous and pious people who have been the pioneers of *tarīqah*.[12] He often opens his writings with a phrase like "relying on Almighty God's assistance, and on the effulgence of the Qur'an, I say this" or something very similar stressing that the *Risale* is rooted in the teachings of the Qur'an and is expressing the same truths of those expressed by the *Salaf* and *Salih* according to the understanding and need of the time.[13]

This is a distinctive feature of the *Risale* that is worth highlighting Nursi aims to enlighten reason with the light of the heart. He believes that only by the joint engagement of the two, can one attain truth. Pointing out the importance of this union, he states: "The religious sciences are the light of the conscience and the modern sciences (lit. "the sciences of civilization") are the light of the reason; the truth becomes manifest through the combining of the two... When they are separated it gives rise to bigotry in the one, and wiles and skepticism in the other."[14]

Realizing that there are numerous ways leading to God, Nursi declares that all true ones are rooted in the Qur'an. He differentiates these ways describing as "some are shorter, safer, and more general than others."[15] Noting that earlier attaining some of the truths of belief or gaining genuine faith through spiritual journeying would take 40 days or up to 40 years, Nursi, trusting in "Almighty God's mercy," claims "there is a way to rise to those truths in 40 minutes."[16] He unfolds a four-step way as one of the paths leading to God, from which he benefited and recommends it to the believer for it is much shorter, safer, and broader. He explains these four steps as reality, rather than *tarīqah*, Sufi order.[17]

---

9   Ibid., 518.

10   Ibid., 86.

11   Ibid., 41.

12   Said Nursi, *Mesnevī-i Nuriye*, Translated from Arabic to Turkish by Ümit Şimşek, (Istanbul: Nesil Press, 2009), 335.

13   *The Words*, Sixteenth Word, p.209, Twentieth Word, Second Station, p. 260.

14   *Munazarat*, 508. As translated by Şükran Vahide in *Islam in Modern Turkey*, 45–56.

15   *The Words*, Twenty-Sixth Word, Addendum, p. 491.

16   *The Letters*, Fifth Letter – p.41.

17   *The Words*, Twenty-Sixth Word, Addendum, p. 491.

The Four Steps in this way of impotence, poverty, compassion, and reflection have been explained in the twenty-six Words so far written, which are concerned with knowledge of reality, the reality of the Shari'a, and the wisdom of the Qur'an. So here we shall allude briefly to only one or two points, as follows:

Indeed, this path is shorter, because it consists of four steps. When impotence removes the hand from the soul, it gives it directly to the All-Powerful One of Glory. Whereas, when the way of ecstatic love, the swiftest way, takes the hand away from the soul, it attaches it to the metaphorical beloved. Only after the beloved is found to be impermanent does it go to the True Beloved.

Also, this path is much safer, because the ravings and high-flown claims of the soul are not present on it. For, apart from impotence, poverty, and defect, the soul possesses nothing so that it oversteps its mark.

Also, this path is much broader and more universal. For, in order to attain to a constant awareness of God's presence, a person is not compelled to imagine the universe to be condemned to non-existence and to declare: "There is no existent but He," like those who believe in "the unity of existence," nor to suppose the universe to be condemned to imprisonment in absolute oblivion and to say, "There is nothing witnessed but He," like those who believe in "the unity of witnessing." Rather, since the Qur'an has most explicitly pardoned the universe and released it from execution and imprisonment, one on this path disregards the above, and dismissing beings from working on their own account and employing them on account of the All-Glorious Creator, and in the duty of manifesting the Most Beautiful Names and being mirrors to them, he considers them from the point of view of signifying something other than themselves; and being saved from absolute heedlessness, he enters the Divine presence permanently; he finds a way leading to the Almighty God in everything.[18]

It is important to mention that Nursi emphasizes the identicalness of the essence and goals of *tarīqah* and the *Risale* that both spring out from the Qur'an and focus on expanding the truths of belief. Difference lies in their methods. Nursi is very cautious in defining the *Risale* and its method in agreement with, and not on the contrary to *tarīqah*. Therefore referring to central figures of *tasavvūf*, he notes:

---

[18]   *The Words*, Twenty-Sixth Word, Addendum, p. 493–494.

my conjecture is that if persons like Shaykh 'Abd al-Qadir Gilani[19] (May God be pleased with him) and Shah Naqshband[20] (May God be pleased with him) and Imam-i Rabbani (May God be pleased with him) were alive at the present time, they would expend all their efforts in strengthening the truths of belief and tenets of Islam. For they are the means to eternal happiness. If there is deficiency in them, it results in eternal misery.[21]

Supporting this claim, he quotes Imam Rabbani Shaykh Ahmad Sirhindi:

In his Letters (*Maktubat*), Imam-i Rabbani[22] (May God be pleased with him), the hero and a sun of the Naqshbandi Order, said: "I prefer the unfolding of a single matter of the truths of belief to thousands of illuminations, ecstasies, and instances of wonder-working."

He also said: "The final point of all the Sufi ways is the clarification and unfolding of the truths of belief."[23]

In his sustained discussion of Sufism, Nursi links spirituality with the quest for sainthood using the Sufi path. He explains that there are two ways. The first of which is the Inner Way:

The Inner Way starts from the self, and drawing the eyes away from the outer world, it looks at the heart. It pierces egotism, opens up a way from the heart, and finds reality. Then it enters to outer world. The outer world now looks luminous. It completes the journey quickly. The reality it sees in the inner world, it sees on a large scale in the outer world. Most of the paths which practice silent recollection take this way. The most important basis of this is to break the ego, give up the desires of the flesh, and kill the evil-commanding soul.[24]

---

[19]   Sayyid 'Abd al-Qadir Gilani (Geylani), known as the Gawth al-A'zam, was the founder of the Qadiri Order and a towering spiritual figure in the history of Islam. He lived 470/1077–561/1166. (Tr.)

[20]   Muhammad Baha'uddin Naqshband. He was the founder of the Naqshbandi Order, and died in 791/1389 in Bukhara. (Tr.)

[21]   *The Letters*, Fifth Letter, p. 41.

[22]   Shaykh Ahmad Sirhindi was also known as Imam-i Rabbani, Ahmad Faruqi, and as the Regenerator of the Second Millenium. He lived in India 971/1563 – 1034/1624, where he purified the religion of Islam of polytheistic accretions and efforts to degenerate it, and reformed Sufism. (Tr.)

[23]   *The Letters*, Fifth Letter, p. 40.

[24]   Said Nursi, 'The Twenty-Ninth Letter – Ninth Section' in *Letters* (Istanbul, 1997), 522.

The picture here is that the act of introspection makes one realize the divine origin of all reality, which then transforms the lens through which one looks at the outer world. The Second Way, Nursi explains thus:

> The Second Way starts from the outer world; it gazes on the reflections of the Divine Names and attributes in their places of manifestation in that greater sphere, then it enters the inner world. It observes those lights on a small scale in the sphere of the heart and opens up the closest way in them. It sees that the heart is the mirror of the Eternally Besoughted One, and becomes united with the goal it was seeking.[25]

In this way, it is as we move from ourselves "up" to God, we are then equipped to recognize in the heart a mirror of the Divine light, which is then united to God.

Spirituality, then, for Nursi involves a fundamental recognition of a link between the Creator and the heart of a person, which then transforms the way in which the person sees the world. Unlike those strands of Islam, which are suspicious of Sufi spirituality, Nursi believes that this account of spirituality is authentically Islamic. Although he has a nuanced view of Sufism, he never deviates from affirming this basic insight.

It is in his criticisms of Sufism that his "grounded spirituality" emerges. It is tempting, explains Nursi, to juxtapose the Sufi spiritual against the observation of the law. He talks of those who are so tempted as people "carried away by the brilliant pleasures of the Sufi path and the way of reality, and since they cannot attain to the pleasures of the truths of the Shari'ah, … they suppose them to be dull formalities and are indifferent towards them."[26] However, this is a temptation that must be resisted. So Nursi writes, "[T]he ways of the Sufi path and of reality are like means, servants, and steps for reaching the truths of the Shari'ah, till at the highest level they are transformed into the meaning of reality and essence of the Sufi way, which are at the heart of the Shari'ah."[27] Therefore the daily prayers are still obligatory, even if the Sufi dervish has experienced the divine. Indeed explains Nursi the ecstatic experience should help the observation of the obligatory prayers. He writes:

> The rules of behavior of the Sufi path and the invocations of Sufism should be a solace and means to true pleasure within those obligatory acts, not themselves be the source. That is, his *tekke* [a Sufi prayer lodge] should be the means to the please and correct performance of the five daily prayers in the mosque; one who hurriedly performs the prayers in the mosque as a formality and thinks he

---

25   Ibid., 522.
26   Ibid., 530.
27   Ibid., 528.

will find his true pleasure and perfection in the *tekke*, is drawing away from reality.[28]

For Nursi, the thrill of the enraptured experience must remain grounded. It cannot and should not displace the ritual obligation. The experience must be firmly located within the Islamic tradition.

This grounded spirituality is a key characteristic of Nursi's account of spirituality. There are four further elements:

1. God has made spirituality possible by creating us complex beings open to the divine.
2. Spirituality makes atheism much harder.
3. Spirituality helps Reason to see the truth.
4. Spirituality is an all-embracing disposition that challenges every area of your life.
5. Spirituality must be grounded in the Qur'an.

Each of these will now be discussed in turn.

On the first, Nursi writes:

> [S]ince man is a comprehensive index of the universe, his heart resembles a map of thousands of worlds. For just as innumerable human sciences and fields of knowledge show that man's brain in his head is a sort of center of the universe, like a telephone and telegraph exchange for innumerable lines, so too the millions of luminous books written by the incalculable saints show that man's heart in his essential being is the place of manifestation of innumerable truths of the universe, and is their means, and seed.

> Thus since the human heart and brain are at this center, and comprise the members of a mighty tree in the form of a seed in which have been encapsulated the parts and components of an eternal, majestic machine pertaining to the hereafter, certainly the heart's Creator willed that the heart should be worked and brought out from the potential to the actual, and developed, and put into action, for that is what He did. Since He willed it, the heart will certainly work like the mind. And the most effective means of working the heart is to be turned towards the truths of belief on the Sufi path through the remembrance of God in the degrees of sainthood.[29]

For Nursi, it is science that is demonstrating the complexity of the mind; and it is the Sufis who are demonstrating the complexity of the heart. In the same way that the Creator requires humanity to use the mind for the purposes of understanding;

---

28   Ibid., 529.
29   Ibid., 518–9

so the Creator requires that we use the heart so that we might experience God. This means that all people (given everyone has a heart) has the capacity to experience God and should be aspiring to enjoy that experience.

Now this is important. This tradition located account of spirituality that Nursi is advocating is not imperialist or insulting to those of us who are not Muslim. For Nursi recognizes that every person has the capacity to sense and experience the Divine. This includes non-Muslims who identify with a different faith tradition. Although his account is located and, as we shall see later, Nursi believes that an accurate description of the experience is found in the Qur'an, it does recognize a universal sense of the transcendent, which has been "hard-wired" into all of us.

On the second, we find a familiar Nursi theme. He was deeply disturbed by the European propensity towards atheism, which he described as "corrupt" due to the "darkness of the philosophy of Naturalism."[30] Safeguarding the faithful from the temptation of atheism is a key theme of the *Risale-i Nur*. Although he is confident that a rational person should see the overwhelming arguments for the truth of theism and, in particular, the divine origin of the Qur'an, he also sees the value of an experience of God. One advantage of the Sufi way, Nursi explains, is that atheism becomes impossible. So he writes:

> A sincere ordinary follower of the Sufi path preserves himself better than a superficial, externalist person with a modern, scientific background. Through the illumination of the Sufi path and the love of the saints, he saves his belief. If he commits grievous sins, he becomes a sinner, but not an unbeliever; he is not easily drawn into atheism. No power at all can refute in his view the chain of shaykhs he accepts, with a strong love and firm belief, to be spiritual poles. And because no power can refute it, his confidence in them cannot be destroyed. And so long as his confidence is not shaken, he cannot accept atheism.[31]

Nursi believes it is important that faith touches both the mind and the heart. One should have good arguments for faith; but one should also have a sense of God made possible through a careful discernment and listening to the Divine.

It is the relationship between reason and experience that makes up the third element of Nursi's account of spirituality. Much of the *Risale-i Nur* comprises proofs for the resurrection,[32] the existence and unity of God,[33] the prophethood of Muhammad,[34] and the miraculousness of the Qur'an.[35] However, despite this robust defense of the intelligibility, coherence, and explanatory power of Islam,

---

[30]   Said Nursi, 'The Seventeenth Flash – Fifth Note' in *The Flashes Collection*, 160.
[31]   Said Nursi, 'The Twenty-Ninth Letter – Ninth Section' in *Letters* 2nd edition, 520–1.
[32]   Said Nursi, 'The Tenth Word' in *The Words* (Istanbul, 1992), 59–131.
[33]   Ibid., 'The Twenty-Second Word', 287–318.
[34]   Ibid., 'The Nineteenth Word', 243–252.
[35]   Ibid., 'The Twenty-Fifth Word', 375–474.

he does concede that reason has its limitations. Given our subject matter is God, Nursi does concede that the human mind is working at the outer limit. It is all so much easier to talk about science or engineering. In a very striking passage, Nursi suggests "witnesses and proofs of knowledge of God are of three sorts."[36] The first resembles water: "it is visible and palpable, but cannot be held with the fingers. For this sort, one has to detach oneself from illusions and submerge oneself in it as a whole."[37] The second resembles air: "it may be perceived, but it is neither visible, nor may be held. You should turn yourself towards it with your face, your mouth, your spirit, and hold yourself before that breeze of mercy."[38] And the third sort resembles light: "it is visible, but it neither palpable nor may it be held. So you should hold yourself before it with the heart's eye and spirit's vision: you should direct your gaze towards it and wait ... For light cannot be held in the hand nor hunted with the fingers; it can be hunted only with the light of insight and intuition."[39]

Nursi wants believers who use their whole body—both their minds and their hearts. We should struggle and formulate good arguments for the positions we hold; but we should also trust and open ourselves to the divine. God ultimately provides the decisive evidence about God by surrounding us with the cosmic, divine love.

The fourth element is the all-embracing aspect of Nursi's spirituality. Spirituality is often criticized as individual and indulgent. It is sometimes set against justice. For Nursi, this is an impossible opposition. Spirituality embraces the obligations to create a just world. This comprehensive sense of spirituality is captured when Nursi shares a text on which he meditates daily. He writes:

I have hung it above my head for the wisdom it teaches. I look at it every morning and evening and receive instruction:

If you want a friend, God is sufficient. Yes, if He is the friend, everything is a friend.

If you want companions, the Qur'an is sufficient. Indeed, for in the imagination one meets with the prophets and angels in it, observes the events in which they were involved, and becomes familiar with them.

If you want possessions, contentment is sufficient. Yes, one who is content is frugal; and one who is frugal, finds the blessing of plenty.

---

[36]   Said Nursi, 'The Seventeenth Flash – Tenth Note' in *The Flashes Collection*, 175.

[37]   Ibid., 175.

[38]   Ibid., 175.

[39]   Ibid., 176.

If you want an enemy, the soul is sufficient. Yes, one who fancies himself is visited with calamities and meets with difficulties. Whereas one who is not fond of himself, finds happiness, and receives mercy.

If you want advice, death is sufficient. Yes, one who thinks of death is saved from love of this world, and works in earnest for the hereafter.[40]

This is an all-embracing outlook, which links together the spiritual with the obligations to live simply. Moving from one's friendship with God, Nursi weaves together the centrality of the Qur'an, the need for a lifestyle of simplicity, the dangers of self-love, and the need to have one's perspective on the life to come. Spirituality for Nursi is not simply an intense experience, but a life-changing disposition.

It is the last element that is vital for Nursi's account of grounded spirituality. When Nursi sets out his definition of the Sufi path, it is firmly located in key Islamic beliefs about the Prophet Muhammad and the Qur'an. Nursi writes:

The aim and goal of the Sufi path is—knowledge of God and the unfolding of the truths of belief—through a spiritual journeying with the feet of the heart under the shadow of the Ascension of Muhammad (PBUH), to manifest the truths of belief and the Qur'an through illumination and certain states, and to a degree by "witnessing"; it is an elevated human mystery and human perfection which is called "the Sufi path" or "Sufism."[41]

As we have already noted, he chides Sufis when they start assuming that their experience of God is more important than ritual obligations. This is because he wants to firmly locate the experience of God in the context of the disclosure of the nature of God in the Qur'an.

One reason why this is so important for Nursi is the correct interpretation of an experience depends on revelation. In the Eighteenth Letter, Nursi muses on the question: why did some great Sufi saints describe the universe in ways that we now know are wrong? Nursi answers: "They are the people of truth and reality. They are also saints and those who witness the realities. They saw correctly what they saw, but since they were not correct in declarations they made while in the state of illumination and witnessing, which is without comprehension, and in their interpretations of their visions, which were like dreams, they were partially incorrect."[42] He then concludes this section by making it clear that the only safeguard against inaccurate interpretations of religious experience is the firm foundation of an infallible and reliable revelation. So he writes: "[T]he

---

[40]   Said Nursi, 'Twenty-third Letter' in *The Letters*, 334.

[41]   Said Nursi, 'The Twenty-Ninth Letter – Ninth Section' in *Letters* 2nd edition, 518.

[42]   Said Nursi, 'The Eighteenth Letter' in *Letters* 2nd edition, 104.

uncomprehending illuminations of some of the saints relying only on "witnessing" do not attain to the statements about the truths of belief of the purified or exact scholars, who are the people of the legacy of prophethood and who rely on the Qur'an and Revelation, not on "witnessing." ... [T]he balance of all illumination, mental states, visions and witnessing are the Book and the *Sunna*."[43]

Although the insights of the Sufi are important (and Nursi always stresses the value of the discoveries of *tasavvuf*), they might be mistaken. Ultimately true knowledge of God depends on God's disclosures to us: God must tell us what God is like. Our mystical experience of the Divine might be mistaken; ultimate certainty depends on trusting God's revelation.

Reflection Questions

1. Is Said Nursi a mystic? What is the significance of this label? To what extent is the label an accurate description of Said Nursi?
2. What is Sufism? How does Nursi relate to this tradition?
3. "A sense of God is at the heart of all faith." Would Said Nursi agree with this assertion?

---

[43] Ibid., 106.

Chapter 4

Nursi's Approach to Disagreement and Pluralism

A primary reason why Bediuzzaman Said Nursi is important is in his attitude to disagreement and pluralism. Humans need to find strategies to cope with disagreement. Too many parts of the world witness to the inability of humanity to live with difference. Many have died because of our inability to handle a disagreement effectively. The north of Ireland, Palestine/Israel, and Lebanon are just three examples where religion has been a factor (among many factors) in a spiral of destructive violence between communities.

In this chapter, we shall summarize briefly the conventional approaches to this topic. For the modern mindset, the choice is simply a religious theocracy (which denies pluralism) or an aggressive secularism (which allows pluralism but only a privatized form of religion). Having looked at the traditional debate, we shall see how Nursi argues for a rich alternative, which affirms diversity yet also remains committed to the public nature of religious traditions. We shall suggest that this Nursi alternative can be called "Grounded pluralism."

The Traditional Options: Theocracy or Secularism

Many religious traditions (perhaps especially those committed to monotheism) have been tempted to advocate a form of theocracy. A theocratic state is one where a group attempt to impose the "rule of God," which in practice involves the "rule of certain religious authorities." It has been a constant temptation for both Christians and Muslims. For Christians, we have Calvin's Geneva, Roman Catholic "Christendom," and, in the modern period, advocates for a "Christian America." For Muslims, we have modern day Iran and Saudi Arabia.

The theocratic temptation has its roots in a certain understanding of religious truth. For both Christians and Muslims, the issues at stake in religion are of eternal importance. They believe that God has revealed the truth to humanity. Accepting that truth is important both because error makes God unhappy and the affirmation or denial of the truth has implications for eternity. It was Augustine of Hippo in the fifth century who took the expression from a parable of Jesus, namely, "compel them to come in," as justification for the use of torture against the heretic. The question "why should the state tolerate those in error?" has haunted countless cultures and societies.

Although even the theocratic examples listed above had to find some way of accommodating diversity (even if it is simply diversity within a faith tradition), the theocratic solution keeps such diversity to a minimum. It strives to use the law to limit the options for the dissenter. Public meetings are difficult; publication of key texts is often prohibited; and all forms of proselytizing are strictly forbidden.

There are plenty of classical defenses of this approach to the state. Even in the twentieth century, there were thoughtful defenders. From the Christian point of view, the best illustration is T.S. Eliot (the gifted English poet). In his *Idea of a Christian Society*, Eliot argues for the necessity of some idea (that is, some underlying worldview) and in England that idea must be Christian. From the Muslim point of view, there are plenty of so-called "Islamists," who are defending a theocratic Muslim state. Israr Ahmed in Pakistan has provided a vision of a state organized around Muslim principles. For Ahmed, this is a state where only Muslims can vote (and hold significant positions of responsibility), the genders must be segregated (with women required to wear the burkha), and various lifestyle options are illegal.

For both Eliot and Ahmed, the primary argument is "truth." Given God has revealed the truth about social organization and given there must be some underpinning worldview in a culture, it is essential that the "right" religion dominate. The problem with these arguments is that in almost every country there are significant minorities who believe differently and would like equality of treatment. This simple point has been the main factor behind the rise of western alternative of secularism.

The secular solution has been entrenched in many countries around the world. Although there are differences, France, America, and India are all secular in their constitution. Provoked by the impact of the protestant reformation, various European theorists in the sixteenth and seventeenth centuries argued that religion cannot and should not dominate the public square. The public square must be strictly neutral. However, under this neutral umbrella, various private and personal worldviews are allowed to coexist.

There are obvious difficulties that the secular project continues to try to resolve. What are the limits of acceptable worldviews? Normally, the classic criterion is that one should allow anything that doesn't impact another person. However, this is a difficult line to draw. What about racism or pedophilia? And if these worldviews are deemed unacceptable, then on what basis are these values being introduced into the state? A further difficulty is that the secular state is a triumph for a particular worldview—a particular'religion', namely the religion of unbelief. The vast majority of people in the world are intensely religious. They do not want to live in a social organization that denies their deepest values. Why should the small minority of atheists and agnostics dominate the public square? It seems to many critics that secularism is incompatible with democracy.

So the quest for an alternative is urgently needed. And this is where Said Nursi is so important and interesting. It is to his "grounded pluralism" that we turn next.

Grounded Pluralism[1]

The key to understanding Said Nursi's alternative is his strong commitment to the human capacity to reason, converse, and persuade.[2] Nursi doesn't want a public square absent of moral and religious conversation (that is, the secular solution). He has a vision of an intense conversation, which is grounded in deep commitment to the particularities of each tradition. In this conversation, one may try and persuade the other. At the same time, he is a realist. Although he believes that Islam is the one true religion, he accepts that it cannot dominate the public square. He draws an analogy with the desire for spring in the middle of winter; he writes:

> Yes, just as I desire and long for the spring during this winter, but I cannot will it nor attempt to bring it, so too, I long for the world to be righted and I pray for it and I want the worldly to be reformed, but I cannot will these things, because I do not have the power. I cannot attempt them in fact, because it is neither my duty, nor do I have the capacity.

At this point, he is especially interesting. He does not want this state of affairs because this is incompatible with his understanding of Islam. In other words, it is because he is a committed Muslim that he accepts pluralism, not despite his commitment to Islam.

The concept of persuasion, which pervades his writing, underpins his resolute commitment to non-violence. As we shall see, for Nursi when a Muslim resorts to violence, then this shows a lack of confidence in the beauty, coherence, and rationality of Islam.

Nursi's attitude to pluralism and disagreement can be summarized in four points. These are as follows:

1. Said Nursi is committed to the truth of Islam and the importance of persuading others of that truth.
2. Nursi finds in his tradition several reasons why it is important to commit to constructive co-existence with other faith traditions.
3. Nursi believes that the resort to violence by Muslims against non-Muslims demonstrates a lack of self-confidence in Islam. Self-confident Muslims who are strong in their faith do not need to resort to violence.
4. Nursi believes that the state needs good citizens and pious believers make good citizens.

---

[1]   Much of the material in this summary of Nursi's views on pluralism and disagreement is taken from Ian Markham, *Engaging with Bediuzzaman Said Nursi: A Model for Interfaith Dialogue*, (Ashgate Publishing, 2010). A fuller discussion of these questions can be found in this volume.

[2]   See Said Nursi, The Damascus Sermon, First Addendum, Third Part, p. 78.

Turning then to the first feature. Islam, for Nursi, is not just a cultural religious option. Instead Islam is the final, definitive, and most elegant description of the nature of God and expectations that God has for humanity. So, for example, when Nursi describes the significance of Muhammad, he writes:

> Peace and blessings be upon our master Muhammed thousands and thousands of times, to the number of the good deeds of his community, to whom was revealed the All-Wise Criterion of Truth and Falsehood, from One Most Merciful, Most Compassionate, from the Sublime Throne; whose Prophethood was foretold by the Torah and Bible, and told of by wondrous signs, the voices of jinn, saints of man, and soothsayers; at whose indication the moon split; our master Muhammed! Peace and blessings be upon him thousands and thousands of times …[3]

It is important to note how embedded in this piety are certain truth claims about the nature of Muhammad and his relationship with the Torah and Bible. In the fourteenth droplet, Said Nursi moves his focus from Muhammad to the Qur'an. Here he writes:

> The All-Wise Qur'an, which makes known to us our Sustainer, is thus: it is the pre-eternal translator of the great Book of the Universe; the discloser of the treasures of the Divine Names concealed in the pages of the earth and heavens; the key to the truths hidden beneath these lines of events; the treasury of the favors of the Most Merciful and pre-eternal addresses, which come forth from the World of the Unseen beyond the veil of this Manifest World; the sun, foundation, and plan of the spiritual world of Islam, and the map of the worlds of the hereafter; the distinct expounder, lucid exposition, articulate proof, and clear translator of the Divine Essence, attributes, and deeds; the instructor, true wisdom, guide and leader of the world of humanity; it is both book of wisdom and law, and a book of prayer and worship, and a book of command and summons, and a book of invocation and Divine knowledge—it is a book for all spiritual needs; and it is a sacred library offering books appropriate to the ways of all the saints and veracious, the purified and the scholars, whose ways and paths are all different.[4]

Said Nursi believes that there are compelling rational arguments for the truth of Islam. There is pervading his writings this constant sense that anyone reading the Qur'an cannot escape acknowledging the divine origin of the text. Indeed the impact of the Qur'an is so great on the reader, that Nursi uses a *reductio ad absurdum* argument to defend its divine origins. After noting how the "common people" cannot help but admit that the Qur'an is totally different from any other book, he explains: "The Qur'an, then, is of a degree either above all of them or

---

[3]   Said Nursi, 'Thirteenth Droplet' in *The Words*, p. 249.

[4]   'Fourteenth Droplet' in *The Words*, p. 250.

below all of them. To be below them is impossible, and no enemy nor the Devil even could accept it. In which case, the Qur'an is above all other books, and is therefore a miracle. Therefore, the Qur'an is the Word of the Creator of the universe. Because there is no point between the two; it is impossible and precluded that there should be."[5]

So, unlike the secularist, Said Nursi starts with a strong commitment to his tradition. Nursi believes that Islam is true. It is not simply true for him, but for the entire world. We do not find anywhere in Nursi's voluminous writings the suggestion that there are many "truths" about God and that the Qur'an is just one such "truth." There is no postmodern cultural relativism in the *Risale-i Nur*. Although Nursi does recognize that there are different ways of understanding the Qur'an, the status of the text remains absolute, even if particular interpretations may be more relative. He makes this explicit when he explains how important it is to convert the "People of the Book." He writes:

> When urging the People of the Book to believe in Islam, the Qur'an shows them in this verse [Qur'an 2:4] a familiar aspect and a facility. That is, it implies: "O People of the Book! There is no difficulty for you in accepting Islam; do not let it appear hard to you. For the Qur'an does not order you to abandon your religion completely, it proposed only that you complete your faith and build it on the fundamentals of religion you already possess. For the Qur'an combines in itself the virtues of all the previous books and the essentials of all the previous religions; it is thus a modifier and a perfector of basic principles.[6]

Because of Said Nursi's commitment that Islam is the truth about the world, we can see two further commitments in this passage. These are a conviction that non-Muslims should be invited to respond to the message of Islam and a sense that the Qur'an "completes" Christianity and Judaism. This "fulfillment theology" is also found in Karl Rahner's description of the relationship of Christianity to non-Christian faiths.

Now this "tradition-constituted" starting point (to use an expression taken from the work of Alasdair MacIntyre) has one major advantage over the secular approach. The advantage is this: the vast majority of Muslims in the world start in

---

5   Ibid., 'The Addendum to the Fifteenth Word' p. 204.

6   Said Nursi, *İşârâtü'l-İ'caz* (Istanbul: Enuar Neşriyat 1995) p. 50 as quoted in Niyazi Beki, 'The Qur'an and Its Method of Guidance' in *A Contemporary Approach to Understanding the Qur'an: The Example of the 'Risale-i Nur'*, (Istanbul: Sözker Neşriyat Ticaret ve Sanayi A.Ş. 2000) p. 105. In the *Letters*, he explains why the Torah and the Bible are not as good as the Qur'an. He writes, 'The words of the Torah, the Bible, and the Psalms do not have the miraculousness of those of the Qur'an. They have been translated again and again, and a great many alien words have become intermingled with them. Also, the words of commentators and their false interpretations have been confused with their verses' (see p. 201).

the same place. The commitment to diversity, conversation, and toleration cannot start from semi-unbelief, but needs to be grounded in the particularities of the faith tradition. We need the "orthodox" believers in each tradition to commit to toleration.

We turn now to the second feature of Said Nursi's position on pluralism and disagreement. This is his recognition that there are many positive reasons, explicitly grounded in the tradition, that encourage a positive attitude to co-existence with non-Muslims. Now given this feature alone could be a substantial discussion in its own right, we shall simply confine ourselves to a small number of illustrations. One major illustration of this feature is Nursi's celebration of the importance of love. So this passage from the "Damascus Sermon" sets the tone well:

> What I am certain of from my experience of social life and have learnt from my life-time of study is the following: the thing most worthy of love is love, and that most deserving of enmity is enmity. That is, love and loving, which renders man's social life secure and lead to happiness are most worthy of love and being loved. Enmity and hostility are ugly and damaging, have overturned man's social life, and more than anything deserve loathing and enmity and to be shunned.[7]

Now for Nursi, this very basic commitment to love does entail a commitment to peaceful coexistence with others.

A good illustration of this has been documented by Thomas Michel.[8] When Kurdish tribesmen in Eastern Anatolia are worried about permitting Greeks and Armenians to be free, Said Nursi is adamant that the "freedom of non-Muslims is a branch of our own freedom."[9] Furthermore the fear about acknowledging the legitimate freedom of the Christian is grounded in Ignorance, Poverty, and Enmity. As Michel puts it: "The message of Said Nursi is as valid for our own day as it was when he wrote these words almost eighty years ago. At the roots of tensions and conflicts between Muslims and Christians today lie not so much the evil nature of the other as our egoistic desires to dominate, control, and retaliate."[10] Nursi is clear; there is a Qur'anic obligation for Muslims to respect the freedom of Christians. Nursi's Qur'anic understanding is grounded in the verse which reads: "No bearer of burdens can bear the burden of another" (Q, 6:164). This is the verse from which Nursi cultivates his understanding of "pure justice."

---

[7]   Said Nursi, *The Damascus Sermon* (Istanbul: Sözler Publications, 1996), p. 49.

[8]   See Thomas Michel, 'Muslim-Christian Dialogue and Co-operation in Bediuzzaman's Thought' in *A Contemporary Approach to Understanding the Qur'an: The Example of the 'Risale-i Nur'*, (Istanbul: Sözler Neşriyat Ticaret ve Sanayi A.Ş. 2000).

[9]   Said Nursi, Munazarat (Istanbul: Sözler Yayinevi 1977), p. 21, as quoted by Thomas Michel, op. cit. p. 557.

[10]   Thomas Michel, op. cit. p. 57.

So we find in Said Nursi's writings, a strong commitment to love, coupled with an equally strong commitment to respecting the liberty of the other. These two dispositions should shape our relationships with non-Muslims. Although he believes it is important to explain to the Christian the truth of Islam, he recognizes that at the end of the age there will be many sincere and good Christians who have not converted to Islam. He cites various passages in the hadith. So Nursi explains in the Fifteenth Letter:

> At that point when the current appears to be very strong, the religion of true Christianity, which comprises the collective personality of Jesus (Upon whom be peace), will emerge. That is, it will descend from the skies of Divine Mercy. Present Christianity will be purified in the face of that reality; it will cast off superstition and distortion, and unite with the truths of Islam. Christianity will in effect be transformed into a sort of Islam.[11]

Although he would love to see all Christians embrace Islam, he recognizes both sociologically and, more importantly, theologically this will not happen until the end of the age. Christians and Jews have roles at the end of the age: for reasons already identified, Muslims have a duty to protect Christian and Jewish communities in the present. They are allies in the argument with the forces of unbelief. So Nursi writes:

> It is even recorded in authentic traditions of the Prophet that at the end of time the truly pious among the Christians will unite with the People of the Qur'an and fight their common enemy, irreligion. And at this time, too, the people of religion and truth need to unite sincerely not only with their own brothers and fellow believers, but also with the truly pious and spiritual ones the Christians, temporarily from the discussion and debate of points of difference in order to combat their joint enemy-aggressive atheism.[12]

The social and political consequences of this theology of the end times are good for coexistence and the root reason for toleration.

Now of course there are more challenging texts in the Qur'an, for example, the verse that seems to prohibit the taking of Jews and Christians as friends (5:51). Said Nursi is interesting here: he concedes the validity of the text, yet insists that it is not a blanket prohibition. Instead it is confined to moments when Jews and Christians are a problem to a Muslim.[13] Nursi explains thus:

---

[11]   Said Nursi, *The Letters*, p. 78.

[12]   Said Nursi, *The Flashes*, p. 203.

[13]   Said Nursi actually writes when Jews and Christians reflect their 'Jewishness and Christianity'. I am interpreting this as an overt antagonism to Islam. For a slightly different interpretation see Thomas Michel, 'Muslim-Christian Dialogue and Co-operation in Bediuzzaman's Thought' in *A Contemporary Approach to Understanding the Qur'an:*

A mighty religious revolution occurred in the time of the Prophet, and because all the people's minds revolved around religion, love and hatred were concentrated on that point and they loved or hated accordingly. For this reason, love for non-Muslims inferred dissembling. But now ... what preoccupies people's minds are progress and this world ... In any event most of them are not so bound to their religions. In which case, our being friendly to them springs from our admiration for their civilization and progress, and our borrowing these. Such friendship is certainly not included in the Qur'anic prohibition.[14]

In other words, friendship is possible when the goals are constructive and appropriate. Said Nursi recognized throughout his life the importance of good relations with the people of the book on the basis of the pure justice. (The Turkish word is *Adalet-i mahza. This is the application by human beings of the "absolute justice" of God, which we are rendering as* "pure justice." When Said Nursi uses the term "pure justice," he is implying the best and complete application of justice by human beings in their interactions with one another and the rest of the creation.)

The net result is a set of arguments, firmly grounded in the Qur'an and hadith, which require Muslims to have positive and constructive relations with non-Muslims based on the criterions of pure justice. These arguments are not intended for the non-Muslims; they assume the truth of the Islamic worldview. But the outcome is that we have in Said Nursi a strong Islamic argument for diversity, conversation, and peaceful co-existence with the other.

This leads to the third feature. Said Nursi is especially interesting in this area. He condemns those who would resort to violence as a form of weakness. It demonstrates a lack of confidence in Islam. For Islam is sufficiently strong that good arguments can bring about victory. Şükran Vahide in her biography of Nursi explains his position thus:

[T]he way of the *Risale-i Nur* was peaceful *jihad* or "*jihad* of the word" (*mânevî jihad*) in the struggle against aggressive atheism and irreligion. By working solely for the spread and strengthening of belief, it was to work also for the preservation of internal order and peace and stability in society in the face of the moral and spiritual destruction of communism and the forces of irreligion which aimed to destabilize society and create anarchy, and to form "a barrier" against them.[15]

The Example of the 'Risale-i Nur', (Istanbul: Sözker Neşriyat Ticaret ve Sanayi A.Ş. 2000), p. 559.

[14]   As quoted in Osman Cilaci, 'Comments on the Holy Bible in the *Risale-i Nur*' in *A Contemporary Approach to Understanding the Qur'an: The Example of the 'Risale-i Nur'*, (Istanbul: Sözker Neşriyat Ticaret ve Sanayi A.Ş. 2000) p. 585.

[15]   Sukhran Vahide, The Biography of Bediuzzaman Said Nursi: the author of the Risale-i Nur, part three.

In other words, Nursi is committed to handling disagreement with peaceful means not because he shares a western skepticism about the truth of religion, but because of the truth of religion. Nursi wants an Islamic renewal; he wants Muslims to realize the power of their tradition. And in so doing, he believes that the power of argument and reason is sufficient to hold those who already belong and attract others who are seeking God. He calls this a *mânevî jihad*, which is a "jihad of the word" or a "non-physical jihad." One of the reasons why Nursi believes the jihad can be non-physical is because he is confident that God will bring about the necessary victory through such a peaceful witness that uses arguments rather than violence. The God Said Nursi believes in can work wonders with the sincere effort of faithful Muslims.

When it comes to secularists and followers of other traditions, Nursi calls for non-violent witness to the beauty and coherence of Islam. Within Islam, Nursi insists that it is an obligation on all faithful Muslims to stand united. So he writes:

> Practice the brotherhood, love and cooperation insistently enjoined by hundreds of Qur'anic verses and traditions of the Prophet! Establish with all of your powers a union with your fellows and brothers in religion that is stronger than the union of the worldly! ... Do not say to yourself, "Instead of spending my valuable time on such petty matters, let me spend it on more valuable things such as the invocation of God and meditation." For precisely what you imagine to be a matter of slight importance in this moral jihad may in fact be very great.[16]

Once again there is an interesting argument embedded in this text. However tempting it might be to evade disagreements and squabbles in the Islamic community by an act of piety, Nursi insists that it would be wrong to do so. Living amongst these arguments is the religious duty; for we do not know what the implications of the disagreement are for the sake of the "moral jihad."

Nursi accepts the reality of pluralism (that is, that there are many religious traditions) and the inevitability of disagreement both within and outside the Islamic community. However, his response is not to call for a "recognition that Islam is just one truth amongst many" (the popular strategy of many western theologians, for example John Hick),[17] but to call for a deeper faith more committed to its distinctive claims and beliefs. For Nursi, part of the renewal he wants amongst Muslims is a greater self-confidence in the arguments for the Islamic faith that enables Muslims to enjoy the pluralist world. Like a much-loved child at home, one can venture into the world unafraid of difference and diversity because one is secure in one's own

---

[16]   Said Nursi, 'On Sincerity' in 'The Twentieth Flash'. From vol. 3 of the *Risale-i Nur*, p. 208.

[17]   John Hick is an advocate of 'pluralism' in the Christian Theology of Other Religions debate. Pluralism entails that each religion should see itself as a way to the Cosmic real, not *the* way. For Hick, see *An Interpretation of Religion* (Basingstoke: Macmillan 1989).

identity. The idea here is that a committed Muslim is one that can enjoy engaging with other traditions because of the power of their arguments.

This leads to the fourth feature. Nursi had plenty of secular critics who were ready to argue that committed Muslims made bad citizens. Again Nursi turns this argument around: instead of sharing the secular assumption that citizenship requires uncommitted religious people, he insists that properly committed Muslims will make model citizens. They are not a threat to the political order; they need not be committed to overthrow of the government. So in the Damascus Sermon, which was delivered in 1911, he explains:

> What we want now is the awakening and attention of believers, for the effect of public attention is undeniable. The aim of the Union and its purpose is to uphold the Word of God, and its way is to wage the "greater *jihad*" with one's own soul, and to guide others. Ninety-nine per cent of the endeavors of this blessed society are not political. They are rather turned towards good morals and moderation, which are the opposite of politics, and other lawful aims.[18]

At every point, Nursi handles the challenge of diversity and disagreement not by resorting to a secular relativism that has shaped many western apologetics for pluralism, but by insisting on a deeper love of God and a greater understanding of the Qur'an. For Nursi, a faith commitment is the best way of handling diversity not semi-agnosticism.

Summary

Nursi's alternative to the tired and entrenched positions of secularism and theocracy is desperately needed. The social consequence is clear: Nursi's commitment to peaceful interaction allows Muslims to be united in a common goal and creates opportunities to share the beauty and cohesion of Islam. One can face disagreement head-on and find resolution peacefully. One can also live faithfully in the midst of religious diversity. Islamic renewal calls Muslims to remain deeply committed to their faith while coexisting with the other. When one is confident in his faith, Nursi argues, one has the freedom and security to embrace and appreciate difference. One should not ignore faith or hide it in the private sphere, rather one should allow it to form a meaningful foundation for one's life and live in harmony with others because of it. In this way Nursi rejects the arguments of secularists that call for non-engagement with faith. Semi-agnosticism does not provide the same preparation for living amongst diversity that a faith commitment does.

---

[18]   Said Nursi, The Damascus Sermon, First Addendum, Third Part, p. 84.

Reflection Question

1. What is a "grounded pluralism"?
2. Some secularists argue that the only safeguard of pluralism in society is to keep religion under control. How would Said Nursi respond?
3. What would Said Nursi say to the person who thinks it is important to forbid other religions in a Muslim country?

EXTRACTS FROM THE WRITINGS OF SAID NURSI

The *Risale-i Nur* collection has a style of its own. The voluminous collection of 130 pieces is a cohesive and all-encompassing work. Among its components, *The Words* is composed of 33 chapters, the last one of which is the second major book of the collection entitled *Letters*. "The Thirtieth Letter" is another book, *Signs of Miraculousness*. Similarly, "The Thirty-First Letter" appears as the third major book of the collection, *The Flashes*. "The Thirty-First Flash" is the fourth major book, *The Rays*. "The Thirty-Third Ray" is the *Seedbed of the Light, Al-Mathnawi al-Nuri*. Seen from this angle, the individual books are as the branches of one major book, which is *The Words*. This is a note to the reader regarding numeric titles of chapters from the *Risale-i Nur* that reflects the collection's order.

In addition, the original language of the *Risale-i Nur* was gender inclusive. Said Nursi uses the word *insan* to refer to humans. He addresses his friends and students as siblings without referring to a specific gender. Although the translation sometimes uses the term "man" or "mankind", the Turkish is inclusive.

These extracts are divided into four sections. The first is beliefs. In this section, we look at the ways in which Nursi argued for belief in God. We will see that Nursi places considerable emphasis on the order of creation and the remarkable significance of human agency, consciousness, and conscience. The second is prophethood. In this section, we look at Nursi's view of the revealing God, the centrality of the Qur'an and the important role prophets play in Islam. The third is the afterlife. We see here that Nursi stresses immortality as a necessary framework for living life in a healthy way. And the final section is justice and worship. This looks at Nursi's social teaching and his attitude to modernity and the west.

Part 1

Belief

Extract One: Difference between Believer and Non-Believer

"The Second Word" explicates the viewpoints of a believer and an unbeliever through an allegorical story of two people, serving as commentary on a Qur'anic verse, defining believers as those who have faith in the unseen. While the former witnesses the joy of existence in everything, the latter dwells in somberness and despair.

In the Name of God, the Merciful, the Compassionate.

Those who believe in the Unseen.[1]

If you want to understand what great happiness and bounty, what great pleasure and ease are to be found in belief in God, listen to this story which is in the form of a comparison:

One time, two men went on a journey for both pleasure and business. One set off in a selfish, inauspicious direction, and the other on a godly, propitious way.

Since the selfish man was both conceited, self-centred, and pessimistic, he ended up in what seemed to him to be a most wicked country due to his pessimism. He looked around and everywhere saw the powerless and the unfortunate lamenting in the grasp of fearsome bullying tyrants, weeping at their destruction. He saw the same grievous, painful situation in all the places he travelled. The whole country took on the form of a house of mourning. Apart from becoming drunk, he could find no way of not noticing this grievous and sombre situation. For everyone seemed to him to be an enemy and foreign. And all around he saw horrible corpses and despairing, weeping orphans. His conscience was in a state of torment.

The other man was godly, devout, fair-minded, and with fine morals so that the country he came to was most excellent in his view. This good man saw universal rejoicing in the land he had entered. Everywhere was a joyful festival, a place for the remembrance of God overflowing with rapture and happiness; everyone seemed to him a friend and relation. Throughout the country he saw

---

[1]   Qur'an, 2:3.

the festive celebrations of a general discharge from duties accompanied by cries of good wishes and thanks. He also heard the sound of a drum and band for the enlistment of soldiers with happy calls of "God is Most Great!" and "There is no god but God!" Rather than being grieved at the suffering of both himself and all the people like the first miserable man, this fortunate man was pleased and happy at both his own joy and that of all the inhabitants. Furthermore, he was able to do some profitable trade. He offered thanks to God.

After some while he returned and came across the other man. He understood his condition, and said to him: "You were out of your mind. The ugliness within you must have been reflected on the outer world so that you imagined laughter to be weeping, and the discharge from duties to be sack and pillage. Come to your senses and purify your heart so that this calamitous veil is raised from your eyes and you can see the truth. For the country of an utterly just, compassionate, beneficent, powerful, order-loving, and kind king could not be as you imagined, nor could a country which demonstrated this number of clear signs of progress and achievement." The unhappy man later came to his senses and repented. He said, "Yes, I was crazy through drink. May God be pleased with you, you have saved me from a hellish state."

O my soul! Know that the first man represents an unbeliever, or someone depraved and heedless. In his view the world is a house of universal mourning. All living creature are orphans weeping at the blows of death and separation. Man and the animals are alone and without ties being ripped apart by the talons of the appointed hour. Mighty beings like the mountains and oceans are like horrendous, lifeless corpses. Many grievous, crushing, terrifying delusions like these arise from his unbelief and misguidance, and torment him.

As for the other man, he is a believer. He recognizes and affirms Almighty God. In his view this world is an abode where the Names of the All-Merciful One are constantly recited, a place of instruction for man and the animals, and a field of examination for man and jinn. All animal and human deaths are a demobilization. Those who have completed their duties of life depart from this transient world for another, happy and trouble-free, world so that place may be made for new officials to come and work. The birth of animals and humans marks their enlistment into the army, their being taken under arms, and the start of their duties. Each living being is a joyful regular soldier, an honest, contented official. And all voices are either glorification of God and the recitation of His Names at the outset of their duties, and the thanks and rejoicing at their ceasing work, or the songs arising from their joy at working. In the view of the believer, all beings are the friendly servants, amicable officials, and agreeable books of his Most Generous Lord and All-Compassionate Owner. Very many more subtle, exalted, pleasurable, and sweet truths like these become manifest and appear from his belief.

That is to say, belief in God bears the seed of what is in effect a Tuba-Tree of Paradise, while unbelief conceals the seed of a Zakkum-Tree of Hell.

That means that salvation and security are only to be found in Islam and belief. In which case, we should continually say, "Praise be to God for the religion of Islam and perfect belief."

The Words, Second Word, p. 27–28.

Extract Two: The Four Channels

Seedbed of the Light, Al-Mathnawi al-Nuri, composed of 12 treatises, is among the early books of the *Risale-i Nur*. "The Eleventh Treatise" contained within this book is about the knowledge of God as explained through four channels, each of which are proofs of God's Existence and Unity. The four channels are: the Prophet Muhammad—his character and witness; the beauty and order of the universe; the Qur'an in all its elegance; and human conscience and consciousness. Notice the way in which Nursi poses questions for him to answer.

The Eleventh Treatise

A point from the light of knowledge of God, exalted is His Majesty

When I enter a garden, I choose its most beautiful flower or fruit. If it is difficult for me to pick it, I take pleasure in looking at it. If I come across to a rotten one, I pretend not to notice it, according to the rule: Take what pleases and leave what does not. This is my style, and I ask my readers to behave in the same way.

...

Our aim and goal is God. *There is no Deity but He, the All-Living, Self-Subsistent* (2:255). Among countless proofs of Him, we give only four here.

- The first proof is Prophet Muhammad, upon him peace and blessings. ...
- The second proof is the universe, the macro-cosmos pr macro-human, the observed, great Book of Creation.
- The third proof is the Qur'an, the book in which there is no doubt and which is the Sacred Word.
- The fourth proof is the human conscience or consciousness, the juncture of the Unseen and the material, visible worlds. A human being's consciousness or conscience influences the intellect from which the ray of belief in Divine Unity issues.

First proof: The Muhammadan Truth²

This proof is furnished with Messengership and Islam. Messengership contains the testimony of the greatest consensus and most comprehensive agreement of all Prophets, and Islam bears the spirit of the Divinely revealed religions and their confirmation based on the Revelation.

The Noble Messenger explains the existence of God and His Unity to humanity. His truthful words are affirmed by his manifest miracles, the Prophets' testimony, and the confirmation of all Divinely revealed religions. The Prophet manifests that light (of Divine Unity) in the name of those purified, excellent men and women who agree on this call. Falsehood cannot have hand in this pure, clear, evident truth, which enjoys such strong confirmation and is discerned by eyes penetrating all truths.

Second Proof: The Book of Creation

All letters and points of this book, individually and collectively and in its particular tongue, say: *There is nothing that does not glorify Him with His praise* (17:44), proclaim the All-Great Creator's Existence and Unity. Every particle testifies truthfully to the All-Wise Creator's necessary Existence. While hesitating among endless possible destinations, if they will constitute building blocks of a being and in what kind of being they will be put, each particle takes a particular route and assumes particular attributes. It is directed to a specific goal in accordance with certain established laws and ends in many amazing purposeful consequences. It strengthens belief in God, which God implanted in our inner faculty so that we may find Him, and which is a sample in us of the unseen worlds.

Does a particle proclaim the purpose of its All-Majestic Maker and His manifest Wisdom in its particular tongue? Through its individual existence, particular attributes, and definite nature, every particle points and testifies to the All-Wise Creator. It acts as a building block in forming compounds; taking a route among countless possibilities, it assumes its proper position in a compound. This position has relations with all other positions, and the particle fulfills many tasks issuing from those relations. As there is a strict balance and perfect harmony among positions, each task the particle fulfills yields numerous, wise fruits.

---

²   The Muhammadan Truth is the truth represented by Prophet Muhammad, upon him be peace and blessings, as a servant and Messenger of God Almighty, as well as the truth of which he is the unique embodiment. (Tr.)

As all of this corroborates the particle's testimony of the Creator, the particle proclaims the proofs of its All-Majestic Maker's necessary Existence and displays its All-Wise Creator's purpose in the tongue of its acts and the tasks it fulfills. IT is as if it recites the verses declaring Divine Unity, just a soldier is charged with particular duties and has relations with all army divisions in respect to those duties.

Then, are the proofs of Almighty God's (Existence and Unity) not more clear than all of creation's particles? The Tradition "The roads leading to God are as many as His creatures breaths" expresses a pure truth.

Question: Why are we unable to find the All-Great Creator with our intellects?

Answer: Because of His manifestation's perfection and His having no opposite.[3]

Reflect upon the lines of the [Book of the] Universe, for they are letters to you from the Highest Realm.

The Book of Creation displays orderliness as clearly as the midday sun and exhibits the Power's miracle in every word or letter. Its composition is so miraculous that, even supposing that each natural cause were a free agent, each cause would prostrate humbly before this miraculousness, acknowledging: "Glory be to you. We have no power. Surely, You are All-Mighty, All-Wise."

This Book's order is so subtle and delicate that inserting a new point in its exacts place requires an absolute power that can create everything, for each letter—especially living ones—has inner relations with sentences and a strong connection with all other words. Thus, whoever created a gnat's eyes created the sun, and whoever ordered a flea's stomach ordered the solar system. Refer to: *Your creation and resurrection are but like (those of) a single soul* (31:28), and see how truthful a witness comes from a bee's tongue, which is only one of the Poser's miracles or represents a small word in this Book.

Ponder over a micro-organism that, although invisible to the naked eye, is a sample of creation. The One Who "wrote" it in that miraculous fashion also "wrote" the universe. If you study it and discern its subtle mechanisms and wonderful systems, you will be convinced that its existence and life cannot be attributed to lifeless, simple, natural causes that cannot distinguish between possibilities. Otherwise you must admit that each particle contains the

---

[3]   Everything is known through its opposite. Only the Almighty God has no equal or opposite. (Tr.)

consciousness of sages, the knowledge of scientists, and they communicate with each other directly. Even the superstitious are ashamed of such a claim.

There is no explanation other than to regard is as a miracle of Divine Power, the invention of the One Who invented and arranged the universe. If this were not so, it would be impossible for two most important natural causes or laws, gravity and repulsion, to come together in an atom. Gravity and repulsion, motion and similar phenomena, are names of Divine principles or ways operating represented as laws. They may be accepted as laws, provided that they are not promoted to being the foundation of an agent nature. Being only names or titles or having nominal existence, they should not be accorded real, external existence.

Question: Why do people believe in matter's eternity and attribute all species' formation to random motions of particles or similar things?

Answer: Reasoning or rational judgment does not always lead to belief, as being rationally convinced does not men believing in God. They cannot perceive their mistake, as their reasoning is based on a superficial view and imitation. If they inquire into the matter closely and pursuit of the truth they will see how illogical and irrational such a belief is. If, despite this, they still hold such a belief, they are heedless of the Creator. Such a strange deviation! How can those who find it hard to accept the eternity of God, the Glorified, and attribute creation to Him—although eternity and creativity are among the Divine Essence's indispensable attributes—attribute eternity and creativity to countless particles and helpless things?

Recall this well-known incident: Once, people were scanning the sky for the new crescent moon to mark the Ramadan's beginning. An old man claimed he had seen it, when what he had really seen was a downward-curving white hair from his eyebrow. It is that hair-like thing that blinds people to the truth. Humanity is of noble character by creation. While pursuing truth, people sometimes encounter falsehood and keep it in their hearts; or while digging out the truth they come across misguidance and, supposing it to be the truth, accept it.

Question: What are those things called "nature," "laws," and "forces," and how are people deceived by them?

Answer: Nature is the comprehensive Divine Shari'a (assembly of laws) established for the order and harmony among everything contained in the visible, material world. This law of creation also is called the "way of God." Nature is the result of all nominal laws in creation. Forces are the principles of this Shari'a, and laws are elements of the same Shari'a. the regularity of its principles and elements leads people to see it as "nature" with a real, external existence, ad after that, as an agent. Although the human heart or mind cannot be conceived that nature is a true agent, those who deny the All-Majestic Creator and refuse to understand the Divine Power's miraculous works may see this blind, ignorant nature as the origin of things.

Nature is something printed, not a printer; a design, not a designer; an object acted on, not an agent; a rule or measure, not an origin; an order, not an orderer. It is principle without power, a set of laws without real or external existence that issues from the Divine Attributes of Will and Power.

Suppose a young person comes to this exquisite world from another one and enters a beautiful, richly adorned palace. No one to whom this building and decoration can be attributed is seen. So this person, after seeing a comprehensive book containing the blueprint and information on how the palace was built and furnished, and due to his o her and ignorance and obsession with the builder, thinks that the book built the palace. In the same way, the heedlessness of some people concerning the All-Majestic Creator allows them to deceive themselves into accepting the natural world as its own originator.

God has two kinds of Shari'a. one issues from the Divine Attribute of Speech and regulates or orders the acts of servants issuing from their free will. The other issues from the Divine Attribute of Will and Power, comprises the Divine commands of creation, and it is the result of the Divine Way of acting. The first one comprises comprehensible laws, while the second one consists of nominal laws, wrongly called "laws of nature." They have no creative or inventive part in existence, for that is unique to the Divine Power.

Everything that exists is connected to all other things; nothing can exist or survive by itself. The one who created a single thing created all things, and can only be the One, Eternally-Besought-of-All. By contrast, natural causes, to which misguided ascribe creativity, are numerous, do not know one another, and are blind. Attributing creativity to them means accepting that innumerable blind, lifeless things have come together by chance and formed this vast, orderly universe, [the existence, order, and harmony of which manifestly require absolute knowledge and will, power and wisdom]. *Then leave them to plunge and play* (6:91).

To sum up: The Book of the Universe's observed order and regularity, and the manifests miraculousness in its composition, are two proofs of Divine Unity showing that the universe and its contents are works of the absolute Power, infinite Knowledge, and eternal Will of God.

Question: How can the order, harmony, and regularity be established?

Answer: Sciences, with function as if humanity's senses, have discovered this order by deduction and induction. Each branch of science is based upon or studies one aspect of existence. Science's universal principles originate in this order, harmony, and regularity. Each branch comprises the universal principles and rules prevalent in the species it studies. Those principles' universality and uniformity point to the order's magnificence, for without it universal rules or what they call laws could not be inferred. Scientists discover that order through science, and by it see that the macro human being (the universe) is as orderly as themselves. There is wisdom in everything, for nothing is purposeless or left to its own devices.

The Book of Creation, with all its systems, worlds of living creatures and particles, proclaims Divine Unity. Altogether they declare: *there is no deity but God.*

Third proof: The Qur'an

When you listen to this articulate proof, you will hear it repeat: *there is no deity but God.* This proof is like an enormous tree whose branches hang down with innumerable, splendid fruits of truth. Since such a tree cannot grow from a rotten seed, all can see that its seed (Divine Unity) is sound and lively.

The branch of this tree stretching into the visible, material world bears fruits of the most sound and realistic commands and rules, while its other great branch, extending into the Unseen, is laden with ripe fruits yielded by Divine Unity and belief in the Unseen.

If this comprehensive proof is studied closely, one will have to admit that the one who communicated it was absolutely certain of its result (Divine Unity), and felt no hesitation about its truth. He based his other claims on this firm result, and made it a criterion to judge whatever exists. Such a basis, established so firmly and bearing a manifest seal of miraculousness, has no need for show and pretension, and is independent of being pronounced true by others. All that is says and declares, and all its tidings, are true.

All six sides of this luminous proof are transparent and clear. On it is the seal of manifest and miraculousness, beneath are logic and evidence, to its right is the assent of intellect, to its left is the testimony of conscience, in front of it is good and happiness in both worlds, and it is founded on pure Revelation. How can doubt enter such a formidable citadel?

There are four paths leading to the throne of perfection, which is knowledge of God:

First: The path Sufis, which is based on purifying carnal soul and spiritual illumination.

Second: The path of theologians who, to prove the Necessarily Existent Being's Existence, depend on the argument that everything comes into existence contingently, in time and space. Thus its existence or non-existence is equally possible, which means that there must be an Eternal One Who prefers their existence and brings them into existence by His Will.

Although both parts are deduced from the Qur'an, their followers have complicated them a bit and thus caused some doubt to enter.

Third: The part of philosophers contaminated with doubt, hesitation, and fancies to sime extent.

Fourth (and best): The path of the Qur'an, which clearly shows the throne of perfection with its numerous eloquence, beautiful style, and incomparable comprehensiveness. It is the most direct and inclusive, as well as the shortest, path to God.

There are four means to reach that throne: inspiration, learning or study, purification, and reflection.

The Qur'an follows two ways to knowledge of God, glory be to Him, and to prove God's unity.

The first is the argument of favoring and purposiveness

All Qur'anic verses that mention the benefits or uses of things, and the wisdom in or purposes for their existence, "weave" this argument and serve as mirrors in which it is reflected. This argument can be summarized as follows: everything is made firmly and artistically. The perfect orderliness in creation, which is for certain purposes and uses and is evident in everything's existence, indicates that the All-Wise Creator created them for a basic purpose. Such clear will leaves no room for chance and coincidence. Any science dealing with creation testifies to this orderliness, points to the uses and fruits hanging from the branches of existence like clusters, and reveals the wisdom and beneficial results behind daily, monthly, and seasonal changes.

Take zoology and botany. The world contains hundreds of thousands (even millions) of plant and animal species, each of which had a first, original ancestor. For humanity this was Adam. Each member of these species is like an exquisite, amazing mechanism. How can one claim that the so called laws of nominal existence and ignorant, blind natural causes could create these innumerable chains of beings? Each species and each member proclaim that they issued from the Hand of the wise, Divine Power.

The Qur'an teaches us this argument: *Then, look again! Can you see any rifts?* (67:3). By commanding us to reflect on creatures and mentioning their uses or benefits as Divine bounties, the Qur'an seeks to establish this argument in the human mind, and then calls upon reason to ponder over them in the conclusions and divisions of verses. It illuminated the role of reason and stirs up conscience in such conclusions as: *Do they not know? Will they not reflect and learn the lesson?*

The second is the argument of invention

God Almighty has given each species and each member an existence particular to the tasks it will fulfill and the perfections it will achieve. No species comes from eternity, because every species has a beginning and its existence is not absolutely necessary. Everything exists by the Necessarily Existent One's will and preference, while it was equally possible for it to exist or not. This truth cannot be changed.

How strange it is that those who deny the All-Majestic Creator's Eternity—although eternity is one of His indispensable Attributes—attribute it to matter, which is contained in time and space. Where can the tiniest blind, ignorant, ad helpless particle find the power, stability, and firmness before which the universe bows in submission and veneration? How can creating and originating, attributes of Divine Power, be attributed to natural causes, the most impotent and weakest of things?

The Qur'an establishes this argument when mentioning creation and invention, and confirms that only God, the One, has creative power. Causes are only veils before the Divine Power and Its Grandeur to prevent the mind from drawing wrong conclusions about the All-Holy Divine Being by seeing with a superficial view the Hand of His Power involved in mundane affairs.

Every thing has two aspects. One is its apparent aspect, which is like a mirror's dense, black face in which opposites—small and great, good and evil, beautiful and ugly—exist side by side. Here, causes display the Almighty's Grandeur and Dignity. The other is the inner, immaterial aspect, which is like a mirror's polished or transparent face. This aspect is pure and absolutely beautiful, and as required by Divine Unity, has no room for causes. Since things like life and spirit, as well as light and existence, were created by the Hand of Power without the "help" of causes, both their outer and inner aspects are beautiful.

Fourth proof: The human conscience (conscious nature)

First: the natural or inborn qualities of things do not lie. A seed has an inclination to grow as if to say: "If I am planted, I will grow and yield fruit." It says the truth. An egg has an inclination toward life as if to say: "I will become a chick," and becomes so. When a handful of water has an inclination to freeze and expand, it says: "I will cover a broader space" and it cracks even iron, despite the latter's hardness and firmness. Such inclinations manifest the commands of creation issuing from Divine Will.

Second: Human senses are not restricted to five known ones. Each person has many "windows" opening from the Unseen, and many other senses of whose nature he or she knows or does not know. For example, *drive* and *energy* are two other senses that do not lie.

Third: Something imagined and only of nominal existence cannot be the origin of external, visible existence. *The point of reliance* (or support) and *the point of seeking help*, both of which people necessarily feel within themselves are two essential aspects of their conscience or conscious nature. The absence of these two points, which is irreconcilable with the wisdom, order, and perfection in creation, would mean that human beings noble creations with an essentially pure spirit, would be reduced to the lowest of the low.

Fourth: Even if reason does not work properly and cannot see the truth, the human conscience does not forget the Creator. Even if one's selfhood denies Him, the conscience sees Him, reflects on Him, and turns toward Him. Intuitive perception stirs it up, and inspiration illuminates it. Love of God urges the conscience to obtain the knowledge of the Almighty. This love, one's strong yearning to Him that issues from a strong desire based on a strong inclination, is innate in the human conscience. The attraction (toward Him) ingrained in this conscience is due to the existence of One Who really attracts.

After these preliminary notes, look into the conscience and see how it is a proof, entrusted to the soul of every person, proclaiming Divine Unity. Just as the heart pumps life throughout the body, knowledge of God, the source of its (spiritual) life, energizes and vitalizes all human ambition and inclinations. It also pours pleasure and joy into them, increases their value, expands and develops, and sharpens them. This is the point of seeking help.

Knowledge of God is a point of support and reliance upon which people base their lives. If people do not believe in the All-Wise Creator, Whose every act contains order and wisdom, but attribute things and events to blind coincidence (which cannot resist misfortune), they will live in a hellish state. This cannot be allowed, for humanity is a noble creation and has the potential to achieve perfection. This also goes against the universe's prevailing, firm order. These two points are necessary for one's spirit, because the All-Munificent Creator uses them to diffuse the light of His knowledge into the conscience of every person. Even if the eyes of reason are blind, the eyes of conscience are always open.

The testimony of these four comprehensive arguments show that the All-Majestic Creator is the Necessarily Existent Being and Eternal, One and Single, Unique and Eternally-Besought-of-All, All-Knowing and All-Powerful, All-Willing and All-Hearing, All-Seeing and All-Speaking, All-Living and Self-Subsistent, He is also qualified with all Attributes of Majesty and Grace. Whatever creatures have in the name of perfection comes from the shadowy manifestation of the Majestic Creator's Perfection. Beauty, Grace, and Perfection are infinitely greater than the sum of the beauty, grace, and perfection shared by creation. Also, the All-Glorified Creator has no defect, for defect originates from the imperfect inborn capacities of material beings. The All-Glorified One is free from materiality, and exempt from the qualities essential to the nature of the created.

There is nothing like Him; He is the Hearing, the All-Seeing. (42:11)

Glory be to Him Who keeps concealed because of the intensity of His manifestation, Who is hidden because of the lack of His opposite, and Who is veiled by natural causes because of His dignity.

Question: What about the doctrine of the Unity of Being (*Wahdat al-Wujud*)?

Answer: Thee doctrine of the Unity of Being comes from absorption in Divine Unity. This is experienced inwardly and deeply and cannot be a matter of theory or thought. Profound absorption in Divine Unity (following belief in God's Unity as Lord and Deity) engenders belief in the Power's unity (only God creates). Belief in the Power's unity engenders belief in the unity of dominion and ruling, which, in turn, ends in seeing what is witnessed as united (Unity of the Witnessed) and finally tin the Unity of Being. This leads to seeing existence as one or united, and then seeing what exists as united.

The ecstatic sayings of some Sufis that go beyond what is really intended must not be taken as proofs for this way's truth. If people who have not saved themselves from the sphere of cause and effect, who organize their lives considering the laws of causality, speak about the Unity of Being (inclusive of created entities), they exceed their limits. Those who really sense and speak about this unity restrict themselves to the Necessarily Existent Being in isolation from the created, and see God as the only truly existent being.

Seeing the result together with or contained in evidence leading to it, that is, the All-Majestic Maker as the only truly existent being, comes from absorbing the view and experience of the Divine Being's existence. It Is the result of seeing or perceiving Divine manifestations in the channels of existence and the flux of Divine effulgences in the inner dimensions of things, and the manifestations of Divine Names and Attributes in the mirrors of creations.

My personal view is as follows: This perception pertains to inner experience and sensing. However, as such belief or inner experience cannot be expressed exactly those who follow the Unity of Being interpret it as pervading Divinity and permeating Life in creatures. Philosophers or those who try to find the truth with their intellects or sense impressions have made this way a philosophical or intellectual topic, and thus a source of false ideas and concepts.

Some materialist, pantheistic philosophers also believe in the Unity of Being. However, both groups understand this phrase in mutually exclusive terms. There are five significant differences between them:

First: Sufi scholars restrict their view to the Necessarily Existent Being and reflect on Him so strongly that they do not accept the universe's existence, for, in their words, only the Necessarily Existent Being truly exists, everything else is illusory. Materialist philosophers and those with weak belief concentrate on matter and are far from perceiving Divinity. They give priority to matter and say that only matter or material things exist. Due to their unbelief, they see Divinity as contained or embodied by matter, or prefer to remain indifferent to Divinity by restricting their view to the universe.

Second: Sufis who believe in the Unity of Being see the universe as something witnessed or only sensed. However, the others regard the universe as really existent and believe in the unity of what exists materially.

Third: The way of Sufi saints pertains to inner experience, while the others follow a purely rationalistic way.

Fourth: Sufi saints are lost in the Truth, the Almighty, and consider the universe from the viewpoint of Divinity. The others are absorbed in creatures and reflect on them for their sake and from within that absorption,

Fifth: Sufi saints worship God and love Him deeply, while the others adore their selves and follow their fancies.

These two ways are as different as the highest heaven and the Earth, bright light and thick darkness.

A mote for further enlightenment

> If Earth were made up of pieces of different-colored glass, each piece would receive sunlight and reflect accordingly. Although what each piece would receive and reflect is neither the sun nor its light itself, if each piece could speak, it would say: "I am a sun." Similarly, if the colors of those smiling, brilliant flowers were to speak, although they are manifestations of the sunlight's seven colors, each would say "The sun resembles me" or "The sun belongs to me exclusively."

Those illusions are traps for saints,

Whereas in reality they are reflections of the radiant-faced in the garden of God.[4]

> Those who believe in the Unity of the Witnessed (or sensed) in the name of existence follow sobriety, wakefulness, and discernment. As the Unity of Being is a way of spiritual intoxication, the Unity of Witnessed is a safer way.

> Think about the bounties and blessings o God. Do not think about His Essence, because you are unable to do that.[5]

> The reality of humanity: While humanity cannot perceive it,

> how can humanity perceive how the Eternal All-Compelling is?

> He is the One Who originated things and built them.

> How can one who is a breath created perceive Him?

> *Seedbed of the Light*, The Eleventh Treatise, p. 367–380.

Extract Three: The Universe as a Book

Considering the universe as a meaningful "book" of God's extensive arts, Nursi illustrated how one could discover God though reading of the pages of this book in an extensive chapter named "The Supreme Sign." One can, argues Nursi, learn so much from the design of the universe about the nature of God. Its lengthy introduction examines the logical basis of faith and denial; particularly the inherent nature of provability of faith and unprovability of denial. It focuses on

---

[4]   Mawlana Jalal al-Din al-Rumi, *Al-Mathnawi al-Kabir*, 1:3.

[5]   A Prophetic Tradition. Tabarani, *Al-Mu'jam as Awsat*, 6456.

"two abysses that shake certainty of faith in this age" and "the means of salvation from them."

Introduction

I created not jinn and mankind except that they might worship me.[6]

According to the meaning of this mighty verse, the purpose for the sending of man to this world and the wisdom implicit in it, consists of recognizing the Creator of all beings and believing in Him and worshipping Him. The primordial duty of man and the obligation incumbent upon him are to know God and believe in Him, to assent to His Being and unity in submission and perfect certainty.

For man, who by nature desires permanent life and immortal existence, whose unlimited hopes are matched by boundless afflictions, any object or accomplishment other than belief in God, knowledge of God and the means for attaining these, which are the fundament and key of eternal life—any such object or accomplishment must be regarded as lowly for man, or even worthless in many cases.

Since this truth has been proven with firm evidence in the Risale-i Nur, we refer exposition of it to that, setting forth here, within the framework of four questions, only two abysses that shake certainty of faith in this age and induce hesitation.

The means for salvation from the first abyss are these two Matters:

The First Matter: As proven in detail in the Thirteenth Flash of the Thirty-First Letter, in general questions denial has no value in the face of proof and is extremely weak. For example, with respect to the sighting of the crescent moon at the beginning of Ramadan the Noble, if two common men prove the crescent to have emerged by their witnessing it, and thousands of nobles and scholars deny it, saying: "We have not seen it," their negation is valueless and without power to convince. When it is a question of proof each person strengthens and supports the other, and consensus results. But when it is a question of negation, there is no difference between one man and a thousand. Each person remains alone and isolated. For the one who affirms looks beyond himself and judges the matter as it is. Thus in the example we have given, if one says "The moon is in the sky," and his friend then points his finger at the moon, the two of them unite and are strengthened.

---

[6]   Qur'an, 51:56.

The one who engages in negation and denial, however, does not regard the matter as it is, and is even unable to do so. For it is a well-known principle that "a non-particularized denial, not directed to a particular locus, cannot be proven."

For example, if I affirm the existence of a thing in the world, and you deny it, I can easily establish its existence with a single indication. But for you to justify your negation, that is to establish the non-existence of the thing—it is necessary to hunt exhaustively through the whole world, and even to examine every aspect of past ages. Only then can you say, "It does not exist, and never has existed."

Since those who negate and deny do not regard the matter as it is but judge rather in the light of their own souls, and their own intelligence and vision, they can in no way strengthen and support each other. For the veils and causes that prevent them from seeing and knowing are various. Anyone can say, "I do not see it; therefore, in my opinion and belief, it does not exist." But none can say, "It does not exist in actuality." If someone says this -particularly in questions of belief, which look to all the universe- it is a lie as vast as the world itself, and he who utters it will be incapable both of speaking the truth and of being corrected.

In Short: The result is one and single in the case of affirmation, and every instance of affirmation supports all other instances.

Negation by contrast is not one, but multiple. Multiplicity arises through each person's saying concerning himself, "In my opinion and view," or "In my belief," and leads to multiplicity of result. Hence each separate instance cannot support all other instances.

Therefore, with respect to the truth with which we began, there is no significance in the multiplicity and apparent predominance of the unbelievers and deniers who oppose belief. Now it is necessary to refrain from introducing any hesitation into the certainty and faith of a believer, but in this age the negations and denials of the philosophers of Europe have induced doubt in a number of unfortunate dupes and thus destroyed their certainty and obliterated their eternal felicity. Death and the coming of one's appointed hour, which afflict thirty thousand men each day, are deprived of their meaning of dismissal from this world and presented as eternal annihilation. The grave with its ever-open door, constantly threatens the denier with annihilation and poisons his life with the bitterest of sorrows. Appreciate then how great a blessing is faith, and the very essence of life.

The Second Matter: With respect to a problem subject to discussion in science or art, those who stand outside that science or art cannot speak authoritatively, however great, learned and accomplished they may be, nor can their judgements be accepted as decisive. They cannot form part of the learned consensus of the science.

For example, the judgement of a great engineer on the diagnosis and cure of a disease does not have the same value as that of the lowliest physician. In particular, the words of denial of a philosopher who is absorbed in the material sphere, who becomes continually more remote from the non-material or spiritual and cruder and more insensitive to light, whose intelligence is restricted to what his eye beholds—the words of such a one are unworthy of consideration and valueless with respect to non-material and spiritual matters.

On matters sacred and spiritual and concerning the Divine unity, there is total accord among the hundreds of thousands of the People of Truth, such as Shaykh Gilani (May his mystery be sanctified), who beheld God's Sublime Throne while still on the earth, who spent ninety years advancing in spiritual work, and who unveiled the truths of belief in all three stations of certainty. This being the case what value have the words of philosophers, who through their absorption in the most diffuse details of the material realm and the most minute aspects of multiplicity are choking and dazed? Are not their denials and objections drowned out like the buzzing of a mosquito by the roaring of thunder?

The essence of the unbelief that opposes the truths of Islam and struggles against them is denial, ignorance, and negation. Even though it may appear to be an affirmation of some kind and a manifestation of being, it is in reality negation and non-being. Whereas belief is knowledge and a manifestation of being; it is affirmation and judgement. Every negating aspect of belief is the gate to a positive truth or the veil covering it. If the unbelievers who struggle against faith attempt, with the utmost difficulty, to affirm and accept their negative beliefs in the form of acceptance and admission of non-being, then their unbelief may be regarded in one respect as a form of mistaken knowledge or erroneous judgement. But as for non-acceptance, denial, and non-admission -something more easily done- it is absolute ignorance and total absence of judgement.

In Short: The convictions underlying unbelief are then of two kinds:

The First pays no regard to the truths of Islam. It is an erroneous admission, a baseless belief and a mistaken acceptance peculiar to itself; it is an unjust judgement. This kind of unbelief is beyond the scope of our discussion. It has no concern with us, nor do we have any concern with it.

The Second Kind opposes the truths of belief and struggles against them. It consists in turn of two varieties.

The First is non-acceptance. It consists simply of not consenting to affirmation. This is a species of ignorance; there is no judgement involved and it occurs easily. It too is beyond the scope of our discussion.

The Second variety is acceptance of non-being. It is to consent to non-being with one's heart, and a judgement is involved. It is a conviction and a taking the part of something. It is on account of this partiality that it is obliged to affirm its negation.

The negation comprises two types:

The First Type says: "A certain thing does not exist at a certain place or in a particular direction." This kind of denial can be proved, and it lies outside of our discussion.

The Second Type consists of negating and denying those doctrinal and sacred matters, general and comprehensive, that concern this world, all beings, the hereafter, and the succession of different ages. This kind of negation cannot in any fashion be substantiated, as we have shown in the First Matter, for what is needed to substantiate such negations is a vision that shall encompass the whole universe, behold the hereafter, and observe every aspect of time without limit.

The Second Abyss and the means for escaping from it: This too consists of two matters.

The First: Intelligences that become narrowed by absorption in neglect of God and in sin, or the material realm, are unable to comprehend vast matters in respect of sublimity, grandeur, and infinity; hence taking pride in such knowledge as they have, they hasten to denial and negation. Since they cannot encompass the extremely vast, profound and comprehensive questions of faith within their straitened and desiccated intellects, their corrupt and spiritually moribund hearts, they cast themselves into unbelief and misguidance, and choke.

If they were able to look at the true nature of their unbelief and the essence of their misguidance they would see that, compared to the reasonable, suitable and indeed necessary sublimity and grandeur that is present in belief, their unbelief conceals and contains manifold absurdity and impossibility. The Risale-i Nur has proven this truth by hundreds of comparisons with the same finality that "two plus two equals four." For example, one who does not accept the Necessary Being, the pre-eternity, and the comprehensiveness of attribute of God Almighty, on account of their grandeur and sublimity, may form a creed of unbelief by assigning that necessary being, pre-eternity, and the attributes of Godhead to an unlimited number of beings, an infinity of atoms. Or like the foolish Sophists, he can abdicate his intelligence by denying and negating both his own existence and that of the universe.

Thus, all the truths of belief and Islam, basing their matters on the grandeur and sublimity which are their requirement, deliver themselves from the awesome absurdities, the fearsome superstitions, and the tenebrous ignorance of unbelief that confront them, and take up their place in sound hearts and straight intellects, through utmost submission and assent.

The constant proclamation of this grandeur and sublimity in the call to prayer, in the prayers themselves and in most of the rites of Islam,

Allahu akbar, God is Most Great!

God is Most Great! God is Most Great!

the declaration of the Sacred Tradition that "Grandeur is My shield and Sublimity My cloak;"[7] and the statement of the Prophet (Peace and blessings be upon him)—his most inspiring communing with God, in the eighty-sixth part of *Jawshan al-Kabir*:[8] *O You other than Whose Kingdom no kingdom exists*;

O You Whose Praise cannot be counted by His slaves [worshippers];

O You Whose Glory cannot be described by His creatures;

O You Whose Perfection lies beyond the range of all vision;

O You Whose Attributes exceed the bounds of all understanding;

O You Whose Grandeur is beyond the reach of all thought;

O You Whose Qualities man cannot fittingly describe;

O You Whose Decree His slaves cannot avert;

O You Whose Signs are manifest in everything

–Be You glorified; there is no god other than You–

Protection, protection, deliver us from the Fire!

all these show that grandeur and sublimity constitute a necessary veil.

The Rays, Seventh Ray (The Supreme Sign), p. 125–129.

---

[7]   *Muslim*, Birr, 136; *Abu Da'ud*, Libas, 25; *Ibn Maja*, Zuhd, 16; *Musnad*, ii, 248, 376, 414, 427, 442; iv, 416; Ibn Hibban, *Sahih*, i, 272; vii, 473; al-Hindi, *Kanz al-'Ummal*, iii, 534.

[8]   The famous supplication revealed to the Prophet Muhammad (PBUH) which, consisting of the Divine Names, is related to possess many merits. [Tr.]

Extract Four: The Supreme Sign

"The Supreme Sign," follows the footsteps of a curious and observant traveler questioning the Maker about the universe. This chapter is a metaphorically rich journey in which the reader finds oneself engaged by the heavens, wind and clouds, the rain, oceans and rivers, mountains and deserts, plants, trees and birds, and other forms of creation, telling of the meaning of their existence. The following is only the beginning of the chapter, including the testimony of the heavens and all they contain along with the testimony of the atmosphere.

The Supreme Sign

The Observations of a Traveller Questioning the Universe Concerning His Maker

In the Name of God, the Merciful, the Compassionate.
The seven heavens and the earth and all that is in them extol and glorify Him, and there is nothing but glorifies Him with praise, but you understand not their glorifying; indeed, He is Most Forebearing, Most Forgiving.[9] ...

Since this sublime verse, like many other Qur'anic verses, mentions first the heavens -that brilliant page proclaiming God's unity, gazed on at all times and by all men with wonder and joy- in its pronouncement of the Creator of this cosmos, let us too begin with a mention of the heavens.

Indeed, every voyager who comes to the hospice and the realm of this world, opens his eyes and wonders who is the master of this fine hospice, which resembles a most generous banquet, a most ingenious exhibition, a most impressive camp and training ground, a most amazing and wondrous place of recreation, a most profound and wise place of instruction. He asks himself too who is the author of this great book, and who is the monarch of this lofty realm. There first presents itself to him the beautiful face of the heavens, inscribed with the gilt lettering of the stars. That face calls him saying, "Look at me, and I shall guide you to what you seek."

He looks then and sees a manifestation of dominicality performing various tasks in the heavens: it holds aloft in the heavens, without any supporting pillar, hundreds of thousands of heavenly bodies, some of which are a thousand times heavier than the earth and revolve seventy times faster than a cannon-ball; it causes them to move in harmony and swiftly without colliding with each other; it causes innumerable lamps to burn constantly, without the use of any oil; it disposes of these great masses without any disturbance or disorder; it sets sun

---

[9]   Qur'an, 17:44.

and moon to work at their respective tasks, without those great bodies ever rebelling; it administers within infinite space -the magnitude of which cannot be measured in figures should they stretch from pole to pole- all that exists, at the same time, with the same strength, in the same fashion, manner and mould, without the least deficiency; it reduces to submissive obedience to its law all the aggressive powers inherent in those bodies; it cleanses and lustrates the face of the heavens, removing all the sweepings and refuse of that vast assembly; it causes those bodies to maneuver like a disciplined army; and then, making the earth revolve, it shows the heavens each night and each year in a different form, like a cinema screen displaying true and imaginative scenes to the audience of creation.

There is within this dominical activity a truth consisting of subjugation, administration, revolution, ordering, cleansing, and employment. This truth, with its grandeur and comprehensiveness, bears witness to the necessary existence and unity of the Creator of the Heavens and testifies to that Existence being more manifest than that of the heavens. Hence it was said in the First Degree of the First Station:

There is no god but God, the Necessary Being, to Whose Necessary Existence in Unity the heavens and all they contain testify, through the testimony of the sublimity of the comprehensiveness of the truth of subjugation, administration, revolution, ordering, cleansing, and employment, a truth vast and perfect, and to be observed.

Then that wondrous place of gathering known as space or the atmosphere begins thunderously to proclaim to that traveller come as a guest to the world, "Look at me! You can discover and find through me the object of your search, the one who sent you here!" The traveller looks at the sour but kind face of the atmosphere, and listening to the awesome but joyous thunderclaps perceives the following.

The clouds, suspended between the sky and the earth, water the garden of the world in the most wise and merciful fashion, furnish the inhabitants of the earth with the water of life, modify the natural heat of life, and hasten to bestow aid wherever it is needed. In addition to fulfilling these and other duties, the vast clouds, capable of filling the heavens sometimes hide themselves, with their parts retiring to rest so that not a trace can be seen, just like a well-disciplined army showing and hiding itself in accordance with sudden orders.

Then, the very instant the command is given to pour down rain, the clouds gather in one hour, or rather in a few minutes; they fill the sky and await further orders from their commander.

Next the traveller looks at the wind in the atmosphere and sees that the air is employed wisely and generously in such numerous tasks that it is as if each of the inanimate atoms of that unconscious air were hearing and noting the orders coming from that monarch of the universe; without neglecting a single one of them, it performs them in ordered fashion and through the power of the monarch. Thereby it gives breath to all beings and conveys to all living things the heat, light, and electricty they need, and transmits sound, as well as aiding in the pollination of plants.

The traveller then looks at the rain and sees that within those delicate, glistening sweet drops, sent from a hidden treasury of mercy, there are so many compassionate gifts and functions contained that it is as if mercy itself were assuming shape and flowing forth from the dominical treasury in the form of drops. It is for this reason that rain has been called "mercy."

The Rays, Seventh Ray (The Supreme Sign), p. 130–132.

Extract Five: God's Unity

The First Station of "The Twenty-Second Word" is on the affirmation of God's unity. It narrates the extraordinariness of the universe in the form of two friends' dialogue. This chapter provides an example of reflective thought and an insightful perspective on how to perceive the existence and unity of God through creation. It has two stations; the second is suggested as further reading. As a sample only, the beginning of the initial station including five of the 12 proofs is included below.

The Twenty-Second Word

First Station

In the Name of God, the Merciful, the Compassionate.

So God sets forth parables for men, so that they may bear [them] in mind.[10] *
Such are the similitudes which we propound to men that they may reflect.[11]

One time two men were washing in a pool. Under some extraordinary influence they lost their senses and when they opened their eyes, they saw that it had transported them to a strange land. It was such that with its perfect order it was like a country, or rather a town, or a palace. They looked around themselves in complete bewilderment: if it was looked at in one way, a vast world was

---

[10] Qur'an, 14:25.
[11] Qur'an, 59:21.

apparent; if in another, a well-ordered country; and if in another, a fine town. And if it was looked at in still another way, it was a palace which comprised a truly magnificent world. Travelling around this strange world, they observed it and saw that creatures of one sort were speaking in a fashion, but they did not understand their language. Nevertheless, it was understood from their signs that they were performing important works and duties.

One of the two men said to his friend: "This strange world must have someone to regulate it, and this orderly country must have a lord, and this fine town, an owner, and this finely made palace, a master builder. We must try to know him, for it is understood that the one who brought us here was he. If we do not recognize him, who will help us? What can we await from these impotent creatures whose language we do not know and who do not heed us? Moreover, surely one who makes a vast world in the form of a country, town, and palace, and fills it from top to bottom with wonderful things, and embellishes it with every sort of adornment, and decks it out with instructive miracles wants something from us and from those that come here. We must get to know him and find out what he wants."

The other man said: "I do not believe it, that there is a person such as the one you speak of, and that he governs this whole world on his own."

His friend replied to him: "If we do not recognize him and remain indifferent towards him, there is no advantage in it at all, and if it is harmful, its harm will be immense. Whereas if we try to recognize him, there is little hardship involved, and if there is benefit, it will be great. Therefore, it is in no way sensible to remain indifferent towards him."

The foolish man said: "I consider all my ease and enjoyment to lie in not thinking of him. Also, I am not going to bother with things that make no sense to me. All these things are the confused objects of chance, they are happening by themselves. What is it to me?"

His intelligent friend replied: "This obstinacy of yours will push me, and a lot of others, into disaster. It sometimes happens that a whole country is laid waste because of one ill-mannered person."

So the foolish man turned to him and said: "Either prove to me decisively that this large country has a single lord and a single maker, or leave me alone."

His friend replied: "Your obstinacy has reached the degree of lunacy, and you will be the cause of some disaster being visited on us. So I shall show you twelve proofs demonstrating that this world which is like a palace, and country which is like town, has a single maker and that it is only he who runs and administers everything. He is completely free of all deficiency. This maker, who does not appear to us, sees us and everything, and hears our words. All his works are miracles and marvels. All these creatures whom we see but whose tongues we do not understand are his officials."

First Proof

A hidden hand is working within all these works. For something which has not even an ounce of strength,[12] something as small as a seed, is raising a load of thousands of pounds. And something that does not have even a particle of consciousness[13] is performing extremely wise and purposeful works. That means they are not working by themselves, but that a hidden possessor of power is causing them to work. If they were independent, it would necessitate all the works which we see everywhere in this land being miracles and everything to be a wonder-working marvel. And that is nonsense.

Second Proof

Come, look carefully at the things which adorn all these plains, fields, and dwellings! There are marks on each telling of that hidden one. Simply, each gives news of Him like a seal or stamp. Look in front of your eyes: what does He make from one ounce of cotton?[14] See how many rolls of cloth, fine linen, and flowered material have come out of it. See how many sugared delights and round sweets are being made. If thousands of people like us were to clothe themselves in them and eat them, they would still be sufficient. And look! He has taken a handful of iron, water, earth, coal, copper, silver, and gold, and made some flesh[15] out of them. Look at that and see! O foolish one! These works are particular to such a one that all this land together with all its parts is under his miraculous power and is submissive to his every wish.

---

[12]   This alludes to seeds, which bear trees on their heads.

[13]   This indicates delicate plants like the grapevine, which themselves cannot climb or bear the weight of fruits, so throwing their delicate arms around other plants or trees and winding themselves around them, they load themselves onto them.

[14]   This indicates a seed. For example, a poppy seed like an atom, the kernel of an apricot stone, and a tiny melon seed, produce from the treasury of mercy woven leaves finer than broadcloth, flowers whiter than linen, and fruits sweeter than sugar and more delicate and delicious than sweets and conserves, and they offer them to us.

[15]   This indicates the creation of animal bodies from the elements, and living creatures from sperm.

Third Proof

Come, look at these mobile works of art![16] Each has been fashioned in such a way that it is simply a miniature sample of the huge palace. Whatever there is in the palace, it is found in these tiny mobile machines. Is it at all possible that someone other than the palace's maker could come and include the wondrous palace in a tiny machine? Also, is it at all possible that although he has included a whole world in a machine the size of a box, there could be anything in it that was purposeless or could be attributed to chance? That means that however many skilfully fashioned machines you can see, each is like a seal of that hidden one. Rather, each is like a herald or proclamation. Through their tongues of disposition they are saying: "We are the art of One Who can make this entire world of ours as easily and simply as He created us."

Fourth Proof

O my stubborn friend! Come, I shall show you something even stranger. Look! All these works and things in this land have changed and are changing. They do not stop in any one state. Note carefully that each of these lifeless bodies and unfeeling boxes has taken on the form of being absolutely dominant. Quite simply it is as though each rules all the others. Look at this machine next to us;[17] it is as though issuing commands; all the necessities and substances necessary for its adornment and functioning come hastening to it from distant places. Look over there: that lifeless body[18] is as though beckoning; it makes the largest bodies serve it and work in its own workplace. Make further analogies in the same way.

Simply, everything subjugates to itself all the beings in this world. If you do not accept the existence of that hidden one, you have to attribute all his skills, arts, and perfections in the stones, earth, animals, and creatures resembling man everywhere in this land to the things themselves. In place of a single wonder-working being, which your mind deems unlikely, you have to accept millions

---

[16] This alludes to animals and humans. For since animals are tiny indexes of the world, and man is a miniature sample of the universe, whatever there is in the world, a sample of it is in man.

[17] The machine indicates fruit-bearing trees. For they bear on their slender branches hundreds of workbenches and factories, and weave, adorn, and cook wonderful leaves, flowers and fruits, and stretch them out to us. And majestic trees like the pine and the cedar, even, set up their workbenches on dry rock, and work.

[18] This alludes to grains, seeds, and the eggs of flies. For example, a fly leaves its eggs on the leaves of the elm. Suddenly the huge tree turns its leaves into a mother's womb and a cradle for the eggs, and into a store full of a food like honey. Simply, in that way the tree, which is not fruit-producing, produces fruits bearing spirits.

like him, who are both opposed to one another, and similar, and one within the other, so they do not cause confusion everywhere and the order be spoiled. Whereas if two fingers meddle in a country, they cause confusion. For if there are two headmen in a village, or two governors in a town, or two kings in a country, the result is chaos. So what about an infinite, absolute ruler?

Fifth Proof

O my sceptical friend! Come, look carefully at the inscriptions of this vast palace, look at all the adornments of the town, see the ordering of this whole land, and reflect on all the works of art in this world! See! If these inscriptions are not worked by the pen of one hidden who possesses infinite miracles and skills, and are attributed to unconscious causes, to blind chance and deaf nature, then every stone and every plant in this land has to be an inscriber so wondrous it can write a thousand books in every letter and include millions of works of art in a single inscription. Because look at the inscription on these stones;[19] in each are the inscriptions of all the palace, and the laws ordering all the town, and the programmes for organizing the whole country. That means that it is as wonderful to make these inscriptions as to make the whole country. In which case, all the inscriptions, all the works of art, are proclamations of that hidden one, and seals of his.

Since a letter cannot exist without showing the one who wrote it, and an artistic inscription cannot exist without making known its inscriber, how is it that an inscriber who writes a huge book in a single letter and inscribes a thousand inscriptions in a single inscription, should not be known through his writing and through his inscribing?

The Words, Twenty-Second Word—First Station, p. 287–291.

Extract Six: God has no Partner

The first section of the "The Thirty-Second Word" is dedicated to Divine unity. Nursi notes that it is written "in the manner of an allegorical conversation and imaginary debate" reflecting on the importance of a phrase that *God has no partner*. This is a good illustration of Nursi's engagement and reflection on the Qur'an.

---

[19]   This alludes to man, the fruit of the tree of creation, and to the fruit which bears its tree's programme and index. For whatever the pen of power has written in the great book of the universe, it has written its summary in man's nature. And whatever the pen of Divine Determining has written in a tree the size of a mountain, it has also included it in its fruit the size of a finger nail.

First Stopping-Place

In the Name of God, the Merciful, the Compassionate.

Had there been in heaven or on earth any deities other than God, there surely would have been confusion in both.[20]

There is no god but God, He is One, He has no partner; His is the dominion and His is the praise; He grants life and deals death, and is living and dies not; all good is in His hand; He is powerful over all things; and with Him all things have their end.[21]

...

Let us suppose one person represents all those things set up as partners to God that all the different varieties of idolators imagine to exist. These idolators are the people of unbelief and misguidance, who worship nature and causes, for example, and assign partners to God. The fictitious person wants to have mastery over one of the beings in the universe, and so claims to be its true owner.

Firstly, that maker of false claims encountered a particle, which is the smallest of those beings, and he spoke to it in the language of Naturalism and philosophy saying that he was to be its master and true owner. But the particle replied to him with the tongue of truth and dominical wisdom, saying:

"I perform innumerable duties. Entering many creatures which are all different I do my work in them. And there are, from among countless particles like me, those that move from place to place[22] and work with me. If you have the knowledge and power to employ me in all those duties, and the authority and

---

[20]   Qur'an, 21:22.

[21]   Bukhari, Adhan 155; Tahajjud 21; 'Umra 12; Jihad 133; Bad' al-Khalq 11; Maghazi 29; Da'wat 18, 52; Riqaq 11; I'tisam 3; Muslim, Dhikr 28, 30, 74, 75, 76; Witr 24; Jihad 158; Adab 101; Tirmidhi, Mawaqit 108; Hajj 104; Da'wat 35, 36; Nasa'i, Sahw 83–6; Manasik 163, 170; Iman 12; Ibn Maja, Tijara 40; Manasik 84; Adab 58; Du'a 10, 14, 16; Abu Da'ud, Manasik 56; Darimi, Salat 88, 90; Manasik 34; Isti'dhan 53, 57; Muwatta', Hajj 127, 243; Qur'an 20, 22; Musnad i, 47; ii, 5; iii, 320; iv, 4; v, 191; al-Hakim, al-Mustadrak i, 538.

[22]   Indeed, every object which is in motion, from minute particles to the planets, displays on itself the stamp of Eternal Besoughtedness and Unity. Also, by reason of its movement, each of them takes possession of all the places in which it travels in the name of Unity, thus including them in the property of its own owner. As for those creatures that are not in motion, they are each of them, from plants to the fixed stars, like a seal of Unity showing the place in which it is situated to be the missive of its own Maker. That is to say, each flower and fruit is a stamp and seal of Unity which demonstrates, in the name of Unity, that its habitat and native place is the missive of its Maker. In short, each thing takes

ability to employ and have at your command all those others as well, and if you are able to be the true owner of and to have total control over the beings of which I become a part in complete order, for example, over red blood-corpuscles, then you can claim to be master over me and ascribe me to something other than God Almighty. But if you cannot do all these things, be silent!

"And in the same way that you cannot have mastery over me, you cannot interfere in any way. For there is such complete orderliness in our duties and motion that one who does not have infinite wisdom and all-encompassing knowledge cannot meddle with us. If he did, it would cause chaos. However, a person like you who is thick, impotent, and unseeing, and is in the clutches of blind chance and nature, could not even begin to stretch out a finger to interfere."

So, just like the Materialists, the one making these claims said: "In that case, own yourself. Why do you say you are working on someone else's account?" To which the particle replied:

"If I had a brain like the sun, and all-embracing knowledge like its light, and all-encompassing power like its heat, and comprehensive senses like the seven colours in its light, and if I had a face that looked to all the places in which I travel and all the beings in which I work, and an eye that looked to them and words that carried authority with them, then perhaps I would indulge in foolishness like you and claim to own myself. Get out! Go away! You won't get anything out of me!"

So, when the representative of those things held to be God's partners despaired of the particle, he hoped to pursue the matter with a red blood—corpuscle. And coming across one he said to it on behalf of causes and in the language of nature and philosophy: "I am your master and owner." And the red corpuscle replied to him through the tongue of truth and Divine wisdom:

"I am not alone. If you are able to own all my fellows in the army of blood whose stamp, nature as officials, and order is the same, and if you have subtle wisdom and mighty power enough to own all the cells of the body in which we travel and are employed with perfect wisdom, and if you can demonstrate this to be the case, then perhaps some meaning might be found in your claim.

"But someone stupified like yourself cannot be owner with your only support being deaf nature and blind force; indeed, you are unable to interfere in so much as an atom. For the order with which we function is so perfect that only one who sees, hears, knows, and does everything can have authority over us." And

---

possession of all things through its motion in the name of Unity. That is, one who does not have all the stars within his grasp cannot have mastery over a single particle.

saying: "So, be silent! My duty is so important and the order so perfect that I have no time to answer garbled rubbish such as yours," it repelled him.

Then, since he was unable to mislead it, the representative left and next came across the little house known as a cell of the body. He said to it in the language of philosophy and nature: "I could not persuade the particle and red corpuscle but perhaps you will be reasonable. Since you have been made of several substances just like a minute house, I am able to make you. You will be my artefact and true property." The cell responded to him through the tongue of wisdom and truth, saying:

"I am only a minute little thing but I have very important duties and very sensitive relations; I am connected to the body as a whole as well as to all its cells. For example, I perform complex and faultless duties in the veins, and in regard to the arteries, the sensory and motor nerves, the powers of attraction and repulsion and procreation, and the imaginative faculty. If you have the knowledge and power to form, arrange, and employ the whole body and all its blood-vessels, nerves and faculties, and if you have comprehensive wisdom and penetrating power with which to control all the body's cells, which are like me, as regards qualities and artistry we are brothers, demonstrate it. Only then can you claim to be able to make me. If you cannot, then off with you!

"The red corpuscles bring my food, while the white ones combat illnesses which attack me. I have work to do, do not distract me! Anyway, an impotent, lifeless, deaf and blind thing like you cannot in any way interfere with us. For we have such an exact, subtle and faultless order[23] that if the one who has authority over

---

[23] The All-Wise Maker has created the human body as though it was a well-arranged city. A number of the blood-vessels perform the duties of telephones and telegraphs, while others of them are like pipes from a fountain through which blood, which is the water of life, flows. As for blood, created within it are two sorts of corpuscles. One of them, known as red corpuscles, distributes nutrients to the cells of the body; it conveys sustenance to the cells according to a Divine law. (Like merchants and food officials.) The other sort are white corpuscles, which are fewer in number than the former. Their duty, like soldiers, is defence against enemies, such as illness. Whenever they undertake that defence, with their two revolutions like Mevlevi dervishes, they take on a swift and wonderful state. As for blood as a whole, it has two general duties; the first is to repair damage done to the body. There are two sorts of blood-vessels, veins and arteries. One of these carry purified blood, they are the channels through which clean blood is conveyed. The others are the channels for the turbid blood which collects the waste-matter; these convey the blood to where breathing occurs; that is, the lungs.

The All-Wise Maker created in the air two elements, nitrogen and oxygen. As for oxygen, when it comes in to contact with the blood in breathing, it drawn to itself, like amber, the impure element, carbon, which is polluting the blood. The two combine and are transformed into matter called carbonic acid gas. Oxygen also maintains the body

us was not Absolutely Wise, Absolutely Powerful and Absolutely Knowing, our order would be broken and our regularity spoilt."

Then the one making the claims despaired of it, too. He encountered the body of a human being and said to it, once again as the Naturalists say, in the language of blind nature and aimless philosophy: "You are mine, it is I who made you; or anyway I have a share in you." The human body answered with the tongue of reality and wisdom and through the eloquence of its order:

"If you possess the power and knowledge to have actual control over the bodies of all human beings, who are the same as me and on whose faces are the stamp of power and seal of creation which are the same, and if you have the wealth and jurisdiction to own, from water and air to plants and animals, the treasuries of my sustenance, and if you have infinite power and boundless wisdom with which to employ me with perfect wisdom and cause me to perform my worship, and the power and wisdom to lodge in a narrow, lowly vessel like me immaterial and subtle faculties like the spirit, heart, and intellect, which are extremely vast and exalted and for which I am merely the sheath, then demonstrate all these and afterwards say that you made me. Otherwise, be silent!

"Moreover, according to the testimony of the perfect order in my body and the indication of the stamp of unity on my face, my Maker is One Who is powerful over all things, knows all things, and sees and hears all things. Someone aimless and impotent like you cannot meddle in His art. You cannot interfere in so much as an atom."

The Words, Thirty-Second Word, pp. 619–623.

---

temperature, and purifies the blood. This is because, in the science of chemistry, the All-Wise Maker bestowed on oxygen and carbon an intense relationship, which might be described as "chemical passion" , whereby, according to this Divine law, when those two elements come close to each other, they combine. It has been established by science that heat is produced by combining, because it is a sort of combustion.

The wisdom in this is as follows: the motion of the particles of those two elements is different. On combining, the particles of one element unite with those of the other, each two particles thereafter moving like a single particle. The other motion is transformed into heat according to a low of the All-Wise Maker. As a matter of a fact, "motion produces heat" is an established principle.

Thus, as a consequence of this fact, by this chemical combination, as carbon is removed from the blood the body temperature of human beings is maintained and at the same time the blood is purified. On inhaling, oxygen both cleanses the body's water of life and kindles the fire of life. On exhaling, it yields, in the mouth, the fruit of words, which are miracles of Divine Power.

GLORY BE UNTO HIM AT WHOSE ART THE MIND IS BEWILDERED.

Extract Seven: Divine Oneness and Works

"The Sixteenth Word" consists of four subchapters each illustrating four different reflections of Divine oneness and works. The first describes Divine oneness and unity through the aspect of God's unlimited and uninterrupted presence and immanence surrounding everywhere at anytime. The second explains the remarkable art, power, and ease as seen in Divine creation. The third section is an interpretation of how to understand the infinite Divine closeness that is mentioned in Qur'anic verses while everything seems to be infinitely distant from Him. The fourth expounds on the intense state of being in the Divine's presence via performance of prescribed worships.

The Sixteenth Word

> *In the Name of God*, **the Merciful, the Compassionate.**
>
> **Indeed, His command when He wills a thing is, "Be!," and it is. * So glory be unto Him in Whose hand is the dominion** *of all things, and to Him will you all be brought back.*[24]

> [This Word was written to afford insight and understanding to my blind soul by pointing out four Rays from the light of the above verse—to dispel the darkness and afford me certainty.]

First Ray

> O my ignorant soul! You say, "The Oneness of the Divine Essence together with the universality of the Divine acts, the Unity of Almighty God's person together with His unassisted comprehensive dominicality, His Singleness together with His unshared all-embracing disposal, His being beyond space and yet present everywhere, His infinite exaltedness together with being close to all things, and His being One and yet Himself holding all matters in His hand, are among the truths of the Qur'an. Yet the Qur'an is All-Wise, and that which is Wise does not impose on the reason things which are unreasonable. And the reason sees an apparent contradiction between these things. I would like an explanation of them which will impel the reason to submit."

> *The Answer*: Since that is the way it is and you want to be certain and reassured, relying on the effulgence of the Qur'an, we say: the Divine Name of Light has solved many of my difficulties. God willing, it will solve this one too. Choosing the way of comparison, which brings clarity to the mind and luminosity to the heart, like Imam-i Rabbani, we say:

---

[24]   1. Qur'an, 36:82–3.

I am neither the night nor a lover of the night;

I am a servant of the Sun; it is of the Sun that I speak.

Since comparison is a most brilliant mirror to the Qur'an's miraculousness, we too shall look at this mystery by means of a comparison. It is as follows:

A single person may gain universality by means of various mirrors. While being a single individual, he becomes like a universal possessing general qualities. For example, while the sun is a single individual, by means of transparent objects, it becomes so universal it fills the face of the earth with its images and reflections. It even has as many manifestations as the number of droplets and shining motes. Although the sun's heat, light, and the seven colours in its light comprehend, encompass, and embrace all the things which confront them, all transparent things also hold in the pupils of their eyes the sun's heat, and its light and seven colours, together with its image. And they make a throne for them in their hearts. That is to say, with regard to Unity, the sun encompasses all the things which confront it, while with regard to Oneness, the sun is present together with many of its attributes in everything through a sort of manifestation of its essence. Since we have passed from the comparison to a discussion of representation, we shall indicate three of the many sorts of representation which will be a means to understanding this matter.

The First: This is the reflection of dense, physical objects. These reflections are both other than the thing reflected; they are not the same, and they are dead, without life. They possess no quality other than their apparent identity. For example, if you enter a store full of mirrors, one Said will become thousands of Said's, but the only living one is you, all the others are dead. They possess none of the characteristics of life.

The Second: This is the reflection of physical luminous objects. This reflection is not the same as the thing reflected, but neither is it other than it. It does not hold the luminous object's nature, but it possesses most of its characteristics, and may be considered as living. For example, the sun entered the world and displayed its reflection in all mirrors. Present in each of the reflections are light and the seven colours in light, which are like the sun's qualities. Let us suppose the sun possessed consciousness, and its heat was pure power; its light, pure knowledge; and its seven colours, the seven attributes: the single sun would be present in all mirrors at one moment, and would be able to make each a throne for itself and a sort of telephone. One mirror would not be an obstacle to another. It would be able to meet with all of us by means of our mirrors. While we are distant from it, it would be closer to us than ourselves.

The Third: This is the reflection of luminous spirits. This reflection is both living, and the same as the spirits. But since it appears in relation to the capacity of the mirrors, it does not hold completely the spirit's essence and nature. For example, at the moment the Angel Gabriel (Peace be upon him) is in the presence of the Prophet in the form of Dihya, he is prostrating with his magnificent wings in the Divine Presence before the Sublime Throne. And at the same moment he is present in innumerable places, and is relaying the Divine commands. One task is not an obstacle to another. Thus, it is through this mystery that the Prophet Muhammad (Peace and blessings be upon him), whose essence is light and nature, luminous, in this world hears at the same time all the benedictions recited for him by all his community, and at the resurrection will meet with all the purified at the same time. One will not be an obstacle to another. In fact, some of the saints who have acquired a high degree of luminosity and are called "substitutes" (*abdal*) have been observed in many places at the same time, and the same person has performed numerous different acts at the same time.

Indeed, just as things like glass and water act as mirrors to physical objects, so the air and ether, and certain beings of the World of Similitudes are like mirrors to spirit beings; they become like means of transport and conveyance of the speed of lightning and imagination. The spirit beings travel in those pure mirrors and subtle dwellings with speed of imagination. They enter thousands of places at the same time. Despite being restricted particulars, through the mystery of luminosity impotent and subjugated creatures like the sun and semi-luminous beings restricted by matter like spirit beings may be present in numerous places while being in one place, thus becoming like absolute universals, and with a limited power of choice being able to perform many matters simultaneously.

Thus, what thing may hide itself from address of Oneness which is within the manifestation of the attributes and acts of the Most Pure and Holy One through His universal will, absolute power, and all-encompassing knowledge? The Most Holy One, Who is far beyond and exalted above matter; free and exempt from any restriction or limitation and the darkness of density; of the sacred lights of Whose Names all these lights and luminous beings are but dense shadows; and of Whose beauty all existence and all life and the World of Spirits and the World of Similitudes are semi-transparent mirrors; Whose attributes are all-encompassing and Whose qualities, universal? What matter could be difficult for Him? What thing can be concealed from Him? What individual can be distant from Him? What person can draw close to Him without acquiring universality?

Although by means of its unrestricted light and immaterial reflection, the sun is closer to you than the pupil of your eye, since you are restricted, you are truly distant from it. In order to draw close to it, you have to transcend numerous restrictions and pass over many universal degrees. Simply, in effect you have to expand to the size of the earth and rise as far as the moon, then you may be able to approach directly to a degree the sun's essential level, and meet with it without veil. In just the same way, the Glorious One of Beauty and Beauteous One of Perfection is infinitely close to you, and you are infinitely distant from Him. If your heart has strength, and your mind, eminence, try to put the points in the comparison into practice.

Second Ray

O my senseless soul! You say that verses like,

Indeed, His command when He wills a thing is, "Be!" and it is,[25]

and,

It will be no more than a single blast, when lo! they will all be brought up before Us![26]

show that the existence of things is instantaneous and merely through a command, and that verses like,

[Such is] the **artistry of God, Who disposes of all things in perfect order,**[27]
and,
Who has created everything *in the best way*[28]

show that existence of things is gradual, through a vast power within knowledge, and a fine art within wisdom. What is the point of agreement between them?

The Answer: Relying on the effulgence of the Qur'an, we say:

Firstly: There is no contradiction. Some are like the former, like primary creation. And some are like the latter, like the repetition of creation.

Secondly: The infinite order and extreme skill, fine art, and perfect creation together with the ease, speed, multiplicity, and extensiveness which are observed in beings testify decisively to the existence of the truths of these two sorts of verses. Since this is so, proving it to be true outside this and making that the point of discussion, is unnecessary. It should rather be asked: "What is the wisdom in them? What is their meaning and purpose?" Thus, we shall point to this wisdom with an analogy in the form of a comparison.

---

[25]   Qur'an, 36:82.

[26]   Qur'an, 36:53.

[27]   Qur'an, 27:88.

[28]   Qur'an, 32:7.

For example, a craftsman like a tailor creates something artistic with much difficulty and employing many skills, and makes a model for it. Then he can make others similar to it quickly and without difficulty. Sometimes, even, it becomes so easy they are as though made at a command, and they acquire a powerful order in that way; like a clock, they function and work as though at the touch of a command. In just the same way, after making this palace of the world and all its contents originally, the All-Wise Maker and All-Knowing Inscriber gave everything, particular and universal, the whole and the parts, a specified measure and proportion through an ordering of Divine Determining, like a model. So, look! Making every century a model, the Pre-Eternal Inscriber clothes them with bejewelled new worlds through the miracles of His power. And making every year a scale, He sews skilfully fashioned new universes through the wonders of His mercy according to their stature. And making every day a line, He writes the decorated, constantly renewed beings in them through the subtleties of His wisdom.

Furthermore, just as that Absolutely Powerful One makes each century, each year, and each day a model, so He makes the face of the earth, and the mountains and plains, gardens and orchards, and trees each a model. He continuously sets up new universes on the earth and creates new worlds. He removes one world and replaces it with another, well-ordered world. Season after season He displays the miracles of His power and gifts of His mercy in all the gardens and orchards. He writes them all as wisdom-displaying books, establishes them as kitchens of His mercy, and clothes them in ever-renewed garments full of art. Every spring He arrays all trees in raiments of brocade and adorns them with fresh jewels like pearls. He fills their hands with the star-like gifts of His mercy.

Thus, the One Who performs these matters with infinitely fine art and perfect order and changes with infinite wisdom, bounty, and perfection of power and art the travelling worlds which follow on one after the other and are attached to the string of time, is certainly All-Powerful and All-Wise. He is All-Seeing and All-Knowing to an infinite degree. Chance cannot interfere in His works. He is the All-Glorious One Who decrees,

Indeed, His command when He wills a thing is, "Be!", and it is,[29]
and,
And the decision of the Hour is as the twinkling of an eye, or even closer,[30]

and both proclaims the perfection of His power, and that in relation to His power the resurrection and Great Gathering are most easy and free of trouble. Since

---

[29] Qur'an, 36:82.
[30] Qur'an, 16:77.

His creational command comprises power and will, and all things are entirely subjugated and obedient to His command, and He creates with no difficulty or hindrance, in order to express the absolute ease in His creating, the Qur'an of Miraculous Exposition decrees that He does this through a mere command.

To Conclude: Some verses proclaim the extremely fine art and infinite perfection of wisdom in beings, especially at the start of their creation. While others describe the extreme ease and speed and infinite obedience and lack of difficulty in the recreation and return of things in particular.

Third Ray

O my soul full of doubts and evil suggestions and exceeding its bounds! You say that verses like,

There is not a moving thing, but He has grasp of its forelock.[31]

and,

In Whose hand is the dominion of all things,[32]

and,

And We are closer to him than his jugular vein,[33]

show that God is infinitely close to us. And yet, the verses,

And to Him shall you return.[34]

and,

The angels ascend to Him in a day the measure of which is fifty thousand years.[35]

and, the Hadith which says: "God is beyond seventy thousand veils,"[36] and truths like the Prophet's Ascension show that we are infinitely distant from Him.

---

[31]   Qur'an, 11:56.

[32]   Qur'an, 36:83.

[33]   Qur'an, 50:16.

[34]   Qur'an, 36:83.

[35]   Qur'an, 70:4.

[36]   al-Ghazali, *Ihya 'Ulum al-Din*, i, 101; *Musnad*, iv, 401, 405.

I would like an explanation which will bring this profound mystery closer to the understanding.

The Answer: Then listen to the following:

Firstly: At the end of the First Ray we said that although with regard to its unrestricted light and immaterial reflection, the sun is closer to you than the pupil of your eye, which is the window of your spirit and its mirror, since you are restricted and imprisoned in materiality, you are extremely distant from it. You can make contact with it only through some of its reflections and shadows, and meet with it through a sort of its minor and particular manifestations, and draw close to its colours, which are like a category of attribute, and to its rays and manifestations, which are like a class of its names. If you want to approach the sun's essential level and meet with the sun's essence directly in person, then you have to transcend very many restrictions and traverse very many levels of universality. Simply, after abstracting yourself from materiality, becoming enlarged to the extent of the earth, expanding in the spirit like the air, rising as far as the moon and resembling the full-moon, only then can you claim to meet with it in person without veil and to draw close to it to any degree.

In just the same way, the All-Glorious One of Perfection, the Peerless One of Beauty, the Necessarily Existent One, the Giver of Existence to All Beings, the Eternal Sun, the Monarch of Pre-Eternity and Post-Eternity, is closer to you than yourself. Yet you are infinitely distant from Him. If you have the power, put the fine points in the comparison into practice.

Secondly: For example, *And God's is the highest similitude*, among many names, a king's name of "Commander" appears in many spheres, one within the other. It has a manifestation and appearance in spheres extensive and narrow, universal and particular, from the universal sphere of Commander-in-Chief, to those of Field Marshal and General, then those of captain and corporal. Now, in his military duties, a private soldier holds as his authority the minor point of commandership manifest in the rank of corporal; he is in touch with and connected to the Commander-in-Chief through this minor manifestation of his name. If he wishes to get in touch with him through his essential name and meet with him through that title, he will have to rise from the corporalship to the universal rank of Commander-in-Chief. That is to say, the king is extremely close to the soldier through his name, decree, law and knowledge, his telephone and regulations, and if he is luminous like a saint who is an *abdal*, with his presence in person. Nothing at all can be an obstacle or obstruction for him. Whereas the soldier is extremely distant. Thousands of degrees form obstructions, and thousands of veils intervene. But sometimes the king is compassionate, and contrary to his practice, receives a soldier into his presence and favours him with his grace.

In just the same way, although the All-Glorious One, the Lord of the command of, "Be!", and it is, for Whom the suns and stars are like His soldiers under orders, is closer to all things than they themselves, all things are infinitely distant from Him. If you want to enter the presence of His grandeur without veil, you have to pass through seventy thousands of veils of darkness and light, that is, material and physical veils and the veils of the Divine Names and attributes, rise through the thousands of particular and universal degrees of manifestation of each Name, pass on through the most elevated levels of His attributes, and ascend as far as the Sublime Throne, which manifests His Greatest Name, and if you are not the object of favour and attraction, work and journey spiritually for thousands of years. For example, if you want to draw close to Him through His Name of Creator, you have to have a relationship through the particularities of your own Creator, then in regard to the Creator of all mankind, then through the title of Creator of all living creatures, then through the Name of Creator of all beings. Otherwise you will remain in shadow and only find a minor manifestation.

A REMINDER: Because of his impotence, the king in the comparison put means like Field Marshal and General in the degrees of his names. But the Absolutely Powerful One, in Whose hand is the dominion of all things, has no need of intermediaries. Intermediaries are only apparent; a veil to His dignity and grandeur. They are heralds and observers of the sovereignty of His dominicality within worship, awe, impotence, and want. They are not His assistants, and cannot be partners in the sovereignty of His dominicality.

Fourth Ray

O my lazy soul! Like the soldier in the previous comparison was received into the royal presence as a pure favour, the reality of the five daily prayers, which are like a sort of Ascension, are a being received into the presence of the All-Glorious One of Beauty, the Beauteous One of Glory, Who is the True Object of Worship, as an instance of pure mercy. Declaring "*God is Most Great!*" it is to traverse the two worlds either in fact, or in the imagination, or by intention, be divested of the restrictions of materiality, pass to a universal degree of worship or a shadow or form of universality, and being honoured with a sort of presence, it is to manifest the address of "*You alone do we worship!*" (everyone according to his own capacity); it is a most elevated attainment. The repetition of "*God is Most Great! God is Most Great!*" in the actions of the prayers indicates rising through the degrees of spiritual progress, and ascending from minor particulars to universal spheres, and is a concise title of the perfections of Divine sublimity which are beyond our knowledge. It is as if each "*God is Most Great!*" indicates traversing a step in the Ascension. To attain to a shadow or a ray of this reality of the prayers either in fact, or by intention, or with the imagination, is a great happiness.

The frequent declaring of "God is Most Great!" during the Hajj is for the above reason. For the blessed Hajj is worship at a universal level for everyone. Just as on a special day like a festival a soldier goes to the king's celebrations like a General in the sphere of General, and receives his favours, in the same way, a Hajji, no matter how lowly, is turned towards his Sustainer under the title Mighty Sustainer of every region of the earth, like a saint who has traversed all the degrees. He is honoured with universal worship. For sure, the universal degrees of dominicality opened with the key of the Hajj, and the horizons of the tremendousness of Godhead which are visible to his eye through its telescope, and the spheres of worship which gradually unfold to his heart and imagination through its observances, and the heat, wonder, awe, and dread of dominicality caused by the levels of sublimity and last stage of manifestation, can only be quieted by "God is Most Great! God is Most Great!", and those observed or imagined unfolded degrees can only be proclaimed by it. After the Hajj, this meaning is found in various exalted and universal degrees in the Festival ('Eid) Prayers, the prayers for rain, and those recited at solar and lunar eclipses, and in prayers performed as a congregation. Thus, the importance of the marks and observances of Islam, also even if of the category of Sunna, lies in this reason.

Glory be unto the One Who has placed His treasuries between the Kaf and the Nun.

So glory be unto Him in Whose hand is the dominion of all things, and to Him will you all be brought back.[37]

Glory be unto You, we have no knowledge save that which You have taught us; indeed You are All-Knowing, All-Wise.[38]

O our Sustainer! Do not take us to task if we forget or unwittingly do wrong![39] *** O our Sustainer! Let not our hearts deviate after You have guided us, and grant us Mercy from Your presence, for You are the Granter of bounties without measure.**[40]

And grant blessings and peace to Your Most Noble Messenger, the manifester of Your Greatest Name, and to his Family, and Companions, and brothers, and followers. Amen. O Most Merciful of the Merciful!

---

[37] Qur'an, 36:83.

[38] Qur'an, 2:32.

[39] Qur'an, 2:286.

[40] Qur'an, 3:8.

A Short Addendum

The All-Powerful and All-Knowing One, the All-Wise Maker, shows His power and His wisdom and that chance can in no way interfere in His works through the system and order His rules and practices in the universe demonstrate in the form of laws. So too, through exceptions to the laws, the wonders of His practices, superficial changes, differences in individual characteristics, and changes in the times of appearance and descent, He shows His volition, will, choice, that He is the Agent with choice, and that He is under no restrictions whatsoever. Thus, rending the veil of monotony, and proclaiming that everything is in need of Him every moment for everything in every way and is obedient to His dominicality, He dispels heedlessness, and turns the gazes of man and jinn from causes to the Producer of Causes. The statements of the Qur'an look to this principle.

For example, in most places some fruit-bearing trees produce fruit one year, that is, it is given to their hands from the treasury of mercy, and they offer it. Then the following year while all apparent causes are present, they do not take it and offer it; that is, they do not produce fruit. Also, for example, contrary to other necessities, the times rain falls are so changeable that it has been included among "the Five Hidden Things."[41] For the most important position in existence is that of life and mercy. And rain is the source of life and pure mercy. Thus, the water of life and rain of mercy does not enter under a monotonous law, which is a veil and leads to heedlessness, rather, the All-Glorious One, Who is Most Merciful and All-Compassionate, and the Bestower of Bounties and Giver of Life, holds it in His hand directly, without veil, so that the doors of supplication and thanks will all the time be left open. And, for example, the giving of sustenance and determining of particular features are works of special favour, and their occurring in unexpected ways shows in excellent fashion the will and choice of the Sustainer. You may make further comparisons with other Divine acts, like the disposals of the air and weather and the subjugation of the clouds.

The Words, Sixteenth Word, p. 209–218.

Extract Eight: There is no god but God

Composed of two sections, "The Twentieth Letter" is about various aspects of the affirmation of God's unity. The following are the introduction and the First Station of the chapter, which explicate the meaning of an 11-phrased sentence of the affirmation of God's unity commonly recited by Muslims. Each of the phrases portrays central Divine qualities mentioned in the Qur'an.

---

[41]   *Bukhari*, ii, 41; ix, 142; Ibn Hibban, i, 144.

The Twentieth Letter

In His Name, be He glorified!

And there is nothing but it glorifies Him with praise. (17:44)

In the Name of God, the Merciful, the Compassionate.

There is no god but God, He is One, He has no partner; His is the dominion, and His is the praise; He alone grants life, and deals death, and He is living and dies not; all good is in His hand, He is powerful over all things, and with Him all things have their end.[42]

[This sentence expressing divine unity, which is recited following the morning and evening prayers, possesses numerous merits[43] and according to an authentic narration bears the degree of the Greatest Name.[44] It consists of eleven phrases each of which conveys both some good tidings, and a degree in the unity of dominicality (*tevhid-i rubûbiyet*), and an aspect of the grandeur and perfection of divine unity from the point of view of a Greatest Name. Referring a full explanation of these vast, elevated truths to other parts of the *Risale-i Nur*, in fulfilment of a promise we shall for now write a brief, index-like summary of them in two "Stations" and an "Introduction."]

Introduction

Be certain of this, that the highest aim of creation and its most important result is belief in God. The most exalted rank in humanity and its highest degree is the knowledge of God contained within belief in God. The most radiant happiness and sweetest bounty for jinn and human beings is the love of God contained within the knowledge of God. And the purest joy for the human spirit and the sheerest delight for man's heart is the rapture of the spirit contained within the love of God. Yes, all true happiness, pure joy, sweet bounties, and untroubled pleasure lie in knowledge of God and love of God; they cannot exist without them.

The person who knows and loves God Almighty may receive endless bounties, happiness, lights, and mysteries. While the one who does not truly know and

---

[42]   Bukhari, Adhan, 155; Tahajjud 21; Muslim, Dhikr, 28, 30, 74, 75, 76; Tirmidhi, Mawaqit, 108; Hajj 104; Nasa'i, Sahw 83–6; Ibn Maja, Du'a 10, 14, 16; Abu Da'ud, Manasik 56; Darimi, Salat 88, 90; Muwatta', Hajj 127, 243; Qur'an 20, 22; Musnad i, 47; ii, 5; iii, 320; iv, 4; v, 191.

[43]   See, Musnad, iv, 60; al-Haythami, Majma' al-Zawa'id, x, 107.

[44]   See, Ibn Maja, Du'a, 9.

love him is afflicted spiritually and materially by endless misery, pain, and fears. Even if such an impotent, miserable person owned the whole world, it would be worth nothing for him, for it would seem to him that he was living a fruitless life among the vagrant human race in a wretched world without owner or protector. Everyone may understand just how forlorn and baffled is man among the aimless human race in this bewildering fleeting world if he does not know his Owner, if he does not discover his Master. But if he does discover and know Him, he will seek refuge in His mercy and will rely on His power. The desolate world will turn into a place of recreation and pleasure, it will become a place of trade for the hereafter.

First Station

Each of the eleven phrases of the above-mentioned sentence affirming divine unity contains some good news. And in the good news lies a cure, while in each of those cures a spiritual pleasure is to be found.

The First Phrase: "There is no god but God"

This phrase conveys the following good news to the human spirit, suffering as it does countless needs and the attacks of innumerable enemies. On the one hand the spirit finds a place of recourse, a source of help, through which is opened to it the door of a treasury of mercy that will guarantee all its needs. While on the other it finds a support and source of strength, for the phrase makes known its Creator and True Object of Worship, who possesses the absolute power to secure it from the evil of all its enemies; it shows its master, and who it is that owns it. Through pointing this out, the phrase saves the heart from utter desolation and the spirit from aching sorrow; it ensures an eternal joy, a perpetual happiness.

The Second Phrase: "He is One"

This phrase announces the following good news, which is both healing and a source of happiness:

Man's spirit and heart, which are connected to most of the creatures in the universe and are almost overwhelmed in misery and confusion on account of this connection, find in the phrase "He is One" a refuge and protector that will deliver them from all the confusion and bewilderment.

That is to say, it is as if "He is One" is saying to man: God is One. Do not wear yourself out having recourse to other things; do not demean yourself and feel indebted to them; do not flatter them and fawn on them and humiliate yourself; do not follow them and make things difficult for yourself; do not fear them and tremble before them; for the Monarch of the universe is One, the key to all things is with Him, the reins of all things are in His hand, everything will be resolved by His command. If you find Him, you will be saved from endless indebtedness, countless fears.

The Third Phrase: "He has no partner"

Just as in His divinity and in His sovereignty God has no partner, He is One and cannot be many; so too He has no partner in His dominicality and in His actions and in His creating. It sometimes happens that a monarch is one, having no partner in his sovereignty, but in the execution of his affairs his officials act as his partners; they prevent everyone from entering his presence, saying: "Apply to us!"

However, God Almighty, the Monarch of Pre-Eternity and Post-Eternity, has no partner in His sovereignty, just as He has no need for partners or helpers in the execution of His dominicality.

If it were not for His command and will, His strength and power, not a single thing could interfere with another. Everyone can have recourse to Him directly. Since He has no partner or helper, no one seeking recourse can be told: "Stop! It is forbidden to enter His presence!"

This phrase, therefore, delivers the following joyful announcement to the human spirit: the human spirit which has attained to faith may, without let or hindrance, opposition or interference, in any state, for any wish, at any time and in any place, enter the presence of the All-Beauteous and Glorious One, the One of power and perfection, who is the Pre-Eternal and Post-Eternal Owner of the treasuries of mercy, the treasuries of bliss, and m ay present its needs. Discovering His mercy and relying on His power, it will find perfect ease and happiness.

The Fourth Phrase: "His is the dominion"

That is to say, ownership is altogether His. As for you, you are both His property, you are owned by Him, and you work in His property. This phrase announces the following joyful and healing news:

O man! Do not suppose that you own yourself, for you have no control over any of the things that concern you; such a load would be heavy. Also, you are unable to protect yourself, to avoid disasters, or to do the things that you must. In which case, do not suffer pain and torment without reason, the ownership is another's. The Owner is both All-Powerful and All-Merciful; rely on His power and do not cast aspersions on His mercy! Put grief behind you, be joyful! Discard your troubles and find serenity!

It also says: You love and are connected to the universe, which is the property of the All-Powerful and Merciful One, yet although it grieves you by its wretchedness, you are unable to put it right. So hand over the property to its Owner, leave it to Him. Attract His pleasure, not His harshness. He is both All-Wise and All-Merciful. He has free disposal over His property and administers it as He wishes. Whenever you take fright, say like İbrahim Hakkı: "Let's see what the Master does; whatever He does, it is best;" understand this thoroughly and do not interfere!

The Fifth Phrase: "His is the praise"

Praise, laudation, and acclaim are proper to Him, are fitting for Him. That is to say, bounties are His; they come from His treasury. And as for the treasury, it is unending. This phrase, therefore, delivers the following good news:

O man! Do not suffer and sorrow when bounties cease, for the treasury of mercy is inexhaustible. Do not dwell on the fleeting nature of pleasure and cry out with pain, because the fruit of the bounty is the fruit of a boundless mercy. Since its tree is undying, when the fruit finishes it is replaced by more. If you thankfully think of there being within the pleasure of the bounty a merciful favour a hundred times more pleasurable, you will be able to increase the pleasure a hundredfold.

An apple an august monarch presents to you holds a pleasure superior to that of a hundred, indeed a thousand, apples, for it is he that has bestowed it on you and made you experience the pleasure of a royal favour. In the same way, through the phrase "His is the praise" will be opened to you the door of a spiritual pleasure a thousand times sweeter than the bounty itself.

For the phrase means to offer praise and thanks; that is to say, to perceive the bestowal of bounty. This in turn means to recognize the Bestower, which is to reflect on the bestowal of bounty, and so finally to ponder over the favour of His compassion and His continuing to bestow bounties.

The Sixth Phrase: "He alone grants life"

That is to say, He is the giver of life. And it is He who causes life to continue by means of sustenance. He also supplies the necessities of life. And it is to Him that the exalted aims of life pertain and its important results look, and His are ninety-nine out of a hundred of its fruits. Thus, this phrase calls out in this way to ephemeral, impotent man, it makes this joyful announcement:

O man! Do not trouble yourself by shouldering the heavy burdens of life. Do not think of the transience of life and start grieving. Do not see only its worldly and unimportant fruits and regret that you came to this world. For the life-machine in the ship of your being belongs to the Ever-Living and Self-Subsistent One, and it is He who provides for all its expenses and requirements. Also, your life has a great many aims and results, and they pertain to Him, too.

As for you, you are just a helmsman on the ship, so do your duty well and take the wage and pleasure that come with it. Think of just how precious is the life-ship and how valuable its benefits; then think of just how Generous and Merciful is the Owner of the ship. So rejoice and give thanks and know that when you perform your duty with integrity, all the results the ship produces will in one respect be transferred to the register of your actions, that they will secure an immortal life for you, will endow you with eternal life.

The Seventh Phrase: "And deals death"

He is the one who causes death. He discharges you from the duty of life, changes your abode from this transitory world, and releases you from the labour of service. That is, He takes you from a transient life to an immortal one. This phrase, then, shouts out the following to ephemeral jinn and man:

Here is good news for you! Death is not destruction, or nothingness, or annihilation; it is not cessation or extinction; it is not eternal separation, or non-existence, or a chance event; it is not authorless obliteration. Rather, it is to be discharged by the Author who is All-Wise and All-Compassionate; it is a change of abode. It is to be despatched to eternal bliss, to your true home. It is the door of union to the Intermediate Realm, which is where you will meet with ninety-nine per cent of your friends.

The Eighth Phrase: "And He is living and dies not"

That is to say, the Possessor of a beauty, perfection, and munificence that are infinitely superior to the beauty, perfection, and munificence to be seen in the creatures of the universe, and that arouse love; and an Eternal Object of Worship, an Everlasting Beloved, a single manifestation of whose beauty is suffcient to replace all other beloveds, has an enduring life through pre-eternity and post-eternity—a life free from any trace of cessation or ephemerality and exempt from any fault, defect, or imperfection. Thus, this phrase proclaims to jinn and man, to all conscious beings, and the people of love and ardour:

Here is good news for you! There exists an Everlasting Beloved who will cure and bind the wounds caused you by countless separations from the ones you love. Since He exists and is undying, whatever happens do not fret over the others. Furthermore, the beauty and generosity, virtue and perfection to be seen in them, the cause of your love, are, passing through many veils, the shadows

of the palest of shadows of the manifestation of the Ever-Enduring Beloved's
ever-enduring beauty. Do not grieve at their disappearance, for they are mirrors
of a sort. The mirrors being changed renews and embellishes the manifestation
of the Beauty's radiance. Since He exists, everything exists.

The Ninth Phrase: "All good is in His hand"

Every good action you perform is transferred to His register. Every righteous
deed you do is recorded with Him. Thus, this phrase calls out to jinn and mankind
with the following good news:

O wretched ones! When you journey to the grave do not cry out in despair,
"Alas! Everything we owned is destroyed, all our efforts are wasted; we have
left the beautiful broad earth and entered the narrow grave," for everything
of yours is preserved, all your actions written down, every service you have
rendered recorded. A Glorious One in whose hand is all good and who is able to
bring all good to fruition, will reward your service: drawing you to Himself, He
will keep you only temporarily under the ground. Later, He will bring you to His
presence. What happiness for those of you who have completed their service and
duty; your labour is finished, you are departing for ease and mercy! Service and
toil are over, you are going to receive your wage!

The All-Powerful One of Glory preserves seeds and grains, which are the pages
of the register of last spring's deeds and the deposit-boxes of its services, and
publishes them the following spring in glittering fashion, indeed, in a manner
a hundred times more plentiful than the originals. The results of your life He is
preserving in the same way, and will reward your service in a truly abundant
fashion.

The Tenth Phrase: "And He is Powerful over all things"

He is One, He is Unique, He has power over everything. Nothing at all is difficult
for Him. To create the spring is as easy for Him as to create a flower, and He
creates Paradise with as much ease as He creates the spring. The innumerable
artefacts which He continuously creates every day, every year, every century,
witness with numberless tongues to His boundless power. Thus, this phrase too
delivers good news:

O man! The service you have offered and the worship you have performed are
not for nothing. A realm of reward, an abode of bliss, has been prepared for you.
An unending Paradise is awaiting you in place of this fleeting world of yours.
Have faith and confidence in the promise of the Glorious Creator whom you
know and whom you worship, for it is impossible for Him to break His promise.
In absolutely no respect is there any deficiency in His power; impotence cannot

impede His works. Just as He creates your tiny garden, so He is able to create Paradise for you, and He has created it and promised it to you. And because He has promised, He shall, of course, admit you to it!

We observe every year on the face of the earth that He gathers together and disperses with perfect order and balance, with perfect timing and ease, more than three hundred thousand species and groups of animals and plants. Most certainly such an All-Powerful One of Glory is capable of carrying out His promise.

Since, being thus absolutely Powerful He creates samples of the resurrection and Paradise in thousands of forms every year; and since, promising eternal bliss through all His revealed scriptures, He gives the glad tidings of Paradise; and since all His actions and deeds are carried out with truth, veracity, and seriousness; and since, through the testimony of all His works of art, all perfections point to and testify to His infinite perfection, there being in absolutely no respect any defect or fault in Him; and since the breaking of a promise, lying, falsehood, and deception are the ugliest of qualities besides being defects and faults; then most decidedly and most certainly that All-Powerful One of Glory, that All-Wise One of Perfection, that All-Merciful One of Beauty, will carry out His promise; He will open the gate to eternal bliss; He will admit you, O people of faith, to Paradise, which was the original home of your forefather Adam.

The Eleventh Phrase: "And with Him all things have their end"

Human beings are sent to this world, the realm of trial and examination, with the important duties of trading and acting as officials. After they have concluded their transactions, accomplished their duties, and completed their service, they will return and meet once more with their Generous Master and Glorious Creator who sent them forth in the first place. Leaving this transient realm, they will be honoured and elevated to the presence of grandeur in the realm of permanence. That is to say, being delivered from the turbulence of causes and from the obscure veils of intermediaries, they will meet with their Merciful Sustainer without veil at the seat of His eternal majesty. Everyone will find his Creator, True Object of Worship, Sustainer, Lord, and Owner and will know Him directly. Thus, this phrase proclaims the following joyful news, which is greater than all the rest:

O man! Do you know where you are going and where you are being driven? As is stated at the end of the Thirty-Second Word, a thousand years of happy life in this world cannot be compared to one hour of life in Paradise. And a thousand years of life in Paradise cannot be compared to one hour's vision of the sheer loveliness of the Beauteous One of Glory. You are going to the realm of His mercy, and to His presence.

The loveliness and beauty in all the creatures of this world and in those worldly beloveds by which you are so stricken and obsessed and for which you are so desirous, are but a sort of shadow of the manifestation of His beauty and of the loveliness of His names; and all Paradise with all of its subtle wonders, a single manifestation of His mercy; and all longing and love and allurement and captivation, but a flash of the love of the Eternal Worshipful One and Everlasting Beloved. You are going to the sphere of His presence. You are being summoned to Paradise, which is an eternal feasting place. Since this is so, you should enter the grave not weeping, but smiling in expectation.

The phrase announces this good news as well: O man! Do not be apprehensive, imagining that you are going to extinction, non-existence, nothingness, darkness, oblivion, decay, and dissolution, and that you will drown in multiplicity. You are going not to extinction, but to permanence. You are being impelled not to non-existence, but to perpetual existence. You are going to enter not darkness, but the world of light. And you are returning to your true owner, to the seat of the Pre-Eternal Monarch. You will not drown in multiplicity, you will take your rest in the realm of unity. You are bound not for separation, but for union."

The Letters, Twentieth Letter, p. 261–268.

For further reading

"The Eighth Word" might be considered as a concise summary of the outlook that is developed in the *Risale-i Nur*. The true nature of this world, function and purpose of religion, belief in God and unbelief along with their consequences are elaborated in the light of an allegory originates in the *suhūf* of Prophet Abraham, the revelations he received.
The Words, Eighth Word, p. 209–218.

The Second Station of "The Twenty-Second Word" focuses on the essence of the affirmation of God's unity and the genuine faith which is gained and confirmed through witnessing signs and stamps of Divine work, some of which are pointed out in this section.
The Words, Twenty-Second Word, Second Station, p. 299–318.

"The Twenty-Third Word" discusses how human beings, who are created in "the most excellent patterns" of creation according to the Qur'an (95:4), can attain their perfection through belief and by manifesting the Divine Names. In this section Nursi focuses on the paradoxical tendencies of human beings and how they journey between good and bad patterns. Defining the world as "an arena of trial," this chapter elaborates on the possible human progress and decline through infinite degrees in this test.

The Words, Twenty-Third Word, p. 319–340.

The third section of the "The Thirty-Second Word" is an example of reading the Divine Names, *asmā al-husnā*, that manifest throughout the universe within one another. The following is an excerpt from the beginning of the third section.
The Words, Thirty-Second Word, 655–682.

Among the important texts of the *Risale-i Nur* on the concepts of the affirmation of God's unity and oneness is the extensive chapter entitled "The Second Ray." Concentrating on the Qur'anic phrase "God, the One," (Qur'an, 112:1) the chapter expresses that understanding oneness manifesting through all entire creation and through all the Divine Names at work in creation is the essence of understanding Divine work and nature. It illustrates Divine unity and its affirmation via examples of apparent Divine beauty and perfection. An well reasoned argument included in this chapter is that due to strong bonds among the beings existent in the universe, the creator of any single being ought to be the creator of all things.
The Rays, Second Ray, p. 13–49.

"The Twelfth Flash" interprets two Qur'anic verses regarding cosmology that are criticised by scientists. (Qur'an, 51:58, 65:12) This chapter provides an example of the *Risale-i Nur*'s responses to doubts of the time and also its explanations according to the understanding of the time.
The Flashes, Twelfth Flash, p. 95–103.

Part 2
Prophethood

Extract One: Need for Prophets

In the "Seeds of Reality," a collection of aphorisms, Nursi concisely states the need for prophethood.

> Pre-eternal power, which does not leave ants without a prince or bees without a queen, certainly does not leave mankind without prophets. ...

> *The Letters*, Seeds of Reality, p. 530.

Extract Two: Foundation of Prophethood

"The Third Part" of *The Reasonings, Muhakemāt* with its original title is one of the early books of the *Risale-i Nur* written in 1911 with, is Said Nursi's response to a group of people from Japan inquiring about the Islamic Proclamation of Testimony declaring Oneness of God and prophethood of Muhammad. The following is the section where Nursi elaborates on the foundation of prophethood. Once again, note how Nursi answers the possible objections.

The Element of Belief

The Second Purpose

Introduction

> *You ask*: You say that the second part of the Proclamation of Testimony—I bear witness that there is no deity but God; and I also bear witness that Muhammad is His servant and Messenger—is a witness for the truth of the first part, and the first part is a witness for the truth of the second part. Is this really so?

> *Answer*: Yes, this is so. The safest and the truest of the ways that lead to knowledge of God, which is the "Ka'ba" of perfections, is the soundest and most radiant one which was built by the holy resident of Madina al-Munawwara, upon him be peace and blessings. That resident, Prophet Muhammad, upon him be peace and blessings, is the spirit of guidance, his heart is the lamp that illuminates the unseen worlds. His truthful tongue, which is the translator of his heart, is the

most articulate and truest of the proofs of the Maker's existence and Oneness. His being and his words are both a light-diffusing proof. Prophet Muhammad, upon him be peace and blessings, is the most decisive and undeniable proof of the Maker, of the institution or mission of Prophethood, of the Resurrection and the afterlife, and of the truth.

A Reminder

It is not necessary to refer to the proofs of the existence and Unity of the Maker in order to prove the truth of that holy being, Prophet Muhammad, upon him be peace and blessings.

An Establishment

Our prophet is a proof for the Maker. So we should analyze this proof from certain, essential viewpoints.

In the Name of God, the All-Merciful, the All-Compassionate.

O God! Bestow blessings and peace upon Muhammad, who bears witness to the absolute necessity of Your existence.

O lover of truth! If you would like to look through the window of conscience or human conscious nature, first do not assume the attitude of intentional opposition, which causes the faculty of heart to be polluted and rust. Also, do not lend an ear to your whims and fancies, nor expect something that should be given by a community to come from every member of that community. Expecting something from every member of that community causes the denial or rejection of the result. This is a point that requires close attention.

In addition, you should purify the mirror of your heart from childish attitudes and enmity, both of which tend to searching for and taking shelter in pretexts. Also, do not look through the eyes of the customer who sees only defects and failings. Furthermore, when you weigh, weigh accurately; compare correctly. What is more, take for evidence and guidance the shining light of truth that comprises all the sign points along your way, so that you can dispel the darkness of groundless doubts and whims that may appear. Finally, listen with attentive, careful ear, and do not object before my words are finished. All that I will utter amounts only to a sentence. When I have said all of it, you can voice your objections, if you have any.

A Reminder

One dimension of this proof is Prophethood in general; the other is the Prophethood of Muhammad, upon him be peace and blessings.

An Indication

The Maker does nothing without a purpose; there are many instances of wisdom in His every act. There is an order in everything in the universe, down to the things that are seemingly most insignificant. Nothing is neglected in creation, and humanity needs a guide on its way to eternity. All these realities demonstrate the necessity of the institution of Prophethood.

If you would like this argument to be explained, then listen:

You can see that there is an order in creation, including the world of humanity, as well as in the animal kingdom, many members of species of which have been put in service of humanity because the reason given to humanity. Humanity's superiority to animals in the following three points is a proof of the necessity for Prophethood:

The *first* is the interesting reality of the fact that the beginning of thought is the end of action and the beginning of action is the end of thought. That is, actions give rise to thoughts, which, in turn, lead to actions. Humanity has the capacity to be able to see the relationship between the cycles of causes and effects. In the light of this relationship, it arrives new combinations and the forms or rules of new thoughts and behavior, as well as what we call laws which appear to be responsible for cause and effect. This is the mechanism of progress and evolution. Science is the ability to analyze those combinations, or to be able to detect the individual elements and causes and effects, which form or lead to them, and the laws that appear to be responsible. Based on these laws, humanity can develop or produce new things. However, its capacity is limited, and its abilities are defective. Thus, together with these defective and limited capacities and abilities, the desire to satisfy all of humanity's needs, and humanity's innate ignorance and powerlessness, as well as the fancies, caprices, suspicions, and whims what pester it constantly, cause us to be in absolute need of the guidance of Prophethood. Only through Prophethood can the perfect orderliness of the universe, with whatever is in it and whatever occurs in it, be perceived adequately. The balance and order of human life depend on the ability to perceive this universal order.

The *second* point is that humanity has been equipped with a great potential and has almost limitless ambitions and tendencies, barely controllable thoughts and conceptions, and the faculties of lust and anger which have not been restricted in origin, but which require education or training and restraint. This essential dimension of human existence also requires Prophethood.

An Indication

Even if a person were given a life that would last millions of years in bliss and pleasure, even if they were allowed to control everything in whatever way that wished, due to the inability of this worldly life to satisfy human desires and potential, they would continue to sigh and regret and wish for more. This dissatisfaction shows that humanity has an innate tendency to eternal life and has been created for eternity so that it can activate its unrestricted potential in an unrestricted realm.

A Reminder

There is nothing without meaning or purpose in existence, and everything is based on a reality. This indicated the fact that in this restricted world, where pleasure is mixed with pain and hindrances intervene; in this world which never lacks in envy and mutual wrongs, it is not possible for humanity to realize the perfections towards which it is innately directed. Therefore, there must be another, more spacious realm where nothing hinders another thing, so that humanity can order its worldly life along the way to perfection and to contribute to the universal order so that it will warn eternal happiness in that spacious, eternal realm.

A Reminder and an Indication

Although it is not the subject here, I have made an indication of the Resurrection. What I want to stress here is that the human innate potential is directed towards eternity. Consider the essence of humanity and the nature of its potential together with what is required to develop it. Then, visit the faculty of imagination which is the simplest and smallest servant of human essence. Ask, "O respected faculty of imagination! I have glad tidings for you. You will be given a million years of happy life in the world. You will be able to control everything in the world as you wish. But following this life, you will be sent to eternal non-existence without being returned to life." What do you think the answer will be? Will it receive your glad tidings happily or utter sighs and regrets? Be sure that the essence of humanity will wail in depths of its conscience, and utter, "Alas! Woe to me that there is no eternal happiness!" It will reprimand the faculty of imagination and say to it: "Do not be content with this transient life!"

O brothers and sisters, look! If this transient happiness, even though it might last millions of years, cannot satisfy the faculty of imagination, which is just one of the servants of the human essence, how can it satisfy the human essence itself, which has many more servants, much greater and more important than the faculty of imagination? The only thing which will satisfy it is eternal happiness that lies in the Resurrection.

The *third* point worth mentioning in relation to the superiority of humanity over animals is the balance in the dispositions of the human, the fineness in its nature, and its tendency to make things better or more beautiful. Humanity has an inborn tendency to live in a way benefitting its essential nature. It must not, and cannot, live like animals. It must lead a life befitting its essential honor. It is because of this unborn tendency that humanity needs to improve and decorate its dwelling place, clothes, and foods, and use science and crafts. It is not possible for an individual to have sufficient knowledge about all such sciences and crafts. Therefore, humans need to live together, cooperate with one another, and exchange their products among themselves. The satisfaction of this need requires justice and the existence of certain rules, as the desires, potentials, and faculties of humanity are not restricted from birth, and so can be the cause of aggression and injustice. Any individual mind or intellect is unable to establish the nature of this justice or rules, as humanity is neither its own creator nor does it have true, all-embracing or universal knowledge about itself, its environment, and its future. So there must be a universal mind or intellect that has this knowledge. This is the Divinely revealed Religion. There must also be a power which can dominate the spirits and consciences of humans, and thus implement the required justice and rules. This power must have some sort of superiority over others. This power is the institutions of Prophethood, which was founded by the Creator of the Universe Himself. It is He Who choose the Prophets and made them distinguished in many respects.

A Prophet inculcates the Creator's grandeur in the minds and the spirits of human beings. The Divinely revealed Religion he communicates requires regular worship, which enables people continuously and increasingly feel the Creator's grandeur. Worship directs thoughts and feelings to the Creator, which, in turn, lead to obedience to Him. Obedience to the Creator, Who is also the Supreme Author of the universal, magnificent order, secures the perfect public order in human life. This perfect public order is based on God's Wisdom. The essence of God's Wisdom is that nothing in the universe is purposeless and meaningless. The universal order, beauty, and harmony bear witness to this Wisdom.

If you have perceived the superiority of humanity over animals in respect to the three points discussed above, you have then understood that Prophethood is the central point of human existence, and that it is around this that human life revolves. Also, consider the following three points:

Firstly, individuals lack sufficient knowledge, accurate viewpoints, and the ability to know themselves in all aspects and dimensions of their existence, and they lack the ability to lead their lives in a proper way that will enable happiness in both their individual and collective lives. In addition, they suffer whims, fancies, and errors, and are often defeated by their carnal impulses which require discipline. Therefore, humans desperately need a perfect guide and teacher; this guise is a Prophet.

Secondly, the laws and systems made by humans cannot satisfy the perennial needs and expectations of humanity, nor properly restrict its innate aggression, train its faculties appropriately, or correctly guide its potential and disposition to development or progress. This latter is inherent in the tendency of the whole creation to achieve perfection. Human laws and systems are almost lifeless and do not last. Even though they are based on the accumulated knowledge and experiences of humanity over the course of history, they are unable to cause the seeds of potential in humanity to grow properly or to yield sound fruit. For this reason, humanity desperately needs a Divine Law, which will enable its happiness both spiritually and intellectually and physically, both in this world and the next. This Law must also guide humanity along the way to the attainment of human perfection through the realization of its potentials. It is the Prophets who brings us this living, life-endowing, everlasting Divine Law.

A Possible Objection: We see that those who do not follow the Divine Religion may enjoy a healthy order.

The answer: If there is any order in their way, this is due to the affirmed or non-affirmed guidance and the effect of the Divine Religion and religions leaders. There has never been a community left completely devoid of the guidance of a Prophet, so even though many people reject the Divine guidance and Religion, they are not able to remain unaffected by the Religion. Any approvable, lasting order observed in any community has its basic source or roots in Divine guidance. With respect to other aspects that are incompatible with Divine guidance, the order of irreligious people or of those who do now follow the Divine Religion is bound to collapse, even though such an order may appear to have brought some sort of worldly happiness to certain people. In addition, a good order must be one which brings only an apparent, transient, superficial happiness to a small minority in the world, whole hurting others into subjection and humiliating misery, cannot be regarded as good, approvable order.

Thirdly, any extremity in human behavior or moral standards destroys human potential, which, in turn, causes purposelessness and vanity. Purposelessness and vanity are absolutely contrary to the Divine universally wisdom, which is clearly observed to pursue purposes and benefits in everything in the universe, from smallest to the greatest.

A False Supposition and a Reminder

On the pretext of giving priority to law and its observance, which have been brought to the attention of humanity after so many disasters and by stirring up public opinion continuously, heretical people suppose there is no need for the Divine Law and that it is possible to replace it with human-made laws. This is a totally false supposition. For the world has grown old and there is still nothing to prove such a supposition. On the contrary, although our old world sees the development of some beauty, new vices and evil appear in even worse and more deceptive forms. Just as the rules of wisdom are not independent of the rules of government, so too is the order of human life increasingly in need of the rules of the Divine Law and virtues that dominate human conscience. In addition, new systems of education and human behavior, which are regarded as having no need for Divine Law, are completely unable to train three basic human faculties—intellect, desire, and anger—properly or to develop them into wisdom, chastity, and moderation or chivalry respectively, nor to sustain them as much. As a result, humanity is in desperate need of Prophethood equipped with the balance of Divine justice, which influences and penetrates human nature and conscience.

An Indication

Thousands of Prophets who appeared among humanity proved their claim to Prophethood with thousands of miracles they worked. These miracles, which form an irrefutable proof and an absolutely true voice, announce and establish the mission and institution of Prophethood. They also function as a proof for the existence and Oneness of the Creator.

A Reminder

Each science has its own principles and laws upon which it is based and each is founded on the orderliness of existence. But for that orderliness in existence, there would have been no laws or sciences. Secondly, certain pleasures and love are found in the basic purposes and benefits appointed for life, such as eating, drinking, and marriage. (For example, the basic purpose of marriage is reproduction, but the pleasures provided by love for one's spouse and love for one's children are the pleasures included in this purpose.) If we can see the Divine favor in this single fact of life, we can easily understand that there is nothing that is useless or extraneous in existence, and we can perceive that Prophethood, upon which the most fundamental purposes of existence and creation are centered, is indispensible for human life and existence. If there were no Prophethood, humanity would have come from a chaotic world and his world would have been thrown into complete chaos.

A Reminder

> O brothers and sisters! If Prophethood, which is the lesser of the two proofs
> for the existence of the Maker, namely the institution of Prophethood and the
> Prophethood of Muhammad, has been inscribed on the page of your minds, then
> we can proceed with the greater one, that is the Prophethood of Muhammad,
> upon him be peace and blessings.

An Indication and a Reminder

> This greater proof is absolutely true. For, if you study the lives and works of
> the Prophets, all of whom have been recorded at the top list of the pride of
> humanity, and consider the meaning and mission of Prophethood, which is the
> basic common point among them, beyond the influences of the considerations
> developed over the course of time, then you can easily understand the following
> reality:

> The rights of the Creator and the created are the lights of Divine favor and
> munificence, and form the rays of abstract beauties in existence. All the Prophets,
> upon them be peace, adopted and strictly observed these as the basic principles
> in their actions. In addition, their treatment of their people, their people's view of
> them, their perfect altruism and selflessness, and many other factors all proved
> that they were Prophets. The attributes essential to Prophethood (truthfulness,
> intellect, trustworthiness, communication of the Divine Message, sinlessness,
> and freedom from physical and mental defects) were found in the most perfect
> form in Prophet Muhammad, upon him be peace and blessings, who appeared
> in the Arabian Peninsula at a time when human kind was at the threshold of its
> maturity, and became the unique source and teacher of all elevated sciences for
> humanity. This inevitably leads us to the conclusion that Prophet Muhammad
> was undoubtedly a Prophet. In addition to these proofs, all the proofs, including
> their miracles, which establish the Prophethood of all the preceding Prophets
> also prove Muhammad's Prophethood, upon him be peace and blessings.

The Reasonings, Third Part, Second Purpose, p. 120–128.

Extract Three: Muhammad the Prophet

"The Nineteenth Word" is a chapter about the prophethood of Muhammad. It
contains 14 subheadings illustrating proof of his authenticity. For Nursi, there are
good arguments for Muhammad's claim to the final prophet from God.

The Nineteenth Word

[About the Messengership of Muhammad (PBUH)]

I could not praise Muhammad with my words; rather, my words were made praiseworthy by Muhammad.

Yes, this Word is beautiful, but what makes it so is the most beautiful of all things, the attributes and qualities of Muhammad (PBUH).

Also being the Fourteenth Flash, this Word consists of fourteen "Droplets."

First Droplet

There are three great and universal things which make known to us our Sustainer. One is the book of the universe, a jot of whose testimony we have heard from the thirteen Flashes together with the Thirteenth Word of the Risale-i Nur. Another is the Seal of the Prophets (Peace and blessings be upon him), the supreme sign of the book of the universe. The other is the Qur'an of Mighty Stature. Now we must become acquainted with the Seal of the Prophets (PBUH), who is the second and articulate proof, and must listen to him.

Yes, consider the collective personality of this proof: the face of the earth has become his mosque, Mecca, his *mihrab*, and Medina, his pulpit. Our Prophet (Peace and blessings be upon him), this clear proof, is leader of all the believers, preacher to all mankind, the chief of all the prophets, lord of all the saints, the leader of a circle for the remembrance of God comprising all the prophets and saints. He is a luminous tree whose living roots are all the prophets, and fresh fruits are all the saints; whose claims all the prophets relying on their miracles and all the saints relying on their wonder-working confirm and corroborate. For he declares and claims: "There is no god but God!" And all on left and right, that is, those luminous reciters of God's Names lined up in the past and the future, repeat the same words, and through their consensus in effect declare: "You speak the truth and what you say is right!" What false idea has the power to meddle in a claim which is thus affirmed and corroborated by thousands?

Second Droplet

Just as that luminous proof of Divine unity is affirmed by the unanimity and consensus of those two wings, so do hundreds of indications in the revealed scriptures, like the Torah and Bible,[45] and the thousands of signs that appeared before the beginning of his mission, and the well-known news given by the voices from the Unseen and the unanimous testimony of the soothsayers, the indications of the thousands of his miracles like the Splitting of the Moon, and the justice of Shari'a all confirm and corroborate him. So too, in his person, his laudable morals, which were at the summit of perfection; and in his duties, his complete confidence and elevated qualities, which were of the highest excellence, and his extraordinary fear of God, worship, seriousness, and fortitude, which demonstrated the strength of his belief, and his total certainty and his complete steadfastness,—these all show as clearly as the sun how utterly faithful he was to his cause.

Third Droplet

If you wish, come! Let us go to Arabian Peninsula, to the Era of Bliss! In our imaginations we shall see him at his duties and visit him. Look! We see a person distinguished by his fine character and beautiful form. In his hand is a miraculous book and on his tongue, a truthful address; he is delivering a pre-eternal sermon to all mankind, indeed, to man, jinn, and the angels, and to all beings. He solves and expounds the strange riddle of the mystery of the world's creation; he discovers and solves the abstruse talisman which is the mystery of the universe; and he provides convincing and satisfying answers to the three awesome and difficult questions that are asked of all beings and have always bewildered and occupied minds: "Where do you come from? What are you doing here? What is your destination?"

Fourth Droplet

See! He spreads such a Light of truth that if you look at the universe as being outside the luminous sphere of his truth and guidance, you see it to be like a place of general mourning, and beings strangers to one another and hostile, and inanimate beings to be like ghastly corpses and living creatures like orphans weeping at the blows of death and separation. Now look! Through the Light he spreads, that place of universal mourning has been transformed into a place where God's Names and praises are recited in joy and ecstasy. The foreign, hostile beings have become friends and brothers. While the dumb, dead inanimate creatures have all become familiar officials and docile servants. And the weeping, complaining orphans are seen to be either reciting God's Names and praises or offering thanks at being released from their duties.

---

[45]   In his *Risale-i Hamidiye*, Husayn Jisri extracted one hundred and fourteen indications from those scriptures. If this many have remained after the texts have become corrupted, there were surely many explicit mentions before.

Fifth Droplet

Also, through his Light, the motion and movement of the universe, and its variations, changes and transformations cease being meaningless, futile, and the playthings of chance; they rise to being dominical missives, pages inscribed with the signs of creation, mirrors to the Divine Names, and the world itself becomes a book of the Eternally Besought One's wisdom. Man's boundless weakness and impotence make him inferior to all other animals and his intelligence, an instrument for conveying grief, sorrow, and sadness, makes him more wretched, yet when he is illumined with that Light, he rises above all animals and all creatures. Through entreaty, his illuminated impotence, poverty, and intelligence make him a petted monarch; due to his complaints, he becomes a spoiled vicegerent of the earth. That is to say, if it was not for his Light, the universe and man, and all things, would be nothing. Yes, certainly such a person is necessary in such a wondrous universe; otherwise the universe and firmaments would not be in existence.

Sixth Droplet

Thus, that Being brings and announces the good news of eternal happiness; he is the discoverer and proclaimer of an infinite mercy, the herald and observer of the beauties of the sovereignty of dominicality, and the discloser and displayer of the treasures of the Divine Names. If you regard him in that way, that is in regard to his being a worshipful servant of God, you will see him to be the model of love, the exemplar of mercy, the glory of mankind, and the most luminous fruit of the tree of creation. While if you look in this way, that is, in regard to his Messengership, you see him to be the proof of God, the lamp of truth, the sun of guidance, and the means to happiness. And look! His Light has lighted up from east to west like dazzling lightning, and half the earth and a fifth of mankind has accepted the gift of his guidance and preserved it like life itself. So how is it that our evil-commanding souls and satans do not accept with all its degrees, the basis of all such a Being claimed, that is, *There is no god but God?*

Seventh Droplet

Now, consider how, eradicating in no time at all their evil, savage customs and habits to which they were fanatically attached, he decked out the various wild, unyielding peoples of that broad peninsula with all the finest virtues, and made them teachers of all the world and masters to the civilized nations. See, it was not an outward domination, he conquered and subjugated their minds, spirits, hearts, and souls. He became the beloved of hearts, the teacher of minds, the trainer of souls, the ruler of spirits.

Eighth Droplet

You know that a small habit like cigarette smoking among a small nation can be removed permanently only by a powerful ruler with great effort. But look! This Being removed numerous ingrained habits from intractable, fanatical large nations with slight outward power and little effort in a short period of time, and in their place he so established exalted qualities that they became as firm as if they had mingled with their very blood. He achieved very many extraordinary feats like this. Thus, we present the Arabian Peninsula as a challenge to those who refuse to see the testimony of the blessed age of the Prophet. Let them each take a hundred philosophers, go there, and strive for a hundred years; would they be able to carry out in that time one hundredth of what he achieved in a year?

Ninth Droplet

Also, you know that an insignificant man of small standing among a small community in a disputed matter of small importance cannot tell a small but shameful lie brazen-faced and without fear without displaying anxiety or disquiet enough to inform the enemies at his side of his deception. Now look at that Being; although he undertook a tremendous task which required an official of great authority and great standing and a situation of great security, can any contradiction at all be found in the words he uttered among a community of great size in the face of great hostility concerning a great cause and matters of great significance, with great ease and freedom, without fear, hesitation, diffidence, or anxiety, with pure sincerity, great seriousness, and in an intense, elevated manner that angered his enemies? Is it at all possible that any trickery should have been involved? God forbid! *It is naught but Revelation inspired.*[46] The truth does not deceive, and one who perceives the truth is not deceived. His way, which is truth, is free of deception. How could a fancy appear to one who sees the truth to be the truth, and deceive him?

Tenth Droplet

Now, look! What curiosity-arousing, attractive, necessary, and awesome truths he shows, what matters he proves!

You know that what impels man most is curiosity. Even, if it was to be said to you: "If you give half of your life and property, someone will come from the Moon and Jupiter and tell you all about them. He will also tell you the truth about your future and what will happen to you," you would be bound to give them if you have any curiosity at all. Whereas that Being tells of a Monarch Who is such that in His realm, the Moon flies round a moth like a fly, and the moth,

---

[46] Qur'an, 53:4.

the earth, flutters round a lamp, and the lamp, the sun, is merely one lamp among thousands in one guest-house out of thousands of that Monarch.

Also, he speaks truly of a world so wondrous and a revolution so momentous that if the earth was a bomb and exploded, it would not be all that strange. Look! Listen to Suras like, *When the sun is folded up*;[47] *When the sky is cleft asunder*;[48] *[The Day] of Noise and Clamour*;[49] which he recites.

Also, he speaks truly about a future in comparison with which the future in this world is like a tiny mirage. And he tells most seriously of a happiness in comparison with which all worldly happiness is but a fleeting flash of lightning in relation to an eternal sun.

Eleventh Droplet

For sure, wonders await us under the apparent veil of the universe which is thus strange and perplexing. So one thus wonderful and extraordinary, a displayer of marvels, is necessary to tell of its wonders. It is apparent from that Being's conduct that he has seen them, and sees them, and says that he has seen them. And he instructs us most soundly concerning what the God of the heavens and the earth, Who nurtures us with His bounties, wants and desires of us. Everyone should therefore leave everything and run to and heed this Being who teaches numerous other necessary and curiosity-arousing truths like these, so how is it that most people are deaf and blind, and mad even, so that they do not see this truth, and they do not listen to it and understand it?

Twelfth Droplet

Thus, just as this Being is an articulate proof and true evidence at the degree of the veracity of the unity of the Creator of beings, so is he a decisive proof and clear evidence for the resurrection of the dead and eternal happiness. Yes, with his guidance he is the reason for eternal happiness coming about and is the means of attaining it; so too through his prayers and supplications, he is the cause of its existence and reason for its creation. We repeat here this mystery, which is mentioned in the Tenth Word, due to its "station".

See! This Being prays with a prayer so supreme that it is as if the Arabian Peninsula and the earth itself performs the prayers through his sublime prayer, and offers entreaties. See, he also entreats in a congregation so vast that it is as if all the luminous and perfected members of mankind from the time of Adam till

---

[47]   Qur'an, 81:1.

[48]   Qur'an, 82:1.

[49]   Qur'an, 101:1.

our age and until the end of time, are following him and saying "Amen" to his supplications. And see! He is beseeching for a need so universal that not only the dwellers of the earth, but also those of the heavens, and all beings, join in his prayer, declaring: "Yes! O our Sustainer!

Grant it to us! We too want it!" And he supplicates with such want, so sorrowfully, in such a loving, yearning, and beseeching fashion that he brings the whole cosmos to tears, leading them to join in his prayer.

And see! The purpose and aim of his prayer is such it raises man and the world, and all creatures, from the lowest of the low, from inferiority, worthlessness, and uselessness to the highest of the high; that is to having value, permanence, and exalted duties. And see! He seeks and pleads for help and mercy in a manner so elevated and sweet, it is as if he makes all beings and the heavens and the earth hear, and bringing them to ecstasy, to exclaim: "Amen, O our God! Amen!" And see! He seeks his needs from One so Powerful, Hearing, and Munificent, One so Knowing, Seeing, and Compassionate, that He sees and hears the most secret need of the most hidden living being and its entreaties, accepts them, and has mercy on it. For He gives what is asked for, if only through the tongue of disposition. And He gives it in so Wise, Seeing, and Compassionate a form that it leaves no doubt that that nurturing and regulation is particular to the All-Hearing and All-Seeing One, the Most Generous and Most Compassionate One.

Thirteenth Droplet

What does he want, this pride of the human race, who taking behind him all the eminent of mankind, stands on top of the world, and raising up his hand, is praying? What is this unique being, who is truly the glory of the cosmos, seeking? Listen! He is seeking eternal happiness. He is asking for eternal life, and to meet with God. He wants Paradise. And he wants all the Sacred Divine Names, which display their beauty and decrees in the mirrors of beings. Even, if it were not for reasons for the fulfilment of those countless requests, like mercy, grace, wisdom, and justice, a single of that Being's prayers would have been sufficient for the construction of Paradise, the creation of which is as easy for Divine power as the creation of the spring. Yes, just as his Messengership was the reason for the opening of this place of examination and trial, so too his worship and servitude to God were the reason for the opening of the next world.

Would the perfect order observed in the universe, which has caused scholars and the intelligent to pronounce: "It is not possible for there to be anything better than what exists;" and the faultless beauty of art within mercy, the incomparable beauty of dominicality,—would these permit the ugliness, the cruelty, the lack of order of its hearing and responding to the least significant, the least important desires and voices, and its considering unimportant the most important, the most necessary wishes, and its not hearing them or understanding them, and not carrying them out? God forbid! A hundred thousand times, God forbid! Such a beauty would not permit such an ugliness; it would not become ugly.

And so, my imaginary friend! That is enough for now, we must return. For if we remain a hundred years in this age in the Arabian Peninsula, we still would only completely comprehend one hundredth of the marvels of that Being's duties and the wonders he carried out, and we would never tire of watching him.

Now, come! We shall look at the centuries, which will turn above us. See how each has opened like a flower through the effulgence it has received from that Sun of Guidance! They have produced millions of enlightened fruits like Abu Hanifa, Shafi'i, Abu Bayazid Bistami, Shah Geylani, Shah Naqshband, Imam Ghazzali, and Imam Rabbani. But postponing the details of our observations to another time, we must recite some benedictions for that displayer of miracles and bringer of guidance, which mention a number of his certain miracles:

Endless peace and blessings be upon our master Muhammad, to the number of the good deeds of his community, to whom was revealed the All-Wise Criterion of Truth and Falsehood, from One Most Merciful, Most Compassionate, from the Sublime Throne; whose Messengership was foretold by the Torah and Bible, and told of by wondrous signs, the voices of jinn, saints of man, and soothsayers; at whose indication the moon split; our master Muhammad! Peace and blessings be upon him thousands and thousands of times, to the number of the breaths of his community; at whose beckoning came the tree, on whose prayer rain swiftly fell; and whom the cloud shaded from the heat; who satisfied a hundred men with his food; from between whose fingers three times flowed water like the Spring of Kawthar; and to whom God made speak the lizard, the gazelle, the wolf, the torso, the arm, the camel, the mountain, the rock, and the clod; the one who made the Ascension and whose eye did not waver; our master and intercessor, Muhammad! Peace and blessings be upon him thousands and thousands of times, to the number of the letters of the Qur'an formed in the words, represented with the permission of the Most Merciful in the mirrors of the airwaves, at the reciting of all the Qur'an's words by all reciters from when it was first revealed to the end of time. And grant us forgiveness and have mercy on us, O God, for each of those blessings. Amen.

[I have described the Evidences for the Prophethood of Muhammad (PBUH) which I have here indicated briefly in a Turkish treatise called *Suaât-i Mârifeti'n-Nebi* and in the Nineteenth Letter (The Miracles of Muhammad). And there too aspects of the All-Wise Qur'an's miraculousness have been mentioned briefly. Again, in a Turkish treatise called *Lemeât* and in the Twenty-Fifth Word (The Miraculousness of the Qur'an) I have explained concisely forty ways in which the Qur'an is a miracle, and indicated forty aspects of its miraculousness. And of those forty aspects, only the eloquence in the word-order, I have written in forty pages in an Arabic commentary called, *Isharat al-I'jaz*. If you have the need, you may refer to those three works.]

Fourteenth Droplet

The All-Wise Qur'an, the treasury of miracles and supreme miracle, proves the Prophethood of Muhammad (PBUH) together with Divine unity so decisively that it leaves no need for further proof. And we shall give its definition and indicate one or two flashes of its miraculousness which have been the cause of criticism.

The All-Wise Qur'an, which makes known to us our Sustainer, is thus: it is the pre-eternal translator of the great book of the universe; the discloser of the treasures of the Divine Names concealed in the pages of the earth and the heavens; the key to the truths hidden beneath these lines of events; the treasury of the favours of the Most Merciful and pre-eternal addresses, which come forth from the World of the Unseen beyond the veil of this Manifest World; the sun, foundation, and plan of the spiritual world of Islam, and the map of the worlds of the hereafter; the distinct expounder, lucid exposition, articulate proof, and clear translator of the Divine Essence, attributes, and deeds; the instructor, true wisdom, guide, and leader of the world of humanity; it is both a book of wisdom and law, and a book of prayer and worship, and a book of command and summons, and a book of invocation and Divine knowledge—it is book for all spiritual needs; and it is a sacred library offering books appropriate to the ways of all the saints and veracious, the purified and the scholars, whose ways and paths are all different.

Consider the flashes of miraculousness in its repetitions, which are imagined to be a fault: since the Qur'an is both a book of invocation, and a book of prayer, and a book of summons, the repetition in it is desirable, indeed, it is essential and most eloquent. It is not as the faulty imagine. For the mark of invocation is illumination through repetition. The mark of prayer is strengthening through repetition. The mark of command and summons is confirmation through repetition. Moreover, everyone is not capable of always reading the whole Qur'an, but is mostly able to read one Sura. Therefore, since the most important purposes of the Qur'an are included in most of the longer Suras, each is like a small Qur'an. That is to say, so that no one should be deprived, certain of its aims like Divine unity, the resurrection of the dead, and the story of Moses, have been repeated. Also, like bodily needs, spiritual needs are various. Man is need of some of them every breath; like the body needs air, the spirit needs the word *Hu* (He). Some he is in need of every hour, like "In the Name of God." And so on. That means the repetition of verses arises from the repetition of need. It makes the repetition in order to point out the need and awaken and incite it, and to arouse desire and appetite.

Also, the Qur'an is a founder; it is the basis of the Clear Religion, and the foundation of the world of Islam. It changed human social life, and is the answer to the repeated questions of its various classes. Repetition is necessary for a founder in order to establish things. Repetition is necessary to corroborate them. Confirmation and repetition are necessary to strengthen them.

Also, it speaks of such mighty matters and minute truths that numerous repetitions are necessary in different forms in order to establish them in everyone's hearts. Nevertheless, they are apparently repetitions, but in reality every verse has numerous meanings, numerous benefits, and many aspects and levels. In each place they are mentioned with a different meaning, for different benefits and purposes.

Also, the Qur'an's being unspecific and concise in certain matters to do with cosmos is a flash of miraculousness for the purpose of guidance. It cannot be the target of criticism and is not a fault, like some atheists imagine.

If you ask: "Why does the All-Wise Qur'an not speak of beings in the same way as philosophy and science? It leaves some matters in brief form, and some it speaks of in a simple and superficial way that is easy in the general view, does not wound general feelings, and does not weary or tax the minds of ordinary people. Why is this?"

By way of answer we say: Philosophy has strayed from the path of truth, that's why. Also, of course you have understood from past Words and what they teach that the All-Wise Qur'an speaks of the universe in order to make known the Divine Essence, attributes, and Names. That is, it explains the meanings of the book of the universe to make known its Creator. That means it looks at beings, not for themselves, but for their Creator. Also, it addresses everyone. But philosophy and science look at beings for themselves, and address scientists in particular. In which case, since the All-Wise Qur'an makes beings evidences and proofs, the evidence has to be superficial so that it will be quickly understood in the general view. And since the Qur'an of Guidance addresses all classes of men, the ordinary people, which form the most numerous class, want guidance which is concise with unnecessary things beings vague, and which brings subtle things close with comparisons, and which does not change things which in their superficial view are obvious into an unnecessary or even harmful form, lest it causes them to fall into error.

For example, it says about the sun: "The sun is a revolving lamp or lantern." For it does not speak of the sun for itself and its nature, but because it is a sort of mainspring of an order and centre of a system, and order and system are mirrors of the Maker's skill. It says:

The sun runs its course.[50]

that is, the sun revolves. Through calling to mind the orderly disposals of Divine power in the revolutions of winter and summer, and day and night with the phrase, The sun revolves, it makes understood the Maker's tremendousness. Thus, whatever the reality of this revolving, it does not affect the order, which is woven and observed, and which is the purpose. It also says,

And set the sun as a lamp.[51]

Through depicting through the word lamp the world in the form of a palace, and the things within it as decorations, necessities, and provisions prepared for man and living beings, and inferring that the sun is also a subjugated candleholder, it makes known the mercy and bestowal of the Creator. Now look and see what this foolish and prattling philosophy says:

"The sun is a vast burning liquid mass. It causes the planets which have been flung off from it to revolve around it. Its mass is such-and-such. It is this, it is that." It does not afford the spirit the satisfaction and fulfilment of true knowledge, just a terrible dread and fearful wonder. It does not speak of it as the Qur'an does. You may understand from this the value of the matters of philosophy, whose inside is hollow and outside, ostentatious. So do not be deceived by its glittering exterior and be disrespectful towards the most miraculous expositions of the Qur'an!

O God! Make the Qur'an healing for us, the writer of this and his peers, from all ills, and a companion to us and to them in our lives and after our deaths, and in this world, and in the grave, and at the Last Judgement an intercessor, and on the Bridge a light, and from the Fire a screen and shield, and in Paradise a friend, and in all good deeds a guide and leader, through Your grace and munificence and beneficence and mercy, O Most Munificent of the Munificent and Most Merciful of the Merciful! Amen.

O God! Grant blessings and peace to the one to whom the All-Wise Qur'an, the Distinguisher between Truth and Falsehood, was re-vealed, and to all his Family and Companions. Amen. Amen.

[NOTE: The Six Drops of the Fourteenth Droplet in the Arabic Risale-i Nur, and especially the Six Points of the Fourth Drop, explain fifteen of the approximately forty sorts of the All-Wise Qur'an's miraculousness. Deeming those to be sufficient, we have limited the discussion here. If you wish, refer to them, and you will find a treasury of miracles.]
The Words, Nineteenth Word, p. 243–252.

---

[50]   Qur'an, 36:38.
[51]   Qur'an, 71:16

Extract Four: Revelation and Philosophy

Composed of four sections, "The Twelfth Word" compares the wisdom of revelation, namely the Qur'an, and philosophy that contradicts religion and revelation. The first section explains two important concepts of the *Risale* namely *mānā-i ismī*, the meaning of things which refer to themselves, and *mānā-i harfī*, the indicative meaning to which things refer. The second and third sections elaborate on the perspectives provided by the Qur'an and philosophy concerning individual and social lives. The last section describes the superiority of Divine revelation.

The Twelfth Word

In the Name of God, the Merciful, the Compassionate.

And he who has been given wisdom has been given great good.[52]

[This Word consists of a brief comparison between the sacred wisdom of the All-Wise Qur'an and the wisdom of philosophy and science, and a concise summary of the instruction and training which Qur'anic wisdom gives to man in his personal life and social life, and an indication of the Qur'an's superiority to other Divine words, and to all speech. There are Four Principles in this Word.]

First Principle

Look through the telescope of the following story which is in the form of a comparison, and see the differences between Qur'anic wisdom and that of philosophy and science:

One time, a renowned Ruler who was both religious and a fine craftsman wanted to write the All-Wise Qur'an in a script worthy of the sacredness in its meaning and the miraculousness in its words, so that its marvel-displaying stature would be arrayed in wondrous apparel. The artist-King therefore wrote the Qur'an in a truly wonderful fashion. He used all his precious jewels in its writing. In order to indicate the great variety of its truths, he wrote some of its embodied letters in diamonds and emeralds, and some in rubies and agate, and other sorts in brilliants and coral, while others he inscribed with silver and gold. He adorned and decorated it in such a way that everyone, those who knew how to read and those who did not, were full of admiration and astonishment when they beheld it. Especially in the view of the people of truth, since the outer beauty was an indication of the brilliant beauty and striking adornment in its meaning, it became a truly precious antique.

---

[52] Qur'an, 2:269.

Then the Ruler showed the artistically wrought and bejewelled Qur'an to a European philosopher and to a Muslim scholar. In order to test them and for reward, he commanded them: "Each of you write a work about the wisdom and purposes of this!" First the philosopher, then the scholar composed a book about it. However, the philosopher's book discussed only the decorations of the letters and their relationships and conditions, and the properties of the jewels, and described them. It did not touch on their meaning at all, for the European had no knowledge of the Arabic script. He did not even know that the embellished Qur'an was a book, a written piece, expressing a meaning. He rather looked on it as an ornamented antique. He did not know any Arabic, but he was a very good engineer, and he described things very aptly, and he was a skilful chemist, and an ingenious jeweller. So this man wrote his work according to those crafts.

As for the Muslim scholar, when he looked at the Qur'an, he understood that it was the Perspicuous Book, the All-Wise Qur'an. This truth-loving person neither attached importance to the external adornments, nor busied himself with the ornamented letters. He became preoccupied with something that was a million times higher, more elevated, more subtle, more noble, more beneficial, and more comprehensive than the matters with which the other man had busied himself. For discussing the sacred truths and lights of the mysteries beneath the veil of the decorations, he wrote a truly fine commentary. Then the two of them took their works and presented them to the Illustrious Ruler. The Ruler first took the philosopher's work. He looked at it and saw that the self-centred and nature-worshipping man had worked very hard, but had written nothing of true wisdom. He had understood nothing of its meaning. Indeed, he had confused it and been disrespectful towards it, and ill-mannered even. For supposing that source of truths, the Qur'an, to be meaningless decoration, he had insulted it as being valueless in regard to meaning. So the Wise Ruler hit him over the head with his work and expelled him from his presence.

Then he looked at the work of the other, the truth-loving, scrupulous scholar, and saw that it was an extremely fine and beneficial commentary, a most wise composition full of guidance. "Congratulations! May God bless you!", he said. Thus, wisdom is this and they call those who possess it knowledgeable and wise. As for the other man, he was a craftsman who had exceeded his mark. Then in reward for the scholar's work, he commanded that in return for each letter ten gold pieces should be given him from his inexhaustible treasury.

If you have understood the comparison, now look and see the reality:

The ornamented Qur'an is this artistically fashioned universe, and the Ruler is the Pre-Eternal All-Wise One. As for the two men, one -the European- represents philosophy and its philosophers, and the other, the Qur'an and its students. Yes, the All-Wise Qur'an is a most elevated expounder, a most eloquent translator of the Mighty Qur'an of the Universe. Yes, it is the Criterion which instructs man and the jinn concerning the signs of creation inscribed by the pen of power on the pages of the universe and on the leaves of time. It regards beings, each of which is a meaningful letter, as bearing the meaning of another, that is, it looks at them on account of their Maker. It says, "How beautifully they have been made! How exquisitely they point to their Maker's beauty!", thus showing the universe's true beauty. But the philosophy they call natural philosophy or science has plunged into the decorations of the letters of beings and into their relationships, and has become bewildered; it has confused the way of reality. While the letters of this mighty book should be looked at as bearing the meaning of another, that is, on account of God, they have not done this; they have looked at beings as signifying themselves. That is, they have looked at beings on account of beings, and have discussed them in that way. Instead of saying, "How beautifully they have been made," they say "How beautiful they are," and have made them ugly. In doing this they have insulted the universe, and made it complain about them. Indeed, *philosophy without religion is a sophistry divorced from reality and an insult to the universe.*

Second Principle

A comparison between the moral training the wisdom of the All-Wise Qur'an gives to personal life and what philosophy and science teach:

The sincere student of philosophy is a pharaoh, but he is a contemptible pharaoh who worships the basest thing for the sake of benefit; he recognizes everything from which he can profit as his "Lord". And that irreligious student is obstinate and refractory, but he is wretched together with his obstinacy and accepts endless abasement for the sake of one pleasure. And he is abject together with his recalcitrance and shows his abasement by kissing the feet of satanic individuals for the sake of some base benefit. And that irreligious student is conceited and domineering, but since he can find no point of support in his heart, he is an utterly impotent blustering tyrant. And that student is a self-centered seeker of benefit whose aim and endeavour is to gratify his animal appetites; a crafty egotist who seeks his personal interests within certain nationalist interests.

However, the sincere student of Qur'anic wisdom is a servant, but he does not stoop to worship even the greatest of creatures; he is an esteemed slave who does not take a supreme benefit like Paradise as the aim of his worship. And its student is humble; he is righteous and mild, yet outside the limits of his Maker's leave, he would not voluntarily lower and abase himself before anything other than his Maker. And he is weak and in want, and he knows his weakness and poverty, but he is self-sufficient due to the wealth which his All-Generous Lord has stored up for him in the hereafter, and he is strong since he relies on his

Master's infinite power. And he acts and strives only for God's sake, for God's pleasure, and for virtue.

Thus, the training the two give may be understood from the comparison of the two students.

Third Principle

The training philosophy and science and Qur'anic wisdom give to human social life is this:

Philosophy accepts "force" as its point of support in the life of society. It considers its aim to be "benefits". The principle of its life it recognizes to be "conflict". It holds the bond between communities to be "racialism and negative nationalism". Its fruits are "gratifying the appetites of the soul and increasing human needs". However, the mark of force is "aggression". The mark of benefit –since they are insufficient for every desire–is "jostling and tussling". While the mark of conflict is "strife". And the mark of racialism -since it is nourished by devouring others- is "aggression". It is for these reasons that it has negated the happiness of mankind.

As for the Qur'anic wisdom, its point of support is "truth" instead of force. It takes "virtue and God's pleasure" as its aims in place of benefits. It takes the principle of "mutual assistance" as the principle of life in place of the principle of conflict. And it takes "the ties of religion, class, and country" to be the ties bonding communities. Its aim is to form a barrier against the lusts of the soul, urge the spirit to sublime matters, satisfy the high emotions, and urging man to the human perfections, make him a true human being. And the mark of "the truth" is accord. The mark of virtue is "solidarity". The mark of mutual assistance is "hastening to assist one another". The mark of religion is "brotherhood" and "attraction". And the mark of reining in and tethering the soul and leaving the spirit free and urging it towards perfections is "happiness in this world and the next".

Fourth Principle

If you want to understand the Qur'an's superiority among all the Divine scriptures and its supremacy over all speech and writings, then consider the following two comparisons:

The First: A king has two forms of speech, two forms of address. One is to speak on his private telephone with a common subject concerning some minor matter, some private need. The other, under the title of sublime sovereignty, supreme vicegerent, and universal rulership, is to speak with an envoy or high official for the purpose of making known and promulgating his commands, to make an utterance through an elevated decree proclaiming his majesty.

The Second: One man holds the mirror he is holding up to the sun. He receives light containing the seven colours according to the capacity of the mirror. He becomes connected to the sun through that relation and converses with it, and if he directs the light-filled mirror towards his dark house or his garden covered by a roof, he will benefit, not in relation to the sun's value, but in accordance with the capacity of the mirror. Another man, however, opens up broad windows out of his house or out of the roof over his garden. He opens up ways to the sun in the sky. He converses with the perpetual light of the actual sun and speaks with it, and says in gratitude through the tongue of his disposition: "O you beauty of the world who gilds the face of the earth with your light and makes the faces of the flowers smile! O beauty of the skies, fine sun! You have furnished my little house and garden with light and heat the same as you have them." Whereas the man with the mirror cannot say that. The reflection and works of the sun under that restriction are limited; they are in accordance with the restriction. Look at the Qur'an through the telescope of these two comparisons and see its miraculousness and understand its sacredness.

The Qur'an says: "If all the trees on the land were to become pens and all the seas ink, and if they were to write the words of Almighty God, they would never come to the end of them." Now, the reason the Qur'an has been given the highest rank among the infinite words of God is this: the Qur'an has come from the Greatest Divine Name and from the greatest level of every Name. It is God's Word in respect of His being Sustainer of All the Worlds; it is His decree through His title of God of All Beings; an address in regard to His being Creator of the Heavens and the Earth; a speech in regard to absolute dominicality; a pre-eternal address on account of universal Divine sovereignty; a note-book of the favours of the Most Merciful One from the point of view of His all-embracing, comprehensive mercy; a collection of communications at the beginnings of which are sometimes ciphers related to the sublime majesty of the Godhead; a wisdom-scattering holy scripture which, descending from the reaches of the Greatest Name, looks to and inspects the all-comprehensive domain of the Supreme Throne. It is for these reasons that the title of Word of God has been given with complete worthiness to the Qur'an.

In respect to the other Divine Words, they are speech which has become evident through a particular regard, a minor title, through the partial manifestation of a particular Name; through a particular dominicality, special sovereignty, a private mercy. Their degrees vary in regard to particularity and universality. Most inspiration is of this sort, but its degrees vary greatly. For example, the most particular and simple is the inspiration of the animals. Then there is the inspiration of the ordinary people; then the inspiration of ordinary angels; then the inspiration of the saints, then the inspiration of the higher angels. Thus, it is for this reason that a saint who offers supplications directly without means by the telephone of the heart says: "My heart tells me news of my Sustainer." He does not say, "It tells me of the Sustainer of All the Worlds." And he says: "My heart is the mirror, the throne, of my Sustainer." He does not say, "It is the throne of the Sustainer of All the Worlds." For he can manifest the address to the extent of its capacity and to the degree nearly seventy thousand veils have been raised. Thus, however much higher and more elevated is the decree of a king promulgated in respect of his supreme sovereignty than the insignificant speech of a common man, and however much more abundantly the effulgence of the sun in the sky may be benefited from than the manifestation of its reflection in the mirror, and however greater is its superiority, to that degree the Qur'an of Mighty Stature is superior to all other speech and all other books.

After the Qur'an, at the second level, the Holy Books and Revealed Scriptures have superiority according to their degree. They have their share from the mystery of that superiority. If all the fine words of all men and jinn which do not issue from the Qur'an were to be gathered together, they still could not attain to the sacred rank of the Qur'an and imitate it. If you want to understand a little of how the Qur'an comes from the Greatest Name and from the greatest level of every Name, consider the universal, elevated statements of *Ayat al-Kursi* and the following verses:

And with Him are the keys of the Unseen.[53]

O God! Lord of All Dominion.[54]

He draws the night as a veil over day, each seeking the other in rapid succession; He created the sun, the moon, and the stars, [all] subject to His command.[55]

O Earth, swallow up your water! And O Sky, withhold your rain![56]

The heavens and the earth and all within them extol and glorify Him.[57]

The creation of you all and the resurrection of you all is but like that of a single soul.[58]

---

[53]   Qur'an, 6:59.
[54]   Qur'an, 3:26.
[55]   Qur'an, 7:54.
[56]   Qur'an, 11:44
[57]   Qur'an, 17:44
[58]   Qur'an, 31:28.

We did indeed offer the Trust to the heavens, and the earth, and the mountains.[59]

The Day that We roll up the heavens like a scroll rolled up for books [completed].[60]

No just estimate have they made of God, such as is due to Him: on the Day of Judgement the whole of the earth will be but His handful.[61]

Had We sent down this Qur'an on a mountain, you would indeed have seen it humble itself and cleave asunder for fear of God.[62]

And study the Suras which begin *al-Hamdulillah*, or *Tusabbihu*, and see the rays of this mighty mystery. Look too at the openings of the *Alif. Lam. Mim.*'s, the *Alif. Lam. Ra.*'s, and the *Ha. Mim.*'s, and understand the Qur'an's importance in the sight of God.

If you have understood the valuable mystery of this Fourth Principle, you have understood that revelation mostly comes to the prophets by means of an angel, and inspiration is mostly without means. You will have also understood the reason why the greatest saint cannot attain to the level of a prophet. And you will have understood too the Qur'an's sublimity and its sacred grandeur and the mystery of its elevated miraculousness. So too you will have understood the mystery of the necessity of the Prophet Muhammad's Ascension, that is, that he went to the heavens, to *the furthest Lote-tree*, to *the distance of two bow-lengths*, offered supplications to the All-Glorious One, Who is *closer to him than his jugular vein*, and in the twinkling of an eye returned whence he came. Indeed, just as the Splitting of the Moon was a miracle of his messengership whereby he demonstrated his prophethood to the jinn and mankind, so the Ascension was a miracle of his worship and servitude to God whereby he demonstrated to the spirits and angels that he was God's Beloved.

O God, grant blessings and peace to him and to his Family as befits Your mercy, and in veneration of him. Amen.

The Words, Twelfth Word, p. 143–149.

---

[59]   Qur'an, 33:72.

[60]   Qur'an, 21:104.

[61]   Qur'an, 39:67

[62]   Qur'an, 59:21.

Extract Five: Humanity, Particles, and the Divine

The following excerpt is from "The Thirtieth Word," which is among the key
chapters of the *Risale-i Nur* and is composed of two parts; one dedicated to the
nature and role of humanity and the human "I," the other on the transformations of
particles, their motion and duties, all of which indicate Divine existence and unity.
This excerpt is from "The First Aim," the chapter discussing origins of the paths of
prophethood and religion as well as various types of philosophy and the outlooks
with which they provide humanity.

> Consider this: in the world of humanity, from the time of Adam up to now, two
> great currents, two lines of thought, have always been and will so continue. Like
> two mighty trees, they have spread out their branches in all directions and in
> every class of humanity. One of them is the line of prophethood and religion, the
> other the line of philosophy in its various forms. Whenever those two lines have
> been in agreement and united, that is to say, if the line of philosophy, having
> joined the line of religion, has been obedient and of service to it, the world of
> humanity has experienced a brilliant happiness and social life. Whereas, when
> they have become separated, goodness and light have been drawn to the side of
> the line of prophethood and religion, and evil and misguidance to the side of
> the line of philosophy. Now let us find the origin and foundations of those two
> lines.
>
> The line of philosophy that does not obey the line of religion, taking the
> form of a tree of Zaqqum, scatters the darkness of ascribing partners to God
> and misguidance on all sides. In the branch of the power of intellect, even, it
> produces the fruit of atheism, Materialism, and Naturalism for the consumption
> of the human intellect. And in the realm of the power of passion, it pours the
> tyrannies of Nimrod, Pharaoh, and Shaddad on mankind.[63] And in the realm of
> the power of animal appetites, it nurtures and bears the fruit of goddesses, idols,
> and those who claim divinity.
>
> The origin of the tree of Zaqqum together with that of the line of prophethood,
> which is like the Tuba-tree of worship, are in the two faces of the "I". The blessed
> branches of the line of prophethood in the garden of the globe of the earth are the
> following: in the branch of the power of intellect, it has nurtured the fruits of the

---

[63]   It was the swamp of Naturalist philosophy that gave birth to idols and established
goddesses in the heads of the ancient Greeks, that nourished and nurtured Nimrods and
Pharaohs. It was again that same Naturalist philosophy that produced the philosophies
of ancient Egypt and Babylon, which either reached the degree of magic or, since they
were represented by the elite, were considered to be magic by the people generally. Most
certainly, if man does not perceive the light of God Almighty because of the veil of Nature,
he will attribute divinity to everything and will thus cause himself nothing but trouble.

prophets, the messengers, and the saints. In the branch of the power of repulsion, it has resulted in angelic kings and just rulers. And in the branch of the power of attraction, it has resulted in people of good character and modest and beautiful manner, both generous and gracious. So the line of prophethood has shown how mankind is the most perfect fruit of the universe. We shall explain the two faces of the "I" as the root and pivot and as a principal seed of those two trees. That is to say, prophethood takes hold of one face of the "I", and philosophy takes hold of the other, causing them to diverge.

The First Face, which is the face of prophethood: It is the origin of sheer worship. That is to say, the "I" knows itself to be a bondsman. It realizes that it serves one other than itself. Its essence has only an indicative meaning. That is, it understands that it carries the meaning of another. Its existence is dependent; that is, it believes that its existence is due only to the existence of another, and that the continuance of its existence is due solely to the creativity of that other. Its ownership is illusory; that is, it knows that with the permission of its owner it has an apparent and temporary ownership. Its reality is shadow-like; that is, a contingent and insignificant shadow that displays the manifestation of a true and necessary reality. As to its function, being a measure and balance for the attributes and functions of its Creator, it is conscious service.

It is in this way that the prophets, and the pure ones and saints who were from the line of the prophets, regarded the "I", they saw it in this regard, and understood the truth. They handed over the sovereignty to the Lord of All Sovereignty and concluded that that Lord of All Glory has no partner or like, neither in His sovereignty, nor in His dominicality, nor in His Divinity. He has no need of assistant or deputy. The key to all things is in His hand. He has absolute power over all things. They also concluded that causes are but an apparent veil; nature is the set of rules of His creation, a collection of His laws, and the way in which He demonstrates His power.

Thus, this shining, luminous, beautiful face is like a living and meaningful seed out of which the Glorious Creator has created a Tuba-tree of worship, the blessed branches of which have adorned with luminous fruits all parts of the world of humanity. By scattering the darkness of all the past, it shows that that long past time is not a place of non-existence and a vast graveyard as philosophy would have it, but is a radiant garden and a place of light for the luminous souls who have departed this world, who have cast off their heavy loads and remain free. It is a luminous, many-runged ascent and an orbit of lights for passing souls in order that they may jump to the future and eternal felicity.

As for the second face, it is represented by philosophy. And as for philosophy, it regards the "I" as carrying no meaning other than its own. That is to say, it declares that the "I" points only to itself, that its meaning is in itself. It considers that the "I" works purely on its own account. It regards its existence as necessary and essential, that is, it says that it exists in itself and of itself. It falsely assumes that the "I" owns its own life and is the real master in its sphere of disposal. It supposes it to be a constant reality. And it considers the *I*'s duty to be perfection of self, which originates from love of self, and likewise, philosophies have constructed their modes of thought on many such corrupt foundations. We have given definite proof in our other treatises, especially in the Words, and more particularly in the Twelfth and Twenty-Fifth Words, of how baseless and rotten these foundations are.

Even men like Plato and Aristotle, Ibn-i Sina and Farabi, who were the most illustrious representatives and authorities of the line of philosophy, said that the ultimate aim of humanity is to liken themselves to the Necessary Being, that is to say, to actually resemble Him. They thus delivered judgement in the manner of Pharaoh, and, by whipping up "I-ness" and allowing polytheism to run free in the valleys, opened the way to numerous different ways of associating partners with God, like worship of causes, idols, nature, and the stars. They closed the doors of impotence and weakness, poverty and need, deficiency and imperfection, which are intrinsic to human beings, thus obstructing the road to worship. Being immersed in Naturalism and being completely incapable of emerging from associating partners with God, they were unable to find the broad gate of thanks.

On the other hand, the line of prophethood considered, in the manner of a worshipper, that the aim of humanity and duty of human beings is to be moulded by God-given ethics and good character, and, by knowing their impotence to seek refuge with Divine power, by seeing their weakness to rely on Divine strength, by realizing their poverty to trust in Divine mercy, by perceiving their need to seek help from Divine riches, by seeing their faults to ask for pardon through Divine forgiveness, and by realizing their deficiency to be glorifiers of Divine perfection.

So, it is because the philosophy which does not obey the line of religion thus lost its way, that the "I" took the reins into its own hands and ran into all sorts of misguidance. And out of the "I" that was in this position, a tree of Zaqqum sprang forth and engulfed more than half of mankind.

Thus, in the branch of power of animal appetites of that tree, the fruits it has presented to mankind are idols and goddesses. Because, according to the principles of philosophy, power is approved. "Might is right" is the norm, even. It says, "All power to the strongest." "The winner takes all," and, "In power there is right."[64] It has given moral support to tyranny, encouraged despots, and urged oppressors to claim divinity.

Also, by appropriating the beauty in works of art and the fineness in the decoration and attributing them to the works of art themselves and their decoration, and by not relating them to the manifestation of the sacred and sheer beauty of the Maker and Fashioner, it says: "How beautiful it is," instead of, "How beautifully made it is," thus regarding each as an idol worthy of worship. Moreover, because it admires a fraudulent, boasting, ostentatious, hypocritical beauty that may be sold to anyone, it has acclaimed the hypocrites, and has made idol-like people monuments for its own worshippers. In the branch of power of passion of that tree, it has nurtured the fruits of greater and lesser Nimrods, Pharaohs, and Shaddads ruling over unfortunate mankind. In the branch of power of intellect, it has produced fruits like atheism, Materialism, and Naturalism in the mind of humanity, and has thrown it into confusion.

The Words, Thirtieth Word, First Aim, p.561–564.

For further reading

"The Twenty-Fifth Word" discusses the miraculousness of the Qur'an based on scholarly principles regarding eloquence. The Qur'anic verses reviewed in this chapter are those often criticized by atheists or that are argued as being contradictory of science.

The Words, Twenty-Fifth Word, p. 375–476.

"The Twentieth Word" is composed of responses to some questions about the Qur'an and various examples of its miraculousness. In the second section of the chapter, discussion about the eloquence of the Qur'an incorporates science and scientific discoveries. It illustrates with examples that miracles of prophets did not only attest that they were spiritual leaders and moral examples of their respective communities, but also their miracles demonstrated pathways to human progress and discoveries. That is to say, by following the natural laws, humankind could draw near to such miracles through technological achievements they attain. Also, in this chapter Nursi claims that each branch of science is related to a Divine Name and is its manifestation.

---

[64]   The principle of prophethood says: "Power is in right; right is not in power." It thus halts tyranny and ensures justice.

The Words, Twentieth Word, p. 253–275.

"The Nineteenth Letter" is about the miracles of Prophet Muhammad. Reporting transmitted traditions, that are considered as strong records by the majority of Muslims, about Prophet Muhammad's miracles concerning different types of creation, this chapter argues the universality his message through his miracles. *The Letters*, Nineteenth Letter, p. 114–262.

"The Fourth Flash" is a chapter on the concept of "*Imamate*," leadership, which is a major point of disagreement between the *Sunni* and *Shi'a*. It is addressed to both parties suggesting a mutual agreement based on the origin of the Prophet's practices. *The Flashes*, Fourth Flash, p. 35–44.

"The Eleventh Flash" is about following the example and traditions of Prophet Muhammad, the *Sunna*, its importance and benefits. *The Flashes*, Eleventh Flash, p. 81–94.

Part 3
Life after Death and Resurrection

Extract One: The Tenth Word

"The Tenth Word," dedicated to resurrection and life after death, was the first portion of the Risale-i Nur collection to be written. For Bediuzzaman Said Nursi, the basis of resurrection is the nature of God, which we learn through the divine names. Hence, this section starts with Nursi looking at the 19 of 99 names of God. Following is only brief extracts from this lengthy Word.

The manifestation of the Name of Sustainer, [Rabb]

> Is it at all possible that the Glory of God's Dominicality and His Divine Sovereignty should create a cosmos such as this, in order to display His perfections, with such lofty aims and elevated purposes, without establishing a reward for those believers who through faith and worship respond to these aims and purposes? Or that He should not punish those misguided ones who treat His purposes with rejection and scorn?

> *The Words*, Tenth Word, First Truth, p. 74.

The Manifestation of the Names of Generous and Merciful [Karīm and Rahīm]

> Is it at all possible that the Lord of this world, Who in His works demonstrates infinite generosity, infinite mercy, infinite splendour and infinite glory, should not give reward in a manner befitting His generosity and mercy, and not punish in a manner befitting His splendour and glory? ...

> Is it at all possible that man should have the most important duty in all of creation and be endowed with the most important capacities; that man's Sustainer should make Himself known to him with all His well-ordered works, and man should then fail to recognize Him in return by way of worship—or that God should make Himself beloved of men through the numerous adorned fruits of His mercy, and man should then fail to make himself beloved of God through worship—or that God should demonstrate His love and mercy to man through His variegated bounties and man should then fail to respect Him with thanks and with praise—is it at all possible that man should remain unpunished, left to his own devices, or that that powerful Possessor of splendour and glory should not make ready for him a realm of requital?

Is it at all possible, on the other hand, that He should not prepare a realm of reward and eternal bliss for those believers who respond to the Merciful and Compassionate One's making Himself known by recognizing Him in faith; to His making Himself beloved by loving Him in worship; and to His mercy by offering thanks and veneration?

The Words, Tenth Word, Second Truth, p. 75–76.

The Manifestation of the Names of Wise and Just [Hakīm and Ādil]

Is it at all possible[65] that the Lord of Glory, Who demonstrates His dominical sovereignty in the wisdom and order, the justice and equilibrium that pervade all things, from the atom to the sun, should not bestow favour on those believers who seek refuge beneath the protective wing of His dominicality, who believe in His Wisdom and Justice, and whose acts are for the purpose of worshipping Him?

Again, is it possible that He should not chastise those rude and discourteous men who disbelieve in His wisdom and justice, and rebel against Him in insolence? Now not even a thousandth part of that wisdom and justice is exercised with respect to man, in this transient world; it is rather deferred. Most of the people of misguidance leave this world unpunished, and most of the people of guidance leave it unrewarded. All things are, then, postponed for a supreme tribunal, an ultimate bliss.

Yes, it is apparent that the Being Who controls this world does so in accordance with an infinite wisdom. Do you require a proof? It is the preservation of interest and benefit in all things. Do you not see that numerous wise benefits are intended in all the limbs, bones and veins of man, even in the cells of his brain and in every particle of his body? Do you not see that from certain limbs wise benefits are to be had as numerous as the fruits of a tree? All of this shows that matters are

---

[65]   The sentence "is it at all possible?" is indeed repeated many times, because it expresses a most significant mystery. Misguidance and lack of belief generally spring from the habit of imagining things to be impossible, far removed from the realm of reason, and therefore denying them. Now in this discussion of resurrection it has been decisively demonstrated that true impossibility, absurdity and irrationality pertain to the path of misbelief and the road of misguidance, whereas true possibility, facility and rationality are characteristics of the path of faith and highway of Islam.

In short, the philosophers tend to unbelief on account of their regarding things as impossible, whereas the Tenth Word (discussion of resurrection), by means of the repeated sentence, "is it at all possible?" shows where impossibility lies, and thus deals them a blow in the mouth.

done in accordance with infinite wisdom. The existence of the utmost regularity in the making of all things is a proof of the same truth.

The compression of the exact programme of development of a beautiful flower into a minute seed, the inscription on a small seed by the pen of destiny of the scroll of deeds of a tree, its life-history and list of equipment, show that a pen of utmost wisdom is at work.

The existence of a high degree of fine artistry in all things proves that there exists also the impress of an infinitely Wise Maker. Further, the inclusion within the minute body of man of an index of all being, of the keys to all the treasuries of mercy, and of the mirrors of all the Divine Names, demonstrates the existence of wisdom within that infinitely fine artistry. Now is it at all possible that the wisdom that thus permeates the workings of dominicality should not wish eternally to favour those who seek refuge beneath the wing of dominicality and who offer obedience in faith?

Do you wish for a proof that all things are done with justice and balance? The fact that all things are endowed with being, given shape and put in their appropriate place in accordance with precise equilibrium and in appropriate measure, shows that all matters are done in accordance with infinite justice and balance.

Similarly, the fact that all things are given their rights in accordance with their disposition, that they receive all the necessities of their being and all the requirements of life in the most fitting form—this too is the sign left by a hand of infinite justice.

Again, the fact that answer is always given to every petition and request made by the tongue of disposition, and of natural need or necessity, demonstrates the existence of infinite justice and wisdom.

Now is it at all possible that the justice and wisdom that hasten to relieve the pettiest need of the smallest of creation should fail to provide immortality, the greatest need of man, the greatest of creatures? That it should fail to respond to his greatest plea and cry for assistance? Or that it should not preserve the dignity of God's dominicality by preserving the rights of His servants? Man, whose life is so brief, cannot experience the true essence of justice in this transient world; it is for this reason that matters are postponed for a supreme tribunal. For true justice requires that man, this apparently petty creature, should be rewarded and punished, not in accordance with his pettiness, but in accordance with the magnitude of his crime, the importance of his nature and the greatness of his function. Since this passing and transient world is far from manifesting such wisdom and justice for man, who is created for eternity, of necessity there will be an eternal Hell and everlasting Paradise of that Just and Awesome Possessor of Beauty, that Wise and Beauteous Possessor of Awe.

The Words, Tenth Word, Third Truth, p. 77–78.

The Manifestation of the Names of Generous and Beautiful [Jawād and Jamīl]

... beauty and fairness desire to see and be seen. Both of these require the existence of yearning witnesses and bewildered admirers. And since beauty and fairness are eternal and everlasting, their witnesses and admirers must have perpetual life. An eternal beauty can never be satisfied with transient admirers. An admirer condemned to irreversible separation will find his love turning to enmity once he conceives of separation. His admiration will yield to ridicule, his respect to contempt. For just as obstinate man is an enemy to what is unknown to him, so too he is opposed to all that lies beyond his reach, and love that is not infinite will respond to a beauty that deserves unending admiration with implicit enmity, hatred and rejection. From this we understand the profound reason for the unbeliever's enmity to God.

So endless generosity and liberality, peerless fairness and beauty, flawless perfection—all these require the existence of eternally grateful and longing supplicants and admirers. But we see in this hospice of the world that everyone quickly leaves and vanishes, having had only a taste of that generosity, enough to whet his appetite but not to satiate him, and having seen only a dim light coming from the perfection, or rather a faint shadow of its light, without in any way being fully satisfied. It follows, then, that men are going toward a place of eternal joy where all will be bestowed on them in full measure.

In short, just as this world, with all its creatures, decisively demonstrates the existence of the Glorious Maker, so too do His sacred attributes and Names indicate, show and logically require, the existence of the hereafter.

The Words, Tenth Word, Fourth Truth, p. 78–79.

The Manifestation of the Names of Answerer of Prayer and Compassionate [Mujīb and Rahīm]

Is it at all possible that a Lord possessing infinite compassion and mercy, Who most compassionately fulfils the smallest need of His lowliest creatures in the most unexpected fashion, Who heeds the muffled plea for help of His most obscure creature, and Who responds to all the petitions He hears, whether vocal or mute—is it at all possible that such a Lord should not pay heed to the greatest petition of the foremost among His servants, the most beloved among his creatures, that He should not hear and grant his most exalted prayer? The kindness and ease manifested in the feeding and nurturing of weak and young animals show that the Monarch of the cosmos exercises his dominicality with infinite mercy.

The Words, Tenth Word, Fifth Truth, p. 81.

The Manifestation of the Names of Glorious and Eternal [Jalīl and Jamīl]

Is it at all possible that the splendour of dominicality that subdues and commands all beings, from suns and trees down to particles, just like obedient soldiers, should concentrate its entire attention on the wretched and transient beings that pass a temporary life in the hospice of this world, and not create an eternal and everlasting sphere of splendour, an unending manifestation of dominicality? The display of Divine splendour in the changing of the seasons, the sublime motions of the planets in the heavens as if they were aeroplanes, the subjugation of all things and the creation of the earth as man's cradle and the sun as his lamp, vast transformations such as the reviving and adornment of the dead and dry globe—all of this shows that behind the veil a sublime dominicality exists, that a splendid monarchy is at work.

... You will understand, too, that all of these transient objects have not been created for the sake of annihilation, in order to appear briefly and then vanish. The purpose for their creation is rather briefly to be assembled in existence and acquire the desired form, so that these may be noted, their images preserved, their meanings known, and their results recorded. This is so that, for example, everlasting spectacles might be wrought for the people of eternity, and that they might serve other purposes in the realm of eternity. You will understand that things have been created for eternity, not for annihilation; and as for apparent annihilation, it has the sense of a completion of duty and a release from service, for every transient thing advances to annihilation with one aspect, but remains eternally with numerous other aspects.

Look, for example, at the flower, a word of God's power; for a short time it smiles and looks at us, and then hides behind the veil of annihilation. It departs just like a word leaving your mouth. But it does so entrusting thousands of its fellows to men's ears. It leaves behind meanings in men's minds as numerous as those minds. The flower, too, expressing its meaning and thus fulfilling its function, goes and departs. But it goes leaving its apparent form in the memory of everything that sees it, its inner essence in every seed. It is as if each memory and seed were a camera to record the adornment of the flower, or a means for its perpetuation. If such be the case with an object at the simplest level of life, it can be readily understood how closely tied to eternity is man, the highest form of life and the possessor of an eternal soul. Again, from the fact that the laws -each resembling a spirit- according to which large flowering and fruit bearing plants are formed and the representations of their forms are preserved and perpetuated in most regular fashion in tiny seeds throughout tempestuous changes—from this fact it can be easily understood how closely tied and related to eternity is the spirit of man, which possesses an extremely exalted and comprehensive nature, and which although clothed in a body, is a conscious and luminous law issuing from the divine command.

The Words, Tenth Word, Sixth Truth, p. 84–88.

The Manifestation of the Names of Preserver and Guardian [Hafiz and Raqīb]

Is it at all possible that God's attribute of Preserver, which protects all things with the utmost order and balance, -things in the heavens and on the earth, on dry land and in the ocean, dry and wet, large and small, commonplace and exalted- and as it were, sifts their results by way of accounting—is it at all possible that this attribute should permit the deeds and acts of man, man who has been given the lofty disposition of humanity, the rank of God's supreme vicegerency, and the duty of bearing the Supreme Trust, not to be recorded, not to be passed through the sieve of accounting, not to be weighed in the balance of justice, not to be punished or rewarded fittingly, even though his acts and deeds closely pertain to God's universal dominicality? No, it is not in any way possible!

...

Do you not see that all the flowers and fruits of the vast spring, the records of their deeds in appropriate form, the laws of their formation, and the images of their forms, are all inscribed into the finite space of a minute seed and are there preserved? The following spring, their record of deeds is set forth, in a form of accounting appropriate to them, and another vast world of spring is brought forth, with the utmost order and wisdom. This demonstrates with what powerful comprehensiveness God's attribute of Preserver exercises itself. Considering that the results of such transient, commonplace, impermanent and insignificant things are preserved, is it at all possible that men's deeds, that yield important fruit in the world of the unseen, the world of the hereafter, and the world of spirits, from the point of view of universal dominicality, is it at all possible that they should not be guarded and preserved, should not be recorded as a matter of importance? No, by no means!

The Words, Tenth Word, Seventh Truth, p. 88–89.

The Manifestation of the Names of Beautiful and Glorious [Jalīl and Jamīl]

Is it at all possible that the Maker of this world, the Possessor of Absolute Knowledge and Absolute Power, should not fulfil the oft-repeated promise and threat that has been proclaimed unanimously by all the prophets and been witnessed in unison by all the veracious and the saints, and thus display weakness and ignorance? God forbid! All that is implied by His promise and threat is not at all difficult for His power to fulfil; it is extremely simple and easy. It is as easy for Him as bringing back next spring the countless beings of last spring, in part identically,[66] in part in simile.[67] It is our need, the need of everything, His own need and the need of His dominical sovereignty, that He should fulfil His promise. For Him to break His promise would be contrary to the dignity of His power, and it would contradict the comprehensiveness of His knowledge. For the breaking of a promise can arise only from ignorance or impotence.

The Words, Tenth Word, Eight Truth, p. 91.

The Manifestation of the Names of Eternally Living and Self-Subsistent, and Giver of Life and Giver of Death [Hayy-e Qayyūm, Muhyī, and Mumīt]

Is it at all possible that the One Who gives life to this vast dead and dry earth; Who in so doing demonstrates His power by deploying more than three hundred thousand different forms of creation, each of them as remarkable as man; Who further demonstrates in this deployment His all-embracing knowledge by the infinite distinctions and differentiations He makes in the complex intermingling of all of those forms; Who directs the gaze of all His slaves to everlasting bliss by promising them resurrection in all of His heavenly decrees; Who demonstrates the splendour of His dominicality by causing all of His creation to collaborate with one another, to revolve within the circle of His command and His will, to aid one another and be submitted to Him; Who shows the importance He has given to man by creating him as the most comprehensive, the most precious and delicate, the most valued and valuable fruit on the tree of creation by addressing him without intermediary and subjugating all things to him;—is it at all possible that so Compassionate and Powerful a One, so Wise and All-Knowing a One, should not bring about resurrection; should not gather His creatures together or be unable to do so; should not restore man to life, or be unable to do so; should not be able to inaugurate His Supreme Court; should not be able to create Heaven and Hell? Nay, indeed, by no means is any of this possible.

---

66   Like trees and the roots of grasses.
67   Like leaves and fruits.

Indeed, the Almighty Disposer of this world's affairs creates in every century, every year and every day, on the narrow and transient face of the globe, numerous signs, examples and indications of the Supreme Gathering and the Plain of Resurrection.

Thus in the gathering that takes place every spring we see that in the course of five or six days more than three hundred thousand different kinds of animal and plant are first gathered together and then dispersed. The roots of all the trees and plants, as well as some animals, are revived and restored exactly as they were. The other animals are recreated in a form so similar as to be almost identical. The seeds which appear, in their outward form, to be so close to each other, nonetheless, in the course of six days or six weeks, become distinct and differentiated from each other, and then with extreme speed, ease and facility, are brought to life in the utmost order and equilibrium. Is it at all possible that for the One Who does all of this anything should be difficult; that He should be unable to create the heavens and the earth in six days; that He should be unable to resurrect men with a single blast? No, by no means is it possible!

...

There is nothing that makes impossible the gathering of resurrection, and much that necessitates it. The glorious and eternal dominicality, the almighty and all embracing sovereignty of the One Who gives life and death to this vast and wondrous earth as if it were a mere animal; Who has made of this earth a pleasing cradle, a fine ship, for man and the animals; Who has made of the sun a lamp furnishing light and heat to the hostelry of the world; Who has made of the planets vehicles for the conveyance of His angels—the dominicality and sovereignty of such a One cannot rest upon and be restricted to the transitory, impermanent, unstable, insignificant, changeable, unlasting, deficient and imperfect affairs of this world. He must, therefore, have another realm, one worthy of Him, permanent, stable, immutable and glorious. Indeed, He does have another kingdom, and it is for the sake of this that He causes us to labour, and to this that He summons us. All those of illumined spirit who have penetrated from outer appearances to truth, and have been ennobled with proximity to the Divine Presence, all the spiritual poles endowed with luminous hearts, all the possessors of lucent intelligence, all bear witness that He will transfer us to that other kingdom. They inform us unanimously that He has prepared for us there reward and requittal, and relate that He is repeatedly giving us firm promises and stern warnings.

As for the breaking of a promise, it is baseless and utter humiliation. It cannot in any way be reconciled with the glory of His sanctity. Similarly, failure to fulfil a threat arises either from forgiveness or powerlessness.

Now unbelief is extreme crime, and cannot be forgiven.[68] The Absolutely Omnipotent One is exempt of and exalted above all powerlessness. Those who bring us their testimony and report, despite all the differences in their methods, temperaments and paths, are totally unanimous and agreed on this basic matter. By their number, they have the authority of unanimity. By their quality, they have the authority of learned consensus. By their rank, each one is a guiding star of mankind, the cherished eye of a people, the object of a nation's veneration. By their importance, each one is an expert and an authority in the matter. In any art or science, two experts are preferred to thousands of non-experts, and two positive affirmers are preferred to thousands of negators in the transmission of a report. For example, the testimony of two men affirming the sighting of the crescent moon at the beginning of Ramadan totally nullifies the negation of thousands of deniers.

In short: In the whole world there is no truer report, no firmer claim, no more apparent truth than this. The world is without doubt a field, and the resurrection a threshing-floor, a harvest. Paradise and Hell are each storehouses for the grain.

The Words, Tenth Word, Ninth Truth, p. 92–95.

The Manifestation of the Names of All-Wise, Generous, Just and Merciful [Hakīm, Karīm, Ādil, and Rahīm]

Is it at all possible that the Glorious Possessor of all Dominion in this impermanent hospice of the world, in this transient place of testing, in this unstable showplace of the earth so manifest a wisdom, so evident a grace, so overwhelming a justice, so comprehensive a mercy,—is it at all possible that in His realm, in the worlds of the outer and inner dimensions of things, there should not exist permanent abodes with eternal inhabitants, everlasting stations with immortal residents, and that as a result all the truths of wisdom, grace, mercy and justice that we now see should decline into nothingness.

---

[68]   Unbelief denounces creation for alleged worthlessness and meaninglessness. It is an insult to all of creation, a denial of the manifestation of the Divine Names in the mirror of beings. It is disrespect to all the Divine Names, and rejection of the witness borne to the Divine Unity by all beings. It is a denial of all creation. It corrupts man's potentialities in such a way that they are incapable of reform and unreceptive to good. Unbelief is also an act of utter injustice, a transgression against all of creation and the rights of God's Names. The preservation of those rights, as well as the unredeemable nature of the unbeliever's soul, make it necessary that unbelief should be unpardonable. The words, "to assign partners to God is verily a great transgression," (Qur'an, 31:13) express this meaning.

Again, is it at all possible that that All-Wise Being should choose man, among all His creation, to receive direct and universal address from Him, should make him a comprehensive mirror to Himself, should permit him to taste, weigh, and become acquainted with, all the contents of His treasuries of mercy, should make Himself known to him with all His Names, should love him and make Himself beloved of him—that He should do all this and then fail to despatch wretched man to that eternal realm, to invite him to that abode of permanent bliss and make him happy there?

Is it at all reasonable that He should impose on every being, even the seed, a task as heavy as a tree, mount in it instances of His wisdom as numerous as the flowers, and beneficial aspects as numerous as the fruits, but assign to that task, to those instances of His wisdom and those beneficial aspects, a purpose pertaining only to this world, one as small as a seed? That He should make that purpose nothing more than the life of this world, something less valuable than a grain of mustard-seed? That He should not make of beings seeds for the world of meaning and tillage for the realm of the hereafter, for them to yield there their true and worthy results? That He should permit such significant alternations to remain without purpose, to be empty and vain? That He should not turn their faces towards the world of meaning and the hereafter, so that they might there reveal their true purposes and fitting results?

Again, is it at all possible that by thus causing things to controvert their own nature He should present His own veracious Names, All-Wise, Generous, Just, Merciful, as being characterized by their opposites -God forbid!- that He should deny the true essences of all those beings that indicate His wisdom and generosity, His justice and mercy, that He should reject the testimony of all creatures, that He should negate the indications made by all things?

...

Since the world exists, and within this world wisdom, beneficence, compassion and justice also exist, with their numerous evidences, of a certainty the hereafter also exists, just as surely as does this world. Since one aspect of everything in this world is turned to that world and is proceeding toward it, to deny that world would be denying this world with all it contains. Just as the allotted hour and the grave await man, so too do Paradise and Hell, anxiously watching for his arrival.

The Words, Tenth Word, Tenth Truth, p. 95–99.

The Manifestation of the Name of Truth [Haqq]

Is it at all possible that God Almighty, He Who is worshipped by right, should create man within creation as the most significant of all of His servants with respect to His absolute dominicality and with respect to His universal dominicality in all of His realms; that He should make him the most thoughtful recipient of His glorious address, the most comprehensive mirror to the manifestation of His Names; that He should create him as the most beautiful miracle of His power in the fairest of forms, in order to receive the manifestation of the Greatest Name, as well as that quality of the Greatest Name inherent in the other Names, in order for him to assess and perceive the contents of His treasuries of mercy; that He should make him an investigator of secrets equipped more than any other creature with balances and instruments; and He should make him the most needy of all creatures with respect to His infinite gifts, the one suffering most from annihilation and the one most desirous of immortality; that He should make him the most delicate, the poorest and neediest of animals, most wretched and subject to pain in his worldly life but most sublime in disposition, in the highest of forms and characters—is it possible that God Almighty should do all this with man and not send him to the Eternal Realm for which he is suited and fitted and for which he is longing? Is it possible that He should thus negate the whole essence of humanity, act in a manner totally contrary to His own veracity, and perform an act of injustice that the eye of truth must deem ugly?

Again, is it at all possible that He Who rules justly, Whose mercy is absolute, should bestow on man such a disposition that he took up the Supreme Trust, from which the heavens and mountains both shrank, in order to measure and know, with his slight and petty measures and crafts, the all encompassing attributes, the universal workings, and the infinite manifestations of the Creator; that He should create him as the most delicate, vulnerable, weak and powerless of beings, while yet entrusting him with the regulation of all the vegetal and animal life upon earth, and causing him to intervene in their modes of worship and glorification of God; that He should cause him to be a representation in miniature of His cosmic processes; that He should cause him to proclaim His glorious dominicality to all beings, in word and deed; that He should prefer him to the angels and give him the rank of vicegerent—is it at all possible that God should bestow all of this on man and not give him eternal bliss, the purpose, result and fruit of all of these duties? That He should cast him down to low degree, as the most wretched, ill-fortuned, humiliated and suffering of all His creatures; or that He should make of intelligence, a gift from His own wisdom and a most blessed and luminous tool for the attainment of happiness, an inauspicious and sombre tool of torment for that wretch, thus acting in total contradiction to His absolute wisdom and in opposition to His absolute mercy? No, it is by no means possible!

...

It is, then, this disposition of man -his desires extending to eternity, his thoughts that embrace all of creation and his wishes that embrace the different varieties of eternal bliss- that demonstrates he has been created for eternity and will indeed proceed to eternity. This world is like a hospice for him, a waiting-room for the hereafter.

The Words, Tenth Word, Eleventh Truth, p. 100–101.

The Manifestation of "In the Name of God, the Merciful, the Compassionate" [Allah, Rahmān, and Rahīm]

Is it at all possible that errant doubts, no stronger than the wing of a fly, could close the path to the hereafter and the gate to Paradise that have been definitively opened by the Most Noble Messenger (Peace and blessings be upon him), with all of his might, relying upon the power of his thousand certified miracles as well as the thousands of decisive verses of the All-Wise Qur'an, a book miraculous in forty different ways—that Messenger whose words are affirmed by all of the other prophets, relying upon their own miracles, whose claim is affirmed by all of the saints, relying upon their visionary and charismatic experiences, and to whose veracity all of the purified scholars bear witness, relying upon their investigations of truth?

The Words, Tenth Word, Twelfth Truth, p. 101.

The verse, *Your creation and resurrection is but like a single soul,*[69] indicates the following meaning: "The creation and resurrection of all men is as easy for God's power as the creation and resurrection of a single man."

The Words, Tenth Word, Conclusion, p. 103.

Extract Two: Benefits of Resurrection

In his illumination of the divine names, Nursi often begins by quoting a relevant Qur'anic verse. Here in the "First Part of the Addendum" to "The Tenth Word," Nursi reflects on the spiritual benefits of the belief in resurrection expanding upon the meaning of life after death and resurrection.

"Look upon the signs of God's mercy, and see how He restores life to the earth after its death. Verily He it is Who shall bring to life the dead, and He is powerful over all things"[70]

---

[69]   Qur'an, 31:28.
[70]   Qur'an, 30:50.

Introduction

[This consists of two Points comprising a concise explanation of one comprehensive result of the numerous spiritual benefits of belief in resurrection and of its vital consequences; a demonstration of how essential it is for human life and especially for the life of society; a summary of one universal proof out of numerous proofs of the tenet of belief in the resurrection; and a statement of how indubitable and self-evident is that tenet of belief.]

First Point

We shall indicate, as a measure, only four out of hundreds of proofs that belief in the hereafter is fundamental to the life of society and to man's personal life, and is the basis of his happiness, prosperity, and achievement.

The First: It is only with the thought of Paradise that children, who form almost a half of mankind, can endure all the deaths around them, which appear to them to be grievous and frightening, and strengthen the morale of their weak and delicate beings. Through Paradise they find hope in their vulnerable spirits, prone to weeping, and may live happily. For example, with the thought of Paradise, one may say: "My little brother or friend has died and become a bird in Paradise. He is flying around Paradise and living more happily than us." The frequent deaths before their unhappy eyes of other children like themselves or of grown-ups will otherwise destroy all their resistance and morale, making their subtle faculties like their spirits, hearts, and minds weep in addition to their eyes; they will either decline utterly or become crazy, wretched animals.

Second Proof: It is only through the life of the hereafter that the elderly, who form half of mankind, can endure the proximity of the grave, and be consoled at the thought that their lives, to which they are firmly attached, will soon be extinguished and their fine worlds come to an end. It is only at the hope of eternal life that they can respond to the grievous despair they feel in their emotional child-like spirits at the thought of death. Those worthy, anxious fathers and mothers, so deserving of compassion and in need of tranquillity and peace of mind, will otherwise feel a terrible spiritual turmoil and distress in their hearts, and this world will become a dark prison for them, and life even, grievous torment.

Third Proof: It is only the thought of Hell-fire that checks the turbulent emotions of youths, the most vigorous element in the life of society, and their violent excesses, restraining them from aggression, oppression, and destruction, and ensuring that the life of society continues tranquilly. If not for fear of Hell, in accordance with the rule "might is right," in pursuing their desires, those drunken youths would turn the worlds of the wretched weak and powerless into Hell, and elevated humanity into base animality.

Fourth Proof: The most comprehensive centre of man's worldly life, and its mainspring, and a paradise, refuge, and fortress of worldly happiness, is the life of the family. Everyone's home is a small world for him. And the life and happiness of his home and family are possible through genuine, earnest, and loyal respect and true, tender, and self-sacrificing compassion. This true respect and genuine kindness may be achieved with the idea of the members of the family having an everlasting companionship and friendship and togetherness, and their parental, filial, brotherly, and friendly relations continuing for all eternity in a limitless life, and their believing this. One says, for example: "My wife will be my constant companion in an everlasting world and eternal life. It does not matter if she is now old and ugly, for she will have an immortal beauty." He will tell himself that he will be as kind and devoted as he can for the sake of that permanent companionship, and treat his elderly wife lovingly and kindly as though she was a beautiful houri. A companionship that was to end in eternal separation after an hour or two of brief, apparent friendship would otherwise afford only superficial, temporary, feigned, animal-like feelings, and false compassion and artificial respect. As with animals, self-interest and other overpowering emotions would prevail over the respect and compassion, transforming that worldly paradise into Hell.

Thus, one of the hundreds of results of belief in resurrection is connected with the life of society. If a comparison is made between the above four proofs out of the hundreds of aspects and benefits of this single consequence and the rest, it will be understood that the realization of the truth of resurrection, and its occurrence, are as certain as the elevated reality of humanity and its universal need. It is clearer even than the evidence for the existence of food offered by the existence of need in man's stomach, and tells of its existence even more clearly. And it proves that if the consequences of the truth of resurrection were to quit humanity, whose nature is extremely significant, lofty, and living, it would descend to being a corrupt corpse fed on by microbes.

The sociologists, politicians, and moralists, who govern mankind and are concerned with its social and moral questions should be aware of this! How do they propose to fill this vacuum? With what can they cure these deep wounds?

The Words, Tenth Word, First Part of the Addendum, p. 109–111.

Resurrection will take place of an absolute certainty. Resurrection will take place, abodes of reward and punishment will open their gates. Then only will the true significance and centrality of the earth, and the true significance and value of man be fulfilled. Then will the justice, wisdom, mercy and sovereignty of the

Wise Ruler, Who is the Creator and Sustainer of earth and man, manifest itself anew. Then will the true friends and ardent lovers of the Eternal Sustainer be delivered from eternal annihilation, and the greatest and most precious of those friends receive the reward for the sacred services with which he gratified the whole cosmos. Then will the perfections of the Sovereign of Eternity claim their exaltation, transcendence and freedom from all defect; His power, its freedom from all foolishness, and His justice, its freedom from all oppression.

In short: Since there is God, certainly there is the hereafter.

The Words, Tenth Word, First Part of the Addendum, p. 116.

The five pillars of faith, together with all of their proofs, indicate and demand the occurrence and existence of resurrection, and the existence and unfolding of the realm of the hereafter. They bear witness to it and necessitate it. It is because there are such imposing and unshakeable supports and proofs for the truth of resurrection, totally worthy of its sublimity, that the Qur'an of Miraculous Exposition devotes about one third of its contents to resurrection, makes of it the foundation stone of all of its truths, and constructs everything on its basis.

The Words, Tenth Word, First Part of the Addendum, p. 118.

As an answer to a question regarding the resurrection of the dead, Nursi wrote in the "Third Part of the Addendum" to "The Tenth Word:"

The frequently repeated verse, *It will be naught but a single cry*,[71] and the verse, *The command of the Hour will be like the glance of the eye*,[72] show that the resurrection of the dead and Great Gathering will occur instantaneously, in a flash. But man's narrow reason requires some tangible example so that it can conceive of this wondrous, extraordinary, and unparalleled event, and accept it.

The Answer: At the resurrection there will be the return of spirits to their bodies, the revivification of the bodies, and the remaking of the bodies. It consists of three matters.

The First Matter: An example for the return of spirits to their bodies is the mustering, at a loud bugle call, of the members of a well-disciplined army after they have dispersed to rest. Yes, the Sur of the Angel Israfil is no less powerful than an army bugle. The spirits, too, who, while in post-eternity, reply with "Yes, we accept" to the question "Am I not your Sustainer?,"[73] which comes from

---

[71]   Qur'an, 36:29,49,53; 38:15; 54:31.

[72]   Qur'an, 16:77.

[73]   Qur'an, 7:172.

pre-eternity, are infinitely more subjugated, disciplined, and obedient than the soldiers of an army. The Thirtieth Word has demonstated with decisive proofs that not only spirits, but all particles, form a Divine army and are its soldiers under command.

Second Matter: An example for the revivification of bodies is the springing to life in an instant of the hundred thousand electric lights of a large city on a festival night, switched on from one centre. It would be possible to light up in the same way a hundred million lamps scattered over the face of the earth from one centre. Since through the training and instruction in regularity and order it has received from its Creator, a creature of Almighty God like electricity -a servant and candleholder in His guest-house- possesses this quality, surely the resurrection of the dead could occur in the twinkling of an eye within the bounds of the regular laws of Divine wisdom which thousands of luminous servants represent, like electricity.

Third Matter: An example for the remaking of bodies instantaneously is the perfect remaking within a few days of all the trees in the spring, which are far more numerous than all humanity, together with all their leaves, in exactly the same way as those of the previous spring; and the bringing into being, again like those of previous springs, all the blossoms, fruits and leaves of the trees with the speed of lightning; and the sudden awakening of the uncountable numbers of seeds, grains, and roots, which are the source of the spring, and their unfolding and being raised to life; and reflecting the meaning of "resurrection after death," the sudden raising to life at a command of the upright skeleton-like corpses of the trees; and the reanimation of the innumerable members of all species of small animals; and the revivification of all the sorts of flying insects, particularly those which, continually cleaning their faces, eyes, and wings, remind us of our ablutions and cleanliness, and caress our faces -the resurrection and remaking of all the members of this tribe within a few days every spring before our very eyes together with all the other species, despite being greater in number than all mankind since the time of Adam, provides not one example of the remaking of all human bodies at the resurrection, but thousands.

Yes, since this world is the realm of wisdom and the hereafter the realm of power, numerous Divine Names like All-Wise, Arranger, Disposer, and Nurturer, and dominical wisdom, require that the creation of things in this world is gradual and in the course of time. In the hereafter, however, power and mercy will be manifested more than wisdom, and there being no need for matter, time, and waiting, things will be made instantaneously. Alluding to the fact that things which are made here in a day or in a year will be made in the hereafter in an instant or a flash, the Qur'an of Miraculous Exposition states:

The command of the Hour will be like the glance of the eye, or briefer.

If you want to be as certain about the occurrence of the resurrection of the dead as you are about the arrival of next spring, study the Tenth and Twenty-Ninth Words carefully, which are about this, and you will see! If you do not then believe that it will occur as you believe the coming of spring, come and stick your finger in my eye!

A Fourth Matter: The death of the world and Doomsday. The sudden collision with this globe, our guest-house, at a dominical command, of a planet or comet, could wipe out this dwelling-place of ours. Like the destruction in a minute of a palace the building of which had taken ten years.

The Words, Tenth Word, Third Part of the Addendum, p. 125–126.

Extract Three: The Concept of Bodily Resurrection

The concept of the after-life for Nursi is a bodily resurrection. This raises several conceptual issues. In this extract, Nursi sets out his response.

Question: What connection with eternity and Paradise has faulty, deficient, changing, unstable, and suffering corporeality? Since the spirit has elevated pleasures, that is sufficient. Why is bodily resurrection necessary for bodily pleasures?

The Answer: Because, just as in relation to water, air, and light, earth is dense and dark, but since it is the source and means of all the varieties of Divine artefacts, in meaning it rises above the other elements; and just as in regard to the mystery of its comprehensiveness and on condition it is purified, the human soul, which is also dense, rises above all the other human subtle faculties; so too corporeality is the richest and most comprehensive and all-embracing mirror to the manifestation of the Divine Names. All the tools and instruments for measuring the contents of the treasuries of mercy and reckoning their balances lie in corporeality. For example, if the sense of taste in the tongue was not the source of scales to the number of the sorts of foods and their pleasures, it could not experience them all and recognize them, and taste and weigh them up. Also, the instruments for experiencing and knowing the manifestations of most of the Divine Names, and tasting and recognizing them, again lie in corporeality. And the faculties for experiencing all the infinitely various pleasures are also in corporeality.

As is proved in the Eleventh Word, it is understood clearly from the disposition of the universe and man's comprehensiveness that the universe's Maker wants to make known all the treasuries of His mercy, and all the manifestations of His Names, and to make experienced all the varieties of His bounties. The abode of bliss, therefore, which is a vast pool formed from the flood of the universe and a great exhibition of the textiles woven on the loom of the universe and an everlasting store of the crops produced in the arable field of this world, will resemble the universe to a degree. And it will preserve all its fundamental matters, both corporeal and spiritual. Its All-Wise Maker, the Most Compassionate One, will also give as recompense for the duties of the physical tools and instruments, pleasures worthy of them; and to His servants, as a wage and reward for the particular worship of each. Otherwise a situation would occur that was contrary to His wisdom, justice, and mercy, which is in no way fitting for the beauty of His mercy and perfection of His justice, and in no way compatible with them.

The Words, Twenty-Seventh Word, Addendum, p. 513–514.

Extract Four: Creation and resurrection

Nursi points out the ease of the continuous act of creation in the cosmos as a proof that creation and resurrection are not difficult for the divine. For Nursi, the evidence of the resurrection is the fact of creation.

It is plain to see that every age within this world an All-Powerful One of Glory creates a new, travelling, orderly universe. Indeed, He makes a new, well-ordered world each day. He perpetually creates and changes with perfect wisdom transient worlds and universes one after the other on the face of the heavens and the earth. He hangs on the string of time regular worlds to the number of the centuries, years, indeed, days, and through them demonstrates the tremendousness of His power. He attaches to the head of the globe the huge flower of spring which he adorns with a hundred thousand embroideries of resurrection as though it was a single flower, and through it displays the perfection of His wisdom and the beauty of His art. Can it be said of such a One, "How can He bring about the resurrection of the dead, and how can He transform this world into the hereafter?" The verse,

Your creation and your resurrection is but like a single soul[74]

proclaims the All-Powerful One's perfect power, that nothing at all is difficult for Him, that like the smallest thing, the greatest presents no difficulties for His power, and that it is as easy for His power to create innumerable individuals as to create as a single one.

The Words, Twenty-Ninth Word, Second Aim, p. 545–546.

---

[74]   Qur'an, 31:28.

Just as there are things necessitating the resurrection of the dead and Great Gathering, and the One Who will bring it about possesses the power to do so, so the world possesses the potential for the resurrection of the dead and Great Gathering. There are four "Matters" in this assertion of mine that "this place is possible."

The First is the possibility of this world's death.

The Second is its actual death.

The Third is the possibility of the destroyed, dead world being reconstructed and resurrected in the form of the hereafter.

The Fourth is its actual reconstruction and resurrection, which are possible.

...

The Words, Twenty-Ninth Word, Second Aim, p. 550.

Extract Five: Divine Name of Ever-Living

"The Thirtieth Flash," focuses on the divine name of Ever-Living. Nursi concludes that resurrection will take place as a necessary manifestation of this divine name.

Since there is life in this world, those who understand the secret of life and do not misuse their lives will manifest eternal life in the realm of eternity and everlasting Paradise. In this we believe!

Shining objects on the face of the earth glistening with the sun's reflection, and bubbles on the surface of the sea sparkling and dying away with flashes of light and the bubbles that follow on after them again acting as mirrors to the imaginary miniature suns, self-evidently show that those flashes are the reflections and manifestations of a single, elevated sun. They recall the sun's existence with various tongues, and point to it with their fingers of light.

In just the same way, through the greatest manifestation of the Ever-Living and Self-Subsistent One's Name of Giver of Life, the living creatures on the earth and in the sea shine through Divine power, and in order to make way for those that follow after them, utter "O Living One!" and vanish behind the veil of the Unseen, thus indicating and testifying to the life and necessary existence of the Ever-Living and Self-Subsistent One, Who possesses eternal life.

So too, all the evidences testifying to Divine knowledge, the effect of which is apparent in the ordering of all creatures; and all the proofs demonstrating the power which has disposal over the universe; and all the evidences proving the will and volition which governs and directs the universe; and all the signs and miracles proving the missions of the prophets, the channels of Divine revelation and dominical speech; and all the evidences attesting to the seven Divine attributes-all these unanimously indicate, denote, and testify to the life of the Ever-Living and Self-Subsistent One.

For if a thing has sight, it also has life; and if it has hearing, that is a sign of life; and if it has speech, it points to the existence of life; and if it has will and choice, it shows life. Thus, attributes like absolute power, comprehensive will, and all-embracing knowledge, the existence of which is clear and certain due to their works and effects in the universe, testify, through all their evidences, to the life and necessary existence of the Ever-Living and Self-Subsistent One, the eternal life which illuminates the whole universe with a single of its shadows, and, through a single of its manifestations gives life to the realm of the Hereafter, even its very particles.

The Flashes, Thirtieth Flash, The Divine Name of Ever-Living, p. 443.

Extract Six: Death as "Bounty" and the Timing of the Last Judgement

The following are Nursi's responses to questions related to death and the occurrence of the Day of Judgement. For Nursi, death is some sense good. And naturally, we are all curious as to the timing of the Last Judgement.

Second Question: Verses like the following in the All-Wise Qur'an, the Criterion of Truth and Falsehood,

Who creates death and life that He may try you, which of you is the best in conduct,

make it understood that "death is created like life; it too is a bounty." Whereas apparently death is dissolution, non-existence, decay, the extinction of life, the annihilator of pleasures; how can it be created and a bounty?

The Answer: As was stated at the end of the answer to the First Question, death is a discharge from the duties of life; it is a rest, a change of residence, a change of existence; it is an invitation to an eternal life, a beginning, the introduction to an immortal life. Just as life comes into the world through an act of creation and a determining, so too departure from the world is through a creation and determining, through a wise and purposeful direction. For the death of plant life, the simplest level of life, shows that it is a more orderly work of art than life. For although the death of fruits, seeds, and grains appear to occur through decay and dissolution, their death is in fact a kneading which comprises an exceedingly well-ordered chemical reaction and well-balanced combining of elements and wise formation of particles; this unseen, orderly and wise death appears through the life of the new shoots. That is to say, the death of the seed is the start of life of the shoot; indeed, since it is like life itself, this death is created and well-ordered as much as is life.

Moreover, the death of the fruits of living beings and animals in the human stomach is the beginning of their rising to the level of human life; it may therefore be said "such a death is more orderly and created than their own life."

Thus, if the death of plant life, the lowest level of life, is thus created, wise, and ordered, so also must be the death that befalls human life, the most elevated level of life. And like a seed sown in the ground becomes a tree in the world of the air, so a man who is laid in the earth will surely produce the shoots of an everlasting life in the Intermediate Realm.

The Letters, First Letter, p. 24.

Second Question: Where will the Great Gathering and Last Judgement take place?

The Answer: The knowledge is with God alone. The elevated instances of wisdom the All-Wise Creator displays in all things, and His even attaching vast instances of wisdom to a single insignificant thing, suggests to the point of being plain that the globe of the earth does not revolve in a circle aimlessly and pointlessly, but revolves around something important; it depicts the circumference of a vast arena. It travels around a huge place of exhibition and hands over its immaterial produce to it; because in the future the produce will be displayed there before the gazes of men. That is to say, it will fill the circle, the circumference of which is a distance of approximately twenty-five thousand years; Syria will be like a seed, according to one narration;[75] the arena of the Great Gathering will be expanded out of that region. All the immaterial produce of the earth is for now sent to the notebooks and tablets of the arena which is beneath the veil of the Unseen, and in the future when the arena is opened up, the earth will also pour its inhabitants into it. Its immaterial produce will also be transposed to the Manifest Realm from that of the Unseen. Yes, like an arable field, a spring, or a measure, the earth has produced crops enough to fill that vast arena, and the creatures that will occupy it have flowed on from the earth, and those that will fill it have departed from it. That is to say, the globe of the earth is a seed, and the arena of the Great

---

[75]   al-Hakim, al-Mustadrak ii, 440; Musnad iv, 447; v, 3, 5.

Gathering, together with those within it, a tree, a shoot, and a store. Indeed, just as a point of light becomes a luminous line or circle on moving at speed, the earth too, through its rapid, purposeful motion is the means of depicting a circle of existence, and together with that circle of existence and its produce, to the formation of the arena of the Great Gathering.

Say, the knowledge of it is with God alone.[76]

The Enduring One, He is the Enduring One!

The Letters, The Tenth Letter, p. 57

Extract Seven: Divine Unity and Humanity

The following two sections are from the first and second stations of "The Twentieth Letter" which interpret a declaration of God's unity. These sections focus on the last phrase of this declaration about humankind's return to their origin and union with their Creator.

The Eleventh Phrase: "And with Him all things have their end"

That is, human beings are sent to this world, which is the realm of trial and examination, with the important duties of trading and acting as officials. After they have concluded their trading, accomplished their duties, and completed their service, they will return and meet once more with their Generous Master and Glorious Creator Who sent them forth in the first place. Leaving this transient realm, they will be honoured and elevated to the presence of grandeur in the realm of permanence. That is to say, being delivered from the turbulence of causes and from the obscure veils of intermediaries, they will meet with their Merciful Sustainer without veil at the seat of His eternal majesty. Everyone will find his Creator, True Object of Worship, Sustainer, Lord, and Owner and will know Him directly. Thus, this phrase proclaims the following joyful news, which is greater than all the rest:

"O mankind! Do you know where you are going and to where you are being impelled? As is stated at the end of the Thirty-Second Word, a thousand years of happy life in this world cannot be compared to one hour of life in Paradise. And a thousand years of life in Paradise cannot be compared to one hour's vision of the sheer loveliness of the Beauteous One of Glory. You are going to the sphere of His mercy, and to His presence.

---

[76]   Qur'an, 67:26.

"The loveliness and beauty in all the creatures of this world and in those metaphorical beloveds by which you are so stricken and obsessed and for which you are so desirous, are but a sort of shadow of the manifestation of His beauty and of the loveliness of His Names; and all Paradise with all of its subtle wonders, a single manifestation of His mercy; and all longing and love and allurement and captivation, but a flash of the love of the Eternal Worshipful One and Everlasting Beloved. And you are going to the sphere of His presence. You are being summoned to Paradise, which is an eternal feasting place. Since this is so, it is not with weeping that you enter the grave, but smiling with expectation."

The phrase announces this good news as well: "O mankind! Do not be apprehensive imagining that you are going to extinction, non-existence, nothingness, darkness, oblivion, decay, and dissolution, and that you will drown in multiplicity. You are going not to extinction, but to permanence. You are being impelled not to non-existence, but to perpetual existence. You are going to enter not darkness, but the world of light. And you are returning to your true owner, to the seat of the Pre-Eternal Monarch. You will not drown in multiplicity, you will take your rest in the sphere of Unity. You are bound not for separation, but for union."

The Letters, The Twentieth Letter, First Station, p. 271.

The Eleventh Phrase: "And with Him all things have their end."

That is, everything will return to the realm of permanence from the transient realm, and will go to the seat of post-eternal sovereignty of the Sempiternal Ever-Enduring One. They will go from the multiplicity of causes to the sphere of power of the All-Glorious One of Unity, and will be transferred from this world to the hereafter. Your place of recourse is His Court, therefore, and your place of refuge, His mercy. And so on.

There are a great many truths which this phrase and those like it state. The one which states that you will return to eternal bliss and Paradise has been proved so decisively by the irrefutable certainty of the twelve arguments of the Tenth Word, and by the six Principles which comprise the numerous cogent proofs of the Twenty-Ninth Word, that no need remains for further explanation. Those two Words have proved, with the certainty of the sun rising on the following morning after setting the previous day, that life too which has the meaning of the sun in this world, will rise in an enduring form in the morning of the resurrection after its setting with the destruction of the world. Since the Tenth and Twenty-Ninth Words have proved this truth to perfection, we refer you to them and here only say this:

Further to what has been proved decisively in the above explanation, the All-Wise Maker of the universe, Who possesses boundless all-embracing power, limitless universal will, and infinite all-encompassing knowlege, the all-Merciful Creator of human beings, has promised with all His heavenly Books and decrees Paradise and eternal bliss to those of mankind who believe in Him. Since He has promised, He will most certainly bring it about, because it is impossible for Him to break His promise. And because, not to carry out a promise is a most ugly fault, and the One of Absolute Perfection is totally exempt and free from all fault. Failure to perform a promise arises either from ignorance or from impotence. However, since it is impossible for there to be any ignorance or impotence pertaining to that Absolutely Powerful One, the One Knowing of All Things, His breaking of a promise is also impossible.

Moreover, first and foremost the Pride of the Worlds (Upon whom be blessings and peace), and all the prophets, saints, purified scholars, and people of belief, continuously request and implore, desire and beseech the All-Generous and Compassionate One for the eternal bliss they have been promised. They beseech it through all His Most Beautiful Names. For foremost His compassion and mercy, and justice and wisdom, His Names of All-Merciful and Compassionate, and All-Just and Wise, and His dominicality and sovereignty, and most of His Names including Sustainer and Allah, require and necessitate the realm of the hereafter and eternal happiness, and they testify and point to its realization. Indeed, all beings with all of their truths point to the hereafter.

The All-Wise Qur'an, the greatest of the revealed Books, also demonstrates and teaches this truth with thousands of its verses; with clear evidences and conclusive, veracious proofs.

The Most Noble Beloved One, too, who is the cause of pride for the human race, relying on thousands of dazzling miracles taught this truth throughout his life, with all his strength; he proved it, proclaimed it, saw it, and demonstrated it.

The Letters, The Twentieth Letter, Second Station, p. 300–301.

Part 4
Justice and Worship

Extract One: Centrality of the Divine Name

A notion expressed throughout the *Risale-i Nur* is to gain knowledge of God from the channels through which God self-reveals. An important path in this journey is to obtain and continuously increase the knowledge of Divine Names that could be witnessed or "read" through their manifestations. "The Thirtieth Flash" is about the six Divine Names "bearing the Greatest Name" of God. The Second Point is on the name All-Just, [*al-'Adl*], explaining that balance, stability, and order of the universe as manifestations of this name. Accordingly, human beings, as the conscious creation, are expected to acknowledge this order and follow it by reflecting the Divine justice in every manner.

The Second Point

The Divine Name All-Just [al-'Adl]

> And there is not a thing but its [sources and] treasures [inexhaustible] are with Us; but We only send down thereof in due and ascertainable measures. (15:21)

> > One point concerning this verse and one manifestation of the name All-Just, which is a greatest name or one of the six lights comprising the Greatest Name, like the First Point, appeared to me from afar while in Eskişehir Prison. In order to bring it closer to the understanding, we say the following; again by means of a comparison:

> > The universe is a palace, but it is such a palace that within it is a city that suffers the upheavals of constant destruction and reconstruction. Within the city is a country that is being continuously agitated by war and emigration. Within the country is a world which is unceasingly revolving amid death and life. But such an astonishing balance, equilibrium and equilibration prevail in the palace, city, country and world that it self-evidently proves that the transformations, and incomings and outgoings apparent in their innumerable beings are being measured and weighed every moment on the scales of a Single Being who sees and supervises the whole universe.

For if it had been otherwise, if causes had been free and unrestrained, which try to destroy the balance and overrun everything, with a single fish laying a thousand eggs and a single flower like the poppy producing twenty thousand seeds, and with the onslaught and violence of change and the elements flowing in floods, or if it had been referred to aimless, purposeless chance, anarchic blind forces, and unconscious dark nature, the equilibrium of beings and balance of the universe would have been so utterly destroyed that within a year, indeed within a day, there would have been chaos. That is to say, the seas would have been filled with wreckage in total disorder and confusion and would have become fetid; the atmosphere would have been poisoned with noxious gases; and as for the earth, it would have turned into a refuse-heap, slaughter-house, and swamp. The world would have suffocated.

Thus, everything from the cells of an animate body, the red and white corpuscles in the blood, the transformations of minute particles, and the mutual proportion and relation of the body's organs, to the incomings and outgoings of the seas, the income and expenditure of springs under the earth, the birth and death of animals and plants, the destruction of autumn and the reconstruction of spring, the duties and motion of the elements and the stars, and the alternations, struggles and clashes of death and life, light and darkness, and heat and cold, are ordered and weighed with so sensitive a balance, so fine a measure, that the human mind can nowhere see any waste or futility, just as human science and philosophy observe everywhere and demonstrate the most perfect order and beautiful symmetry. Indeed, human science and philosophy are a manifestation and interpreter of that order and symmetry.

So, come and consider the balance and equilibrium of the sun and its twelve planets. Does it not point as clearly as the sun to the All-Glorious One who is All-Just and All-Powerful? Especially our ship, that is, the globe of the earth, which is one of the planets; it travels an orbit of twenty-four thousand years in one year, not scattering or shaking the things stored up and stacked on its face, despite its extraordinary speed, nor throwing them off into space. If its speed had been increased or reduced just a little, it would have thrown its inhabitants off into the atmosphere, and scattered them through space. And if its balance was to be destroyed for a minute, or even a second, it would destroy the world. Indeed, it would clash with another body and doomsday would break forth.

Especially the compassionate balance on the face of the earth of the births, deaths, livelihoods, and lives of the four hundred thousand plant and animal species; it shows a single Just and Compassionate One, as clearly as light shows the sun.

Especially the members, faculties, and senses of a single of the innumerable members of those species; they are related to each other with so fine a balance and equilibrium that their balance and mutual proportion show an All-Wise and Just Maker so clearly as to be self-evident.

Especially the cells and blood-vessels in the bodies of animals, and the corpuscles in the blood and particles in the corpuscles; they have such a fine, sensitive, and wondrous balance that it self-evidently proves that they are being nurtured and administered through the balance, law, and order of a single All-Just and Wise Creator who holds the reins of all things, has the key to all things, for whom nothing is an obstacle to anything else, and directs all things as easily as a single thing.

If someone who does not believe or deems it unlikely that the deeds of jinn and men will be weighed up on the supreme scales of justice at the Last Judgement notes carefully this vast balance, which he can observe in this world with his own eyes, he will surely no longer consider it unlikely.

O wasteful, prodigal. wrongful, unjust. dirty, unclean. wretched man! You have not acted in accordance with the economy, cleanliness, and justice that are the principles by which the whole universe and all beings act, and are therefore in effect the object of their anger and disgust. On what do you rely that through your wrongdoing and disequilibrium, your wastefulness and uncleanliness, you make all beings angry? Yes, the universal wisdom of the universe, which is the greatest manifestation of the divine name of All-Wise, turns on economy and lack of waste. It commands frugality. And the total justice in the universe proceeding from the greatest manifestation of the Name All-Just, administers the balance of all things and enjoins justice on man. Mentioning the word balance four times, the verses in Sura al-Rahman,

And the firmament has He raised high, and He has set up the balance [of justice], * In order that you may not transgress [due] balance. * So establish weight with justice and fall not short in the balance, (35:7–9)

indicate four degrees and four sorts of balance, showing its immensity and supreme importance in the universe. Yes, just as there is no wastefulness in anything, so in nothing is there true injustice or imbalance.

The cleanliness and purification proceeding from the name Most Holy cleans and makes beautiful all the beings in the universe. So long as man's dirty hand does not interfere, there is no true uncleanliness or ugliness in anything.

So you may understand how basic to human life are the principles of justice, frugality, and cleanliness, which are truths of the Qur'an and Islamic principles. And know how closely connected with the universe are the injunctions of the

Qur'an, having spread their firm roots everywhere, and that it is as impossible to destroy those truths as it is to destroy the universe and change its form.

Is it at all possible that although hundreds of comprehensive truths like these three vast lights, such as mercy, grace, and preservation, require and necessitate the resurrection of the dead and the hereafter, such powerful and all-encompassing truths as mercy, favour, justice, wisdom, frugality, and cleanliness, which govern in the universe and all beings, should be transformed into unkindness, tyranny, lack of wisdom, wastefulness, uncleanliness, and futility, by there being no hereafter and the resurrection not occurring?

God forbid, a hundred thousand times, God forbid! Would a mercy and wisdom which compassionately preserve the rights of life of a fly violate the countless rights of life of all conscious beings and the numberless rights of numberless beings, by not bringing about the resurrection? And if one may say so, would a splendid dominicality which displays infinite sensitivity and care in its mercy and compassion and justice and wisdom, and a divine sovereignty which adorns the universe with His endless wondrous arts and bounties in order to display His perfections and make himself known and loved, permit there to be no resurrection, which would reduce to nothing the value of creatures and all their perfections, and make them denied? God forbid! Such an absolute beauty clearly would not permit such absolute ugliness.

Yes, the person who wants to deny the hereafter must first deny all the world and all its truths. Otherwise the world together with all its truths will give him the lie with a hundred thousand tongues, proving the compounded nature of his lie. The Tenth Word proves with certain evidences that the existence of the hereafter is as definite and indubitable as the existence of this world.

The Flashes, Thirtieth Flash, Second Point, p. 397–400.

Extract Two: Human Tendencies That Need Justice

According to Said Nursi, certain tendencies embedded in human nature make justice necessary. He defines three unlimited human powers that need to be trained and controlled by each individual. They are the human tendency of appetite, *kuvve-i şeheviye*, referring to the tendency to obtain anything wanted; anger, *kuvve-i gadabiye*, the tendency to avoid anything unwanted; and intellect, *kuvve-i akliye*. Nursi notes that it is part of humankind's test in the earthly life to train and control these powers. Uncontrolled usage of these tendencies causes injustices among human encounters and in their attitude toward the rest of the creation. Though the translation refers these inclinations as "powers," a preferred alternative would be understanding them as "tendencies."

*"The Straight Path (*al-Ṣirāṭ al-mustaqīm*)"* (1:4)

Know that the Straight Path is justice, consisting of the blending and summary of wisdom (ḥikma), chastity ('iffa), and courage (shajā'a), which are the mean or middle way of the three degrees of man's three powers.

To explain: when Allah (May He be exalted and glorified!) housed spirit (rūḥ) in man's body, which is changing, needy, and exposed to dangers, He deposited three powers in it to ensure its continued existence.

The First: the power of animal appetites to attract benefits.

The Second: the power of savage passion to repulse harmful and destructive things.

The Third: the power of angelic intellect to distinguish between benefit and harm.

However, since His wisdom necessitated that humanity should achieve perfection through the mystery of competition, Allah placed no innate limitation on these powers, as He did on those of other living beings. He did however limit them through the Shari'a, for it prohibits excess (*ifrāṭ*) and deficiency (*tafrīṭ*) and enjoins the middle way (*wasaṭ*). This is what is inferred by the verse *"Pursue then the right course as you have been bidden."* (11:112) In the absence of any innate limitation, three degrees arise in the three powers: the degree of deficiency, which is negligence; the degree of superabundance, which is excess; and the middle way, which is justice.

Thus, deficiency in the power of intellect is stupidity and foolishness, and its excess, perfidious deception and over-meticulousness in trivialities, and its middle way is wisdom. *"He who has been given wisdom, has been given great good."* (2:269)

Know that just as the power varies in these degrees, so does each of its branches vary. For example, in the question of the creation of actions, the middle way is that of the *Sunni* School between the *Jabriyya* and the *Mu'tazila*, and in the question of doctrine, the school of divine unity is the middle way between the denial of the divine attributes (*ta'ṭīl*) and anthropomorphism (*tashbīh*). You can make further examples in the same way.

Deficiency in the power of animal appetites is apathy and want of appetite, while its excess is profligacy, which is to desire whatever is encountered whether lawful or unlawful. Its middle way is uprightness, which is desiring what is licit and shunning what is illicit. You may apply the principle applied to this power to any of its branches, such as eating, drinking, dressing, and so on.

Deficiency in the power of savage passion is cowardice, that is, fear of what is not to be feared and delusive imagining. Its excess is uncontrolled anger, which is the progenitor of despotism, domination, and tyranny. And its middle way is courage, which is giving freely of oneself with love and eagerness for the defence of the laws of Islam and the upholding of the Word of divine unity. Apply this same principle to each of its branches.

The six extremes are thus tyranny and the three middle ways are justice, which is the Straight Path and is to act in act in accordance with *"Pursue then the right course as you have been bidden."* (11:112) …

Signs of Miraculousness, p. 29–30.

Extract Three: The Nature and Purpose of the Worship of God

The following is the introduction of a commentary of the Qur'anic verses 2:21, 22 about worship from the *Signs of Miraculousness*. Relating worship to the creation of humans, human nature along with the unlimited human tendencies explained in the extract above, and much needed application of justice in humans' social interactions; Nursi expounds on the nature and purpose of worship and describes it as "the cause of personal attainment and perfection."

> *"0 you people'. Worship your Lord and Sustainer, who has created you and those [who lived] before you, so that you might remain conscious of Him; * Who has made the earth a resting-place for you and the sky a canopy, and has sent down water from the sky and thereby brought forth fruits for your sustenance: then set not up rivals to Allah, when you know [the truth]." (2:21,22)*

Introduction

You should know that it is worship that instils the tenets of belief [in the believers] making them a very part of their character. For if matters pertaining to the conscience and reason are not nurtured and strengthened by worship, which consists of carrying out Allah's commands and abstaining from His prohibitions, they remain ineffectual and weak. The present state of the Islamic world testifies to this.

Know too that worship is the cause of happiness in this world and the next, and is a means of ordering life here and there, and a cause of attainment and perfection, both individual and collective. It is an exalted, esteemed relation between Creator and bondsman.

There are several reasons worship is the cause of happiness and prosperity in this world, which is the tillage of the hereafter:

Firstly: Man has been created with a strange, subtle nature distinguishing him from all other living beings and making him an exception to them. By virtue of this there have arisen in him the desire to choose, and the wish for the most beautiful things and for fine decoration, and a natural desire to have a livelihood and position befitting humanity.

For his food, dress, and accommodation—the need for which arises due to the above-mentioned desires—to be prepared proficiently man has need of multiple arts and crafts, but he is incapable of practising all of these on his own. He needs therefore to mix with his fellow-men and to cooperate with them, and for all of them to assist each other and exchange the fruits of their labour. However, since so as to allow men's progress by means of the mainspring of the will the All-Wise Maker placed no innate limits on the [three] human powers of appetite, anger, and intellect—as with the animals and their limited powers—tyranny and aggression have arisen. And since no limit has been placed on them, the powers [tend to] aggression and the [human] community is in need of justice when exchanging the fruits of its labour. But because the intellects of single members of society are incapable of comprehending justice, the human race as a whole needs a general or universal intellect [to establish] justice from which all may benefit. And that intellect is the universal law, and that law is the Shari'a. Then in order to preserve the effectiveness of the Shari'a and its enforcement, a law-maker is necessary, someone to lay claim to it and promulgate it, an authority, and that is the Prophet (Upon whom be blessings and peace).

Then in order to perpetuate his outward and inward domination over [people's] minds and hearts the Prophet needs to be eminently superior both physically and spiritually and morally, and in conduct and appearance, and by nature and in character. He is in need too of proof of the strength of his relations with the Lord of All Sovereignty, the Master of the World, and such a proof is his miracles. Then in order to secure obedience to [its] commands and avoidance of [its] prohibitions he is in need of perpetuating the idea of the Maker's grandeur, the Master of all Sovereignty, and that is [possible] through the manifestation of the tenets of belief. Then in order to perpetuate this idea and fix the tenets of belief firmly in their minds, he needs a constantly repeated reminder and renewed act, and that reminder is nothing but worship.

Secondly: The purpose of worship is to turn minds towards the All-Wise Maker. And this turning towards induces obedience and submission, and this includes [the worshippers] under the perfect order [in the universe] and binds them to it. To follow this order leads to the realization of the mystery of wisdom, and the wisdom is testified to by the perfect art in the universe.

Thirdly: Man resembles a pole to the top of which are joined electric cables, for attached to his head are the tips of all the laws of creation; the natural laws extend to him, and the rays of the divine laws and principles in the universe are reflected and centred on him. So man has to complete them and adhere to them and cling on to them to facilitate the general current lest his foot slips and he falls and is crushed under the wheels of the machinery turning in the levels [of the world]. And this is achieved through worship, which consists of conforming to the commands and prohibitions.

Fourthly: By complying with the commands and prohibitions numerous connections are formed for a person with the many levels of society, and the individual becomes like a species. For many of the commands, especially those that touch on the marks [of Islam] and the general good, resemble threads to which are tied [people's] honour and through which their rights are set in order. If it were not for them, all those rights and duties would be torn up and scattered to the wind.

Fifthly: The Muslim has firm relations with all other Muslims and there are strong bonds between them. By reason of the tenets of belief and [the Muslims'] Islamic traits these relations give rise to unshakeable brotherhood and true love. And it is worship that makes manifest the tenets of belief and renders them effective, and roots them firmly in the pysche.

How Worship Is the Cause of Personal Attainment and Perfection

Consider this: together with being physically small, weak, and powerless, and being one of the animals, man bears within him an exalted spirit, and has vast potentiality, unrestricted desires, infinite hopes, uncountable ideas, and unlimited powers, and he has a nature so strange he is as though an index of all the species and all the worlds. As for worship, it expands his spirit and raises his value; it causes his abilities to unfold and develop, allowing him to become worthy of eternal happiness. Worship is also a means of rectifying and purifying his inclinations, and of realizing his hopes and making them fruitful, and of marshalling his ideas and setting them in order, and also of reining in and limiting his [three] powers [of appetite, anger, and intellect]. Worship also removes the rust of nature from his members, physical and spiritual, each of which when transparent is like a window onto his private world and that of humankind. Also, when performed with both conscience and mind and heart and body, worship raises man to the dignity of which he is worthy and to his appointed perfection. It is a subtle, elevated relation, an illustrious lofty connection between the bondsman and the One Worshipped. This relation constitutes the utmost degree of human perfection.

Sincerity in worship is this, that it is performed only because it is commanded, although it comprises numerous instances of wisdom [and benefits]. Each of these may be a reason ('ilia) for performing worship, but sincerity makes it imperative that the [true] reason be the command to perform it. If the wisdom or benefit is made the reason, the worship is null and void, but if it merely encourages the person to perform the worship, it is permissible.

When those addressed hear the words "O you people! worship," they ask through the tongue of disposition: "Why and for what reason? What is the wisdom in it? Why should we? And what for?" You learnt the wisdom in the introduction above; concerning the reason ('illa), the Qur'an replies with proof of the Maker and His unity with the words: "Your Lord and Sus-tainer who created you." Then with the verse: "If you are in doubt about what We have revealed" (2:23) it proves prophethood.

Signs of Miraculousness, p.160–163.

Extract Four: The Importance of Daily Prayer

"The Eleventh Word" is about wisdom of the creation of the universe and humankind, wisdom of worship and the relationship between humans and God. The initial part of this Word is included in the first chapter of this section among the selections on belief. Here is the remaining of this Word as it focuses on the importance of daily prayers and worship.

The Eleventh Word

In the Name of God, the Merciful, the Compassionate.

By the sun and its glorious splendour; * By the moon as it follows it; * By the day as it shows [the sun's] glory; * By the night as it conceals it; * By the firmament and its wonderful structure; * By the earth and its wide expanse; * By the soul and the order and proportion given it.[77]

Brother! If you want to understand a little about the talisman of the wisdom of the world and the riddle of man's creation and the mystery of the reality of the

---

[77]   Qur'an, 91:1–7.

prescribed prayers, then consider this short comparison together with my own soul.

One time there was a king. As wealth he had numerous treasuries containing diamonds and emeralds and jewels of every kind. Besides these he had other, hidden, wondrous treasures. By way of attainment he had consummate skill in strange arts, and encompassing knowledge of innumerable wondrous sciences, and great erudition in endless branches of abstruse learning. Now, like every possessor of beauty and perfection wants to see and display his own beauty and perfection, that glorious king wanted to open up an exhibition and set out displays within it in order to make manifest and display in the view of the people the majesty of his rule, his glittering wealth, the wonders of his art, and the marvels of his knowledge, and so that he could behold his beauty and perfection in two respects:

The First Respect: so that he himself could behold them with his own discerning eye.

The Other: so that he could look through the view of others.

With this purpose in mind, the king started to construct a vast and majestic palace. He divided it into magnificent apartments and dwellings, and decorated it with every sort of jewel from his treasuries, and with his own hand so full of art adorned it with the finest and most beautiful works. He ordered it with the subtlest of the arts of his wisdom, and decked it out with the miraculous works of his knowledge. Then after completing it, he set up in the palace broad tables containing the most delicious of every kind of food and every sort of bounty. He specified an appropriate table for each group. He set out such a munificent and artful banquet that it was as though the boundless priceless bounties he spread out had come into existence through the works of a hundred subtle arts. Then he invited his people and subjects from all the regions of his lands to feast and behold the spectacle.

Later the king appointed a Supreme Commander (PBUH) as teacher, to make known the purposes of the palace and the meanings of its contents; to describe its Maker and its contents to the people, make known the secrets of the palace's embellishments, teach what the arts within it were pointing to, and to explain what the well-set jewels were, and the harmonious embroideries; and to explain to those who entered the palace the way in which they indicated the perfections and arts of the palace's owner, and to inform them of the correct conduct in beholding them, and to explain the official ceremonies as the king, who did not appear, wished them to be. The teacher and instructor had an assistant in each area of the palace, while he himself remained in the largest apartment among his students, making the following announcement to all the spectators. He told them:

"O people! By making this palace and displaying these things our lord, who is the king of the palace, wants to make himself known to you. You therefore should recognize Him and try to get to know Him. And with these adornments He wants to make Himself loved by you. Also, He shows His love for you through these bounties that you see, so you should love Him too by obeying Him. And through these bounties and gifts which are to be seen He shows His compassion and kindness for you, so you should show your respect for Him by offering thanks. And through these works of His perfection He wants to display His transcendent beauty to you, so you should show your eagerness to see Him and gain His regard. And through placing a particular stamp and special seal and an inimitable signet on every one of these adorned works of art that you see, He wants to show that everything is particular to Him, and is the work of His own hand, and that He is single and unique and independent and removed. You therefore should recognize that He is single and alone, and without peer or like or match, and accept that He is such." He spoke further fitting words to the spectators like these concerning the King and this station. Then the people who had entered the palace separated into two groups.

The First Group: Since these people had self-knowledge, were intelligent, and their hearts were in the right place, when they looked at the wonders inside the palace, they declared: "There are great matters afoot here!" They understood that it was not in vain or some trifling plaything. They were curious, and while wondering: "I wonder what the talisman to this is and what it contains," they suddenly heard the speech the Master and Instructor was giving, and they realized that the keys to all the mysteries were with him. So they approached him and said: "Peace be upon you, O Master! By rights, a truthful and exact instructor like you is necessary for a magnificent palace such as this. Please tell us what our Lord has made known to you!" First of all the Master repeated the speech to them. They listened carefully, and accepting it, profited greatly. They acted as the King wished. And because the King was pleased at their becoming conduct and manners, he invited them to another special, elevated, ineffable palace. And he bestowed it on them in a way worthy of such a munificent king, and fitting for such obedient subjects, and suitable for such well-mannered guests, and appropriate to such an elevated palace. He made them permanently happy.

As for the Second Group, because their minds were corrupted and their hearts extinguished, when they entered the palace, they were defeated by their evil-commanding souls and took notice of nothing apart from the delicious foods; they closed their eyes to all the virtues and stopped up their ears to the guidance of the Master (PBUH) and the warnings of his students. They stuffed themselves like animals then sank into sleep. They quaffed elixirs which had been prepared for certain other matters and were not to have been consumed. Then they became drunk and started shouting so much they greatly upset the other spectating guests. They were ill-mannered in the face of the Glorious Maker's rules. So the soldiers of the palace's owner arrested them, and cast them into a prison appropriate to such unmannerly people.

O friend who is listening to this story with me! Of course you have understood that the Glorious Creator built this palace for the above-mentioned aims. The achievement of these aims is dependent on two things:

The First: The existence of the Master (PBUH) whom we saw and whose speech we heard. Because if it was not for him, all these aims would be in vain. For if an incomprehensible book has no author, it consists only of meaningless paper.

The Second is the people listening the Master's words and accepting them. That is to say, the Master's existence is the cause of the palace's existence, and the people's listening to him is the cause of the continuation of the palace's existence. In which case it can be said that if it was not for the Master (PBUH), the Glorious King would not have built the palace. And again it may be said that when the people do not heed the Master's (PBUH) instructions, the palace will of a certainty be transformed and changed.

Friend! The story ends here. If you have understood the meaning of the comparison, come and behold its reality.

The palace is this world. Its roof is the heavens illuminated with smiling stars, and its floor, the face of the earth adorned from east to west with multifarious flowers. As for the King, he is the Most Holy One, the Pre-Eternal and Post-Eternal Monarch, Whom all things in the seven heavens and the earth glorify and extol, each with its particular tongue. He is a king so powerful He created the heavens and earth in six days, then abided on the Throne. One of Power and Majesty, Who, alternating night and day like two threads, one white and one black, writes His signs of the page of the universe; One to Whose command the sun, moon, and stars are subjugated. The apartments of the palace are the eighteen thousand worlds, each of which has been set in order and decorated in a fashion suitable to it. The strange arts you saw in the palace are the miracles of Divine power you see in this world, and the foods you saw there allude to the wonderful fruits of Divine mercy in this world, especially in summer, and above all in the gardens of Barla. The stove and kitchen there is the earth here, which has fire in its heart, and the face of the earth. While the jewels of the hidden treasuries you saw in the comparison are the similitudes of the manifestations of the sacred Divine Names. And the embroideries there, and the signs of the embroideries, are the well-ordered and finely worked beings and the harmonious impresses of the pen of power which adorn this world and point to the Names of the All-Powerful One of Glory.

As for the Master, he is our Master Muhammad (Peace and blessings be upon him). His assistants are the prophets (Peace be upon them), and his students, the saints and purified scholars. The ruler's servants in the palace indicate the angels (Peace be upon them) in this world. And the guests invited to the banquet to spectate in the comparison are the jinn and mankind in this guest-house of the world, and the animals, who are the servants of mankind. As for the two groups, one of them here consists of the people of belief, who are the students of the All-Wise Qur'an, the interpreter of the verses and signs of the book of the universe. The other group are the people of unbelief and rebellion, who follow Satan and their evil-commanding souls; deaf and dumb, like animals, or even lower, they form the group of the misguided, who recognize the life of this world only.

First Group: These are the felicitous and the good, who listened to the Master, "the Possessor of Two Wings." He is both the worshipping servant of God; in regard to worship he describes his Sustainer so that he is like the envoy of his community at the Court of Almighty God. And he is also God's Messenger; with regard to Messengership he conveys his Sustainer's decrees to men and the jinn by means of the Qur'an.

This happy community heeded the Messenger and listened to the Qur'an. They saw themselves invested with the prescribed prayers, which are the index of all the varieties of worship, and numerous subtle duties within elevated stations. Indeed, they saw in detail the duties and stations which the prayers point to with their various formulas and actions. It was like this:

Firstly: Since they observed the Divine works, and in the form of a transaction in the absence of the person concerned, saw themselves in the station of observing the wonders of the sovereignty of dominicality, they performed the duty of extolling and glorifying God, declaring: "*God is Most Great!*"

Secondly: Through being seen in the station of herald of His brilliant and wonderful works, which are the manifestations of the sacred Divine Names, exclaiming: "*Glory be to God! All praise be to God!*," they performed the duty of hallowing and praising God.

Thirdly: In the station of perceiving and understanding with their inner and outer senses the bounties stored up in the treasuries of Divine mercy, they started to carry out the duty of thanks and praise.

Fourthly: In the station of weighing up with the scales of their spiritual faculties the jewels in the treasuries of the Divine Names, they began the duty of praise and declaring God to be free of all fault.

Fifthly: In the station of studying the Sustainer's missives, written with the pen of power on the plan of Divine Determining, they began the duty of contemplation and appreciation.

Sixthly: With beholding the subtle, delicate, fine beauties in the creation of things and in the art in beings, in the station of declaring God to be free of all defect, they took up the duty of love and yearning for their All-Glorious Creator, their All-Beauteous Maker. That is to say, after looking at the universe and works and performing the duties in the above-mentioned stations through transactions in the object of worship's absence, they rose to the degree of also beholding the transactions and acts of the All-Wise Maker, whereby, in the form of a transaction in the presence of the person concerned, they responded with knowledge and wonder in the face of the All-Glorious Creator's making Himself known to conscious beings through the miracles of His art, and declared: "Glory be unto You! How can we truly know you? What makes You known are the miracles of the works of Your art!"

Then, they responded with love and passion to that Most Merciful One's making Himself loved through the beautiful fruits of His mercy. "*You alone do we worship and from You alone do we seek help!*," [Qur'an, 1:5] they declared.

Then they responded with thanks and praise to the True Bestower's showing His mercy and compassion through His sweet bounties, and exclaimed: "Glory be unto You! All praise is Yours! How can we thank You as is Your due? You are utterly worthy of thanks! For all Your bounties spread through all the universe hymn Your praises and thanks through the clear tongues of their beings. All Your bounties lined up in the market of the world and scattered over the face of the earth proclaim Your praises and extol You. Through testifying to Your munificence and generosity, all the well-ordered and well-proportioned fruits of Your mercy and bounty offer You thanks before the gazes of Your creatures."

Then they responded, saying: "*God is Most Great!*" before the manifestation of Divine beauty, glory, perfection, and majesty in the mirrors of beings, ever changing on the face of the universe; they bowed reverently in their impotence, and prostrated in humility with love and wonder.

Then announcing their poverty and need, they responded with supplication and beseeching to the Possessor of Absolute Riches' displaying the abundance of His wealth and breadth of His mercy, and declared: "From You alone do we seek help!"

Then they responded appreciatively to the All-Glorious Maker's displaying the subtleties and wonders of His antique art in the exhibition of creatures, exclaiming: "What wonders God has willed!" Observing and applauding them, they declared, "How beautifully they have been made! What blessings God has bestowed!" Holding everyone witness, they said in wonder: "Come! Look at these! Hasten to the prayers and to prosperity!"

And they responded with submission and obedience to the Monarch of Pre-Eternity and Post-Eternity's proclamation of the sovereignty of His dominicality in every corner of the universe and the manifestation of His unity. Declaring: "We hear and we obey!," they affirmed His unity.

Then, before the manifestation of the Godhead of that Sustainer of All the Worlds, they responded with worship and humble veneration, which consists of proclaiming their poverty within need, and with the prescribed prayers, which are the summary of worship. Thus, through performing their various duties of worship in the mighty mosque known as the abode of this world, they carried out the obligations and duties of their lives, and assumed "the finest of forms." They ascended to a rank above all creatures by which, through the auspiciousness of belief and assurance and "the Trust," they became trustworthy Vicegerents of God on the Earth. And after this field of trial and place of examination, their Munificent Sustainer invited them to eternal happiness in recompense for their belief, and to the Abode of Peace in reward for their adhering to His religion of Islam. There, He bestowed on them out of His mercy bounties so dazzling that no eye has seen them, nor ear heard them, nor have they occurred to the heart of man[78]—and so He does bestow these on them, and He gave them eternity and everlasting life. For the desirous, mirror-bearing lovers of an eternal, abiding beauty who gaze upon it will certainly not perish, but will go to eternity. The final state of the Qur'an's students is thus. May Almighty God include us among them, Amen!

As for the other group, the sinners and the wicked, when they entered the palace of this world at the age of discretion, they responded with unbelief to all the evidences of Divine unity, and with ingratitude towards all the bounties, and by accusing all creatures of being valueless, insulted them in an unbelieving manner. And since they rejected and denied all the manifestations of the Divine Names, they committed a boundless crime in a short time and became deserving of endless punishment. For the capital of life and the human faculties were given to man for the duties mentioned above.

---

[78]   Bukhari, Bad'ul-Khalq, 8; Tafsir al-Sura, xxxii, 1;Tawhid, 35; Muslim, Iman, 312.

O my senseless soul and foolish friend! Do you suppose your life's duty is restricted to following the good life according to the requisites of civilization, and, if you will excuse the expression, to gratifying the physical appetites? Do you suppose the sole aim of the delicate and subtle senses, the sensitive faculties and members, the well-ordered limbs and systems, the inquisitive feelings and senses included in the machine of your life is restricted to satisfying the low desires of the base soul in this fleeting life? God forbid! There are two main aims in their creation and inclusion in your essential being:

The First consists of making known to you all the varieties of the True Bestower's bounties, and causing you to offer Him thanks. You should be aware of this, and offer Him thanks and worship.

The Second is to make known to you by means of your faculties all the sorts of the manifestations of the sacred Divine Names manifested in the world and to cause you to experience them. And you, by recognizing them through experiencing them, should come to believe in them.

Thus, man develops and is perfected through the achievement of these two basic aims. Through them, man becomes a true human being.

Look through the meaning of the following comparison, and see that the human faculties were not given in order to gain worldly life like an animal.

For example, someone gave one of his servants twenty gold pieces, telling him to have a suit of clothes made out of a particular cloth. The servant went and got himself a fine suit out of the highest grade of the cloth, and put it on. Then he saw that his employer had given another of his servants a thousand gold pieces, and putting in the servant's pocket a piece of paper with some things written on it, had sent him to conclude some business. Now, anyone with any sense would know that the capital was not for getting a suit of clothes, for, since the first servant had bought a suit of the finest cloth with twenty gold pieces, the thousand gold pieces were certainly not to be spent on that. Since the second servant had not read the paper in his pocket, and looking at the first servant, had given all the money to a shopkeeper for a suit of clothes, and then received the very lowest grade of cloth and a suit fifty times worse that his friend's, his employer was bound to reprimand him severely for his utter stupidity, and punish him angrily.

O my soul and my friend! Come to your senses! Do not spend the capital and potentialities of your life on pleasures of the flesh and this fleeting life like an animal, or even lower. Otherwise, although you are fifty times superior with regard to capital than the highest animal, you will fall fifty times lower than the lowest.

O my heedless soul! If you want to understand to a degree both the aim of your life and its nature, and the form of your life, and the true meaning of your life, and its perfect happiness, then look! The summary of the aims of your life consists of nine matters:

The First is this: To weigh up on the scales of the senses put in your being the bounties stored up in the treasuries of Divine mercy, and to offer universal thanks.

The Second: To open with the keys of the faculties placed in your nature the hidden treasuries of the sacred Divine Names.

The Third: To consciously display and make known through your life in the view of the creatures in this exhibition of the world the wondrous arts and subtle manifestations which the Divine Names have attached to you.

The Fourth: To proclaim your worship to the Court of the Creator's dominicality verbally and through the tongue of your disposition.

The Fifth: Like on ceremonial occasions a soldier wears all the decorations he has received from his king, and through appearing before the him, displays the marks of his favour towards him, this is to consciously adorn yourself in the jewels of the subtle senses which the manifestations of the Divine Names have given you, and to appear in the observant view of the Pre-Eternal Witness.

The Sixth: To consciously observe the salutations of living beings to their Creator, known as the manifestations of life, and their glorifications of their Maker, known as the signs of life, and their worship of the Bestower of Life, known as the aims of life, and by reflecting on them to see them, and through testifying to them to display them.

The Seventh: Through taking as units of measurement the small samples of attributes like the partial knowledge, power, and will given to your life, it is to know through those measures the absolute attributes and sacred qualities of the All-Glorious Creator. For example, since, through your partial power, knowledge, and will, you have made your house in well-ordered fashion, you should know that the Maker of the palace of the world is its Disposer, and Powerful, Knowing, and Wise to the degree it is greater than your house.

The Eighth: To understand the words concerning the Creator's unity and Maker's dominicality uttered by each of the beings in the world in its particular tongue.

The Ninth: To understand through your impotence and weakness, your poverty and need, the degrees of the Divine power and dominical riches. Just as the pleasure and degrees and varieties of food are understood through the degrees of hunger and the sorts of need, so you should understand the degrees of the infinite Divine power and riches through your infinite impotence and poverty. The aims of your life, then, briefly, are matters like these. Now consider the nature of your life; its summary is this:

It is an index of wonders pertaining to the Divine Names; a scale for measuring the Divine attributes; a balance of the worlds within the universe; a list of the mighty world; a map of the cosmos; a summary of the vast book of the universe; a bunch of keys with which to open the hidden treasuries of Divine power; and a most excellent pattern of the perfections scattered over beings and attached to time. The nature of your life consists of matters like these.

Now, the form of your life and the manner of its duty is this: your life is an inscribed word, a wisdom-displaying word written by the pen of power. Seen and heard, it points to the Divine Names. The form of your life consists of matters like these.

Now the true meaning of your life is this: its acting as a mirror to the manifestation of Divine oneness and the manifestation of the Eternally Besought One. That is to say, through a comprehensiveness as though being the point of focus for all the Divine Names manifested in the world, it is its being a mirror to the Single and Eternally Besought One.

Now, as for the perfection of your life, it is to perceive the lights of the Pre-Eternal Sun which are depicted in the mirror of your life, and to love them. It is to display ardour for Him as a conscious being. It is to pass beyond yourself with love of Him. It is to establish the reflection of His light in the centre of your heart. It is due to this mystery that the Hadith Qudsi was uttered, which is expressed by the following lines, and will raise you to the highest of the high:

The heavens and the earth contain me not;

Yet, how strange! I am contained in the hearts of believers.[79]

And so, my soul! Since your life is turned towards such elevated aims and gathers together such priceless treasures, is it at all worthy of reason and fairness that you should spend it on temporary gratification of the instinctual soul and fleeting worldly pleasures, and waste it? If you do not want to fritter away your life, ponder over the oaths in this Sura of the Qur'an, which allude to the above comparison and truths, and act accordingly:

---

[79]   See, al-'Ajluni, Kashf al-Khafa, ii, 165; Ghazzali, Ihya'l-'Ulum al-Din, iii, 14.

By the sun and its [glorious] splendour; * By the moon as it follows it; * By the day as it shows up [the sun's] glory; * By the night as it conceals it; * By the firmament and its [wonderful] structure; * By the earth and its [wide] expanse; * By the soul and the order and proportion given it; * And its enlightenment to its wrong and its right. * Truly he succeeds that purifies it, * And he fails that corrupts it.[80]

O God, grant blessings and peace to the Sun of the Skies of Messengership, the Moon of the Constellation of Prophethood, and to his Family and Companions, the stars of guidance, and grant mercy to us and to all believing men and all believing women. Amen. Amen. Amen.

The Words, Eleventh Word, p. 134–142.

Extract Five: The Damascus Sermon

Said Nursi delivered the Damascus Sermon in 1911 responding the insistent requests of *ulemā*, religious scholars, of Damascus to give sermon for a Friday prayer at the momentous Umayyad Mosque. The Sermon was delivered to an audience of approximately ten thousand together with about a hundred scholars. Its impact was notable that it was printed twice in the same week there. Later on, Said Nursi published its translation to Turkish. At a time close to the start of the World War I and when the Muslim world was fragmented due colonial occupation, the sermon focused on the analysis of the problems and their solutions. Without blaming outer forces, Nursi preferred a self-critical look at the Muslim world, identifying "six dare sicknesses" and suggested them six solutions, or "remedies," each based on a Qur'anic concept. Illnesses he notes are as it follows:

> In the conditions of the present time in these lands, I have learnt a lesson in the school of mankind's social life and I have realized that what has allowed foreigners, Europeans, to fly towards the future on progress while it arrested us and kept us, in respect of material development, in the Middle Ages, are six dire sicknesses. The sicknesses are these:
>
> *Firstly*: The rising to life of despair and hopelessness in social life.
>
> *Secondly*: The death of truthfulness in social and political life.
>
> *Thirdly*: Love of enmity.

---

[80]   Qur'an, 91:1–10.

Fourthly: Not knowing the luminous bonds that bind the believers to one another.

Fifthly: Despotism, which spreads, becoming widespread as though it was various contagious diseases.

Sixthly: Restricting endeavour to what is personally beneficial.

I shall explain, by means of six "Words," the lesson I have learnt from the pharmacy of the Qur'an, which is like a faculty of medicine. This lesson constitutes the medicine to cure our social life of those six dire sicknesses.

The Damascus Sermon, p. 26–27.

For the Muslim world still has not fully recovered of these severe problems, *The Damascus Sermon* continues to be read and seen as an important work. Within the limits of this section, we will only be able to provide little abstracts of the Sermon. The following extract is on love and enmity:

The thing most worthy of love is love, and that most deserving of enmity is enmity. That is, love and loving, which render man's social life secure and lead to happiness are most worthy of love and being loved. Enmity and hostility are ugly and damaging, have overturned man's social life, and more than anything deserve loathing and enmity and to be shunned.

The Damascus Sermon, p. 49–50.

An advocate of freedom, Said Nursi supported constitutionalism. In 1910, he voyaged through eastern Anatolia to inform tribes living there about social, and civilizational benefits of freedom and constitutionalism and to respond their questions of rejection. Composed of his responses to questions about freedom, minority rights, and related political concerns were published in 1913 as *Münāzarat*, *The Debates*, which is a book its translation to English is yet to be completed. Several selections from Şükran Vahide's *Intellectual Biography of Bediüzzaman Said Nursi: Islam in Modern Turkey*, as her translation are below.

Despotism is oppression. It is dealing with others in an arbitrary fashion. It is compulsion relying on force. It is the opinion of one person. It provides extremely favorable ground for exploitation. It is the basis of tyranny. It annihilates humanity. It is despotism that reduces man to the most abject valleys of abasement, has caused the Islamic world to sink into abjection and degradation, which arouses animosity and malice, has poisoned Islam—and in fact shows its poison everywhere by contagion, and has caused endless conflict within Islam …

Constitutionalism is ... the manifestation of the Qur'anic verses "And consult them in affairs [of public concern]" (3:158) and "Whose rule in consultation among themselves" (42:38). It is the consultation enjoyed be the Sharī'ah. This luminous body of life is truth, instead of force. Its hearth is knowledge; its tongue, love. Its mind is the law, not an individual. Indeed, constitutionalism is the sovereignty of the nation ...

Münāzarat in Asar-ı Bedi'iyye, p. 406–407, and *Islam in Modern Turkey*, p. 85.

Delicate manners of freedom is instructed and adorned by the good manners of the Sharī'ah. Freedom to be dissolute and behave scandalously is not freedom; it is animality; it is the tyranny of the devil; it is to be the slave of the evil commanding soul. General freedom is the product of the portions of individual freedoms. The characteristic of freedom is that one harms neither oneself not others.

...

Freedom is this: apart from the law of justice and punishment, no one can dominate anyone else. Everybody's rights are protected. In their legitimate actions, everyone is royally free. The prohibition: "Take not one from among yourselves as Lord over you apart from God" (Qur'ān 3:64) is manifested.

...

Freedom springs from the belief in God. ... belief requires not degrading others through tyranny and oppression, and abasing them, and not abasing oneself before oppressors. Someone who is a true slave of God cannot be slave to others. ... That is to say, however perfect belief is, Freedom will shine to that degree.

...

Münāzarat, p. 15–19, and *Islam in Modern Turkey*, p. 86–87.

Further Readings

Translated books from the Risale-i Nur Collection are available from different publishers:

The Words
The Letters
The Flashes
The Rays
The Reasonings
The Gleams
Signs of Miraculousness
The Damascus Sermon
Al-Mathnawi Al-Nuri
The Staff of Moses: Reflections of Islamic Belief, and Divine Existence and Unity
Humanity's Encounter with the Divine Series *and similar selected text.*

Books on Said Nursi

Engaging with Bediuzzaman Said Nursi: A Model of Interfaith Dialogue by Ian Markham, (England: Ashgate Publishing, 2009).

Said Nursi by Colin Turner and Hasan Horkuc, (London: I.B. Tauris, 2009).

Theodicy and Justice in Modern Islamic Thought: The Case of Said Nursi edited by Ibrahim Abu-Rabi, (England, Ashgate Publishing, 2009). *Spiritual Dimensions of Bediuzzaman Said Nursi's Risale-i Nur,* edited by Ibrahim Abu-Rabi, (New York: State University of New York Press, 2008).

Islam in Modern Turkey: An Intellectual Biography of Bediüzzaman Said Nursi by Şükran Vahide, (New York: State University of New York Press, 2005). An earlier version of Şükran Vahide's biography is available with the title *Bediüzzaman Said Nursi: The Author of the Risale-i Nur,* (Istanbul: Sözler Publications, 1992).

Globalization, Ethics and Islam: The Case of Bediuzzaman Said Nursi edited by Ian Markham and Ibrahim Ozdemir. (England: Ashgate, 2005).

Said Nursi's Veiews on Muslim-Christian Understanding by Thomas Michel, (Istanbul: Söz Press, 2005).

Islam at the Crossroads: On the Life and Thought of Bediuzzaman Said Nursi edited by Ibrahim M. Abu-Rabi, (New York: State University of New York Press, 2003).

Islamic Political Identity in Turkey by M. Hakan Yavuz (Oxford: Oxford University Press, 2003).

Anatolia Junction: A Journey into Hidden Turkey by Fred Reed, (Canada: Talonbooks, 1999).

Religion and Social Change in Modern Turkey The Case of Bediüzzaman Said Nursi by Şerif Mardin, (New York: State University of New York Press, 1989).

Doctoral Dissertations:

"Some Aspects of Religious Identity: The Nurcu Movement in Turkey Today" by Ali Mermer

"Said Nursi's Ideal for Human Society: Moral and Social Reform in the Risale-i Nur" by Hasan Horkuc

"The Islamic Constitutional Societal Model in Bediuzzaman Said Nursi's Works For Confronting Dictatorship, Anarchy or Chaos" by Abdul-Muhsin Alkonawi

Online resources:

An up-to-date reference website regarding information and news on Nursi Studies: http://www.nursistudies.com/

Risale-i Nur Studies at Durham University: http://www.dur.ac.uk/sgia/imeis/risale/

Said Nursi Chair at John Carroll University: http://www.jcu.edu/religion/nursi/about.htm

Glossary

Agnosticism: The belief that one cannot be certain of the existence of God.

Atheism: Belief that there is no god.

Bediüzzaman: title meaning nonpareil or wonder of the age.

Bible: The holy book of Christianity.

Burkha: A loose outer garment worn by Muslim women in few Islamic nations which covers their entire body, including the head, leaving only the eyes exposed.

Caliph / Caliphate: According to *Sunni* school of thought, Caliph was a title given to Muslim leaders. Early Caliphs, the Four Rightly Guided Ones, were considered both as spiritual leaders and head of the Islamic state known as *Caliphate*. Late Caliphs mostly dealt with political leadership and state affairs. In Ottoman, *Caliphs* were supervised by *sheikh al-Islam*, a leading religious scholar given the highest authority of legislation and guidance.

Damascus Sermon: Delivered by Said Nursi in 1911 at Umayyad Mosque in Damascus, it outlined six problems Muslim world faced and offered solutions.

Dominicality: The understanding that God has dominion (or power) over all things.

Fulfillment theology: Reports of sayings and deeds of Prophet Muhammad and his companions. Each *hadith* is preceded by an isnad, a list or chain of those who passed the report on. *Hadith* are a primary source of Islam, secondary to the scripture of the religion, the Qur'an.

Hadith: A term used by Muslims to refer to the traditions of the prophet and his companions. Each hadith is preceded by an isnad, a list, of those who passed the story on. The hadith literature is an important source of Islamic law.

Houri: A special creation particular to the Paradise manifesting many different Divine art and beauties simultaneously, satisfying the recipient human faculties.

Imam: Derived from Arabic, it literally means 'leader.' It's used to refer to the person leading a congregational prayer, a community or a spiritual leader, a scholar, and similar. In Shi'a Islam, Imams are successors to Prophet Muhammad and are spiritual and political leaders.

Jihad: An Arabic word means 'struggle.' Said Nursi explains it as spiritual struggle or struggle with ideas and words.

Jinn: refers to a spirit created from fire before man was created from clay (Qur'an 15:27). Jinn are conscious and responsible beings. (Qur'an, 51:56).

Medrese [Medāris]: Schooling focused on religion and Islamic teaching.

Mekteb [Mekātib]: Schooling focused on the teaching of science, law and other vocations.

Ottoman Empire: The Turkish Empire that ran from the twelfth century until the end of the First World War stretched from Turkey to eastern Europe and across central Asia to the Middle East.

People of the Book: Primarily Jews and Christians. Persons of faith traditions that are centred around Divinely revealed scriptures.

Pluralism: The belief that truth can be found in many religions.

Qur'an: The holy book of Islam

Ramadan: The ninth month of the Muslim lunar calendar, believed to be the time when the revelation of the Qur'an began. Muslims are required to fast during this month. .

Reductio ad absurdum: An argument which proves its point by reducing the alternative to an absurd or illogical conclusion.

Risale-i Nur / Risale: The Epistle of Light, an approximately six-thousand-page commentary on the Qur'an written by Said Nursi. The work is divided into sections such as: the Words, the Rays, the Flashes, the Miracles, the Signs, and Letters.

Shari'ah: The sacred, ethical law, derived from the Qur'an and *Hadith*, around which Muslims structure their lives.

Shaykh: An Arabic word referred to people of knowledge and wisdom. It is commonly used for scholars.

Shi'a: Followers or the party of Ali. It is the second largest group in Islam with a belief in *Imamate*, that Ali ibn Abi Talib and *Imams* coming from his descendants were true successors to Prophet Muhammad.

Shiite: From Shia—the party of Ali. Muslims divide into two groups, with the Shiite group believing that Ali should have succeeded Muhammad.

Sufism: Known as tasavvuf, it is a discipline requiring cleansing of one's heart from the worldly and transient things in order dedicate it to love of God.

Sunna: An Islamic term referring to sayings, practices, and silent approvals of Prophet Muhammad.

Sunni: Followers of Prophet Muhammad's *Sunna*. It is the largest group in Islam.

Tanzimat: The period between 1839–1876 known as a time of reorganization or reform of the Ottoman Empire.

Torah: The holy book of Judaism.

Ulemā: Plural for ālim, scholar, in Arabic. Commonly used to refer religious scholars.

Ummah: It is the Arabic word for community or nation. It refers to the Muslim community or people throughout the world.

Vicegerent: Means a deputy. In the Qur'an, human beings are depicted as vicegerents of God (Qur'an, 2:30).

Index